MARGARET MITCHELL: REPORTER

D1470515

Margaret Mitchell
REPORTER

Edited by Patrick Allen

THE UNIVERSITY OF SOUTH CAROLINA PRESS

© 2000 by Hill Street Press LLC.

Originally published by and reprinted by arrangement with Hill Street Press LLC
Paperback edition published in Columbia, South Carolina,
by the University of South Carolina Press, 2010

www.sc.edu/uscpress

Manufactured in the United States of America

19 18 17 16 15 14 13 12 11 10   10 9 8 7 6 5 4 3 2 1

Library of Congress Cataloging-in-Publication Data
Mitchell, Margaret, 1900–1949.
Margaret Mitchell : reporter / edited by Patrick Allen.
p. cm.
Originally published: Athens, Ga. : Hill Street Press, c2000.
Columns written for the Atlanta Journal Sunday Magazine from
1922 to 1926.
ISBN 978-1-57003-937-9 (pbk : alk. paper)
I. Allen, Patrick, 1965– II. Title.
PS3525.I972A6 2010
814'.52—dc22
2009048778

The columns appearing herein originally appeared in the *Atlanta Journal.*
Reprinted with the consent of the *Atlanta Journal-Constitution.*
Photographs reprinted courtesy of the Atlanta History Center, the *Atlanta
Journal-Constitution,* DeKalb Historical Society, and the Hargrett Rare Book
and Manuscript Library of the University of Georgia Libraries.

Text and cover design by Anne Richmond Boston

This book was printed on Glatfelter Natures, a recycled paper
with 30 percent postconsumer waste content.

Contents

Introduction

Early in December of 1922, the same year famed reporter Nellie Bly died, Margaret Mitchell approached *Atlanta Journal* city editor Harlee Branch about a position at the newspaper. Although Branch was impressed by Mitchell—perhaps more by her demeanor and family name than the few Smith College compositions she brought as writing samples—there were no openings on the society and women's pages, and Branch felt that the *Journal* was not then ready for women in "hard news" reporting.

The following week Mitchell finagled an interview with Angus Perkerson for a staff job on the *Atlanta Journal Sunday Magazine*. Even at the interview, Mitchell showed the ingenuity and pluck, if not the veracity, which would mark her career at the *Journal*. In a 1936 letter to former *Journal Magazine* colleague and then *Chattanooga Times* reporter Julia Collier Harris, Mitchell gave an account of how she talked her way into the newspaper: ". . . Mother died when I was in my freshman year and there was no one to keep house for Father and [brother] Stephens so I came home. I made my debut and then went onto the Magazine Section of the *Journal*, somewhat to the consternation of my father. I had had no newspaper experience and had never had my hands on a typewriter, but by telling poor Angus Perkerson outrageous lies about how I had worked on the *Springfield Republican* (How could I? And all my people good Democrats?) and swearing I was a speed demon on a Remington, I got the job."

Mitchell could obviously talk a good game, because Perkerson, purportedly the epitome of the hard-nosed, hard-drinking news-paperman, hired her over his own small flutterings of doubt. "I was a little bit worried about putting her on the staff," Perkerson said in a 1950 interview, "because she was a society girl, and I said to [his wife and *Journal Magazine* contributing editor] Medora, 'Medora, I reckon we'll always be waiting for her to get to work.' But I was wrong there—she was always waiting for us when we got there in the morning, because she came to town on the street car and had to leave home before the cook got there. So she ate breakfast in the little café in the building—the *Journal* folks called it 'The Roachery'—and then she sort of opened up the office."

The world of the daily journalist of the era, from the office environment to the work itself, was different from the white-shoe world in which Mitchell had grown up. The five-story brick building which housed the newspaper, already slightly de-crepit in 1922, was in the Five Points section of Atlanta, so-named because five major roads intersected there beside vast and busy railyards. The newspaper's masthead proclaimed "The *Journal* Covers Dixie Like the Dew," but an ever-present cloud of coal soot covered the *Journal's* Forsyth Street offices like a dank blanket. In those pre-air conditioning days, it was not un-common for a stray coal cinder to land on a *Journal* staffer's desk through an open window.

The *Journal* had strong, long-standing competition for read-ers from Hearst's Atlanta *Georgia* and *Sunday American.* (John Marsh, Mitchell's second husband, worked at the former.) News radio was only just nascent, and breaking news was still rushed into special editions and hawked by newsboys on street corners shouting "Extra! Extra!" to passersby. The *Journal* cost five cents on weekdays, double that on Sundays. Notables on the staff included Roark Bradford, Erskine Caldwell, Frances Newman, and Grantland Rice, among others.

Reporters' hours are not debutantes' hours. *Journal* staffers were expected to work at least eight hours a day, six days a week. Reporters might be given two night assignments a week and were required to stay late every other Saturday to get out the Sunday paper. They were also expected to frequent the bar at the Kimball House Hotel near the *Journal* offices for copious drinking and swearing.

Mitchell took her place at her desk beside Medora Field Perkerson in the magazine's third-floor back office, a room Mitchell dubbed "The Black Hole of Calcutta." Her Underwood typewriter lacked a backspace key and the legs of her desk and office chair had to be cut down by a *Journal* maintenance man to fit the petite Mitchell. The staff of six shared a single telephone.

True to his desire to exploit Mitchell's social connections, Perkerson's first assignment to Mitchell was to interview Mary Hines Gunsaulus, an Atlanta socialite recently returned from the European couture shows, about the latest trends on the catwalk. The story, which ran under the title "Atlanta Girl Sees Italian Revolution" on December 31, 1922, with the byline Margaret Mitchell Upshaw, was well written and contained the requisite fashion forecast for which her editor was looking. Mitchell recalled her first experience as a professional writer:

Would skirts be short again anytime soon? That was the story I was told to get, and I darn well got it. Mrs. Gunsaulus posed for photographs in her Paris frocks and mentioned incidentally that she had been in Rome the day the Fascisti marched in, black shirts and all, and Mussolini took over the government.

Mussolini was not even a name to me then, but it sounded interesting and I listened and asked questions while Mrs. Gunsaulus told more. I came back and wrote my story about skirts and tacked all this other incident onto the end.

You know what happened. Angus—I called him Mr.

Perkerson then—turned the story hindside before and featured the eyewitness account of Mussolini taking over the Italian government.

Married to Berrien "Red" Upshaw less than four months before her hire, Mitchell wrote two stories under the byline Margaret Mitchell Upshaw. She then requested of her editors that her family name appear as her byline, and continued to write as Peggy Mitchell even after her second marriage to John R. Marsh in the summer of 1925.

In 1945 Mitchell reflected on her assignments at the *Journal Magazine:*

> A lot of the things we wrote about were topical, of course. Could a girl be virtuous and bob her hair? Could she have a home and husband and children and a job, too? Should she roll her stockings, park her corsets, be allowed a latchkey? These questions are all as dead as the bloomer girl now, but they were hot stuff then. Between the younger and older generation, swords were drawn. Practically anybody could get publicity by criticizing young people. There was a passionate interest on the part of both old and young as to what prominent people had to say on these issues. They aren't issues any longer and they are dead because they were victories won by the younger generation of the 1920s.

Occasionally her stories generated either a hail of controversy or a shower of praise. Mitchell conceived of and completed a four-part series of profiles of women in Georgia history. Her research was conducted at the Carnegie Public Library, the same library which would later provide much material for *Gone With the Wind,* and was completed on her own time. The profiles, which appear in this volume, were of Rebecca Latimer Felton, the first woman to become a United

State senator; Lucy Mathilde Kenney, who dressed as a man to serve in the Civil War; Mary Musgrove, the famous Creek Indian; and Mary Hart, who killed a British soldier in the Revolutionary War. Shortly after the profiles appeared under the title "Georgia's Empress and Woman Soldiers" on May 20, 1923, Perkerson called Mitchell into his office to show her a sheaf of angry readers' letters charging her with, as Mitchell biographer Anne Edwards summarizes, "everything from defaming Georgian womanhood to bastardizing history to sell newspapers."

Mitchell had much better luck with readers when she profiled several of Georgia's Civil War generals in a series of articles which ran from November–December, 1925. It had been announced that each Southern state would be represented by five of its generals in a Confederate memorial being carved into the face of the granite outcropping of Stone Mountain, Georgia, by sculptor Gutzon Borglum. The *Journal* originally planned to do only two articles, but reader response was so immediate and enthusiastic that Perkerson extended the series to four parts and to an unusually lengthy three thousand to four thousand words per story.

Angus Perkerson, reflecting in 1945 on Mitchell's tenure at the magazine he edited for decades, said, "One thing I liked about her was that she was always ready to take on any story— she never looked down on any story. And she wrote like a man. . . . Her stories did not require much editing. They ran as she wrote them."

In addition to her regular features on the magazine, Mitchell had many other responsibilities.

She was sometimes drafted by city editor Harlee Branch, over the objections of Angus Perkerson, to do features for the news section of the daily *Journal,* several of which ran with her byline. She also contributed, for no additional pay, book reviews to the "News of Books and Writers" department of the magazine, including what might have been the earliest review of Faulkner's first novel, *Soldiers' Pay.* Also, she was sometimes called into service as an advice columnist in the "Courtship, Marriage, and Manners" column begun by Frances Newman.

Like all *Journal Magazine* staffers, Mitchell was responsible for proofreading part of the magazine. Mitchell proofed the religion columns of Bishop Warren A. Candler and Dr. Cary B. Wilmer, whose subjects included comments on the explosive Scopes trial and the rise of radio preachers, and she was also responsible for correcting the long serial stories which ran in the Sunday magazine nearly every week. The first installment of each story, by writers such as Arthur Conan Doyle, P. G. Wodehouse, Wallace Irwin, Fannie Hurst, and Willie Snow Etheridge, ran on Sunday and additional chapters continued throughout the week. Frequently, the daily installments got jumbled or even lost, and Mitchell often told the story that when an entire chapter of a bodice-ripping romance disappeared, she simply wrote a new installment to fill its place.

Mitchell, like the rest of the magazine staff, was responsible for editing and producing the Sunday rotogravure picture section of the Sunday *Journal*—the "brown section," as it was called. The staffers' responsibilities involved selecting and writing captions for staff and wire service photos. Mitchell was in charge of selecting baby photos for the brown section. Much of the job involved assuaging the hurt feelings of parents whose bundle of joy was not selected for inclusion in the paper.

Despite her long work hours, the famously gregarious young Mitchell maintained an active social life. In their early courting, Mitchell wrote future husband John Marsh love letters from her desk at the magazine. She began her letters not with a salutation such as "Darling" or "Dear John," but with the typesetter's code "14 ems 8 pt. sun mag.," a ruse she devised in case her eagle-eyed editor walked past her desk.

When she was off the clock, Mitchell often entertained a boisterous, fun-loving crowd at her family house at 1401 Peachtree Street. With the exception of long-time friend Augusta Dearborn and a few others, many of her friends from Atlanta "society" eschewed the group, which included Roy Flannagan, William S. Howland, O. B. Keeler, and Allan Taylor and their wives and girlfriends. The closest knit of the group dubbed themselves the Peachtree Yacht Club. The land-locked social club's name was perfectly logical, according to Mitchell's brother Stephens, given that "there are no athletes at the Athletic Club and no one drives at the Driving Club. Why should there be yachts at the Yacht Club?"

Mitchell's career as a journalist came to a somewhat abrupt end in early 1926. Mitchell badly sprained her ankle—the same ankle previously injured in riding accidents in 1911 and 1920—and doctors' diagnoses wavered between arthritis and rheumatism. In intense pain, Mitchell resigned from the *Journal* and her last story, "Pigeons to Race from Havana to Atlanta," ran on May 9, 1926.

In four years and four months, Mitchell turned out 129 features, many of them cover stories; eighty-five news stories, and several book reviews. Mitchell had received her first paycheck—written to Peggy Mitchell Upshaw—on January 22, 1923, in the amount of twenty-five dollars. (Although Mitchell's first story appeared on December 31, 1922, she probably received her pay for her first two weeks by voucher, rather than check.) Her final paycheck was dated May 3, 1926, and was for thirty dollars. She earned two raises while at the paper, both of two dollars and fifty cents each.

After she quit, she commenced to write (probably on May 16, 1926), at home, a Sunday magazine column of society chitchat called "Elizabeth Bennet's Gossip," a column begun by Frances Newman and named after Jane Austen's heroine. She found the work loathsome and discontinued it upon Newman's return to Atlanta in August of the same year.

Mitchell continued her many friendships with Atlanta journalists throughout her life, was a longtime member of the Atlanta Women's Press Club, and continued to attend the annual convention of Georgia journalists until her death in 1949. It was through the introduction of Medora Field Perkerson, whose desk was beside Mitchell's at the magazine and who was herself a novelist well known in the South, that editor Harold Latham was able to pursue Mitchell for her manuscript of *Gone With the Wind*. Mitchell gave her only radio interview to Perkerson after the publication of the novel.

Journal Magazine editor Angus Perkerson thought he knew what he was getting when he hired Margaret Mitchell as a staff writer in 1922—a well-raised debutante who would report on fashion and the Southern smart set until she either got bored or got married. Instead, cub reporter Margaret Mitchell took the responsibilities of a working journalist seriously, seeking out interesting stories, doing research, fighting for cover placement, and pounding out her weekly stories on a raggedy Underwood typewriter.

Mitchell recognized that her years of newspapering made her a stronger, better person. In a 1945 interview in the same *Journal Magazine* which began her career as a working writer, Mitchell reflected on her time spent as a reporter.

Being a reporter was a liberal education. If more women, when they were girls, were in a position to see—as a newspaper girl is—the insides of jails, the horrible things Travelers' Aid discovers, the emergency rooms of Grady Hospital, and those sad, desolate sections which used to be fine homes but now are rookeries and rabbit warrens— if more people knew the sad things and the horrible things that go on in the world, there would be a darned sight less complacency and probably not so many of these sad sights and horrible things. It is not so much that people are cold-hearted and selfish, it is just that they have not seen. And what eye has not seen, heart cannot feel. Nowadays, girls do get out more, people do know more, but even so, one good whiff of the police station on a hot July day would do a lot for a lot of people.

The tendency to draw parallels between the biographies of the real-life Margaret Mitchell and her fictional heroine are irresistible. Likewise, in this collection there are new and rich insights into Mitchell's sensibilities, passions, and opinions. Even as a putatively neutral reporter, whether she is reporting on first-time women voters or describing life in a circus sideshow or conducting a jailhouse interview, the irrepressible personae of the observer shines through. Like the fictional Scarlett of *Gone With the Wind*, the real Margaret of this collection of her journalism from 1922–1926 can show both an extravagant femininity and a directness once thought appropriate only for men, both old-fashioned eloquence and modern sharpness of tongue, both the demureness of a bridge-playing deb and the mania of a shimmy-dancing flapper.

Taken as a whole, Margaret Mitchell's journalism transcends the who, what, when, and where of the reporter's trade to give a portrait of the artist as a young woman.

—◦◦◦—

Sources

Books

Caldwell, Erskine. *Call It Experience: The Years of Learning How to Write* (Athens, Ga.: University of Georgia Press, 1996), 40–41.

Edwards, Ann. *Road to Tara* (New Haven and New York: Ticknor and Fields, 1983), 5–6, 81–91.

Farr, Finis. *Margaret Mitchell of Atlanta* (New York: Morrow, 1965), 59–78.

Mitchell to Katharine Brown, 18 November 1936, *"Gone With the Wind"*
Letters, 1936–1949, ed. Richard Harwell (New York: Macmillan, 1976).

Mitchell to Julia Collier Harris, 28 April 1936, *"Gone With the Wind" Letters,*
1936–1949, ed. Richard Harwell (New York: Macmillan, 1976).

Mitchell to James S. Pope, 22 September 1942, *"Gone With the Wind" Letters,*
1936–1949, ed. Richard Harwell (New York: Macmillan, 1976).

Periodicals

Abbott, Reginald. "'Folks Gwine Talk Sumpin' Scan'lous': Margaret Mitchell,
Frances Newman, and the Art of Gossip," *The Southern Quarterly* 37, nos.
3–4 (Spring–Summer 1999), 221–37.

Abrams, Harvey Dan. "Medora Field Perkerson," *Atlanta Historical Bulletin*
11, no.3 (September 1966), 7–30.

Bledsoe, Erik. "Margaret Mitchell's Review of Soldiers' Pay," *Mississippi*
Quarterly 49 (Summer 1996): 591–93.

Howland, William S. "Peggy Mitchell, Newspaperman," *Atlanta Historical*
Bulletin 9, no.34 (May 1950), 47–64.

Mitchell, Margaret. "Margaret Mitchell, Girl Reporter," interview by Medora
Field Perkerson, *Atlanta Journal Sunday Magazine,* 7 January 1945.

Mitchell Chronology

1900   Born Margaret Munnerlyn Mitchell to May Belle Stephens and Eugene Mitchell in Atlanta on November 8.

1903   Begins wearing boy's clothes after her dress catches fire; her attire earns her the nickname "Jimmy."

1911   After being thrown from a horse, suffers the first of a series of ankle injuries that plague her throughout her life.

1912   Moves from childhood home on Jackson Hill in southeast Atlanta to a white-columned mansion at 1149 Peachtree Street.

1914–1918   Attends Atlanta's Washington Seminary for girls; becomes involved in the drama club and literary societies.

1917   Publishes first two stories in the school yearbook *Facts and Fancies* under the name "Peggy."

1918   Falls in love with Lt. Clifford Henry, a wealthy Harvard man stationed at Camp Gordon, Georgia, in the summer. Enrolls in Smith College with plans to study medicine. Henry is wounded on the battlefields of France and dies on October 16.

1919   May Belle Mitchell dies of influenza on January 23. Mitchell withdraws from school in May and returns to Atlanta to keep house for her father and brother Stephens.

1920   Suffers another ankle injury in February after being thrown from her horse. The accident renders Mitchell immobile until July. Makes her début to Atlanta "society" during the winter season.

1922   Marries Berrien "Red" Upshaw on September 2 against her father's wishes; the couple separates in December. Accepts a job at the *Atlanta Journal Sunday Magazine* and publishes her first story on December 31, "Atlanta Girl Sees Italian Revolution."

1924   Files for divorce, citing Upshaw's drinking and physical abuse, and it is granted by the court on October 16, 1924.

1925   Weds journalist John Marsh on July 4.

1926   Publishes her last story for the *Journal Magazine,* "Pigeons Race from Havana to Atlanta," on May 9. Quits the magazine after suffering another sprained ankle. Rests at home and begins in earnest research on the novel that would become *Gone With the Wind.*

1929   Finishes the bulk of the novel and shows her work to only her husband and a close friend at the Macmillan Publishing Company, Lois Cole.

1932   The Marshes move from their Crescent Avenue apartment to the Russell Apartments at Peachtree and Seventeenth streets in Atlanta.

1935   At Cole's insistence, Mitchell shows the *GWTW* manuscript to editor Harold S. Latham in April. He accepts it in July, and advances Mitchell five hundred dollars. She spends the rest of the year rewriting, editing, and checking the historical accuracy of the text with John's input.

1936   *GWTW* is published in June, and by October the novel sells over one million copies. Producer David O. Selznick purchases the film rights for fifty thousand dollars.

1937   Receives the Pulitzer Prize, the National Book Award, and the annual award of the American Booksellers Association.

1938   After twenty-one months, *GWTW* goes off the best-seller list on April 8.

1939   The film version of *GWTW* premières at Loew's Grand Theatre in Atlanta on December 15. The film goes on to win ten Academy Awards, including best picture. Mitchell receives an honorary master's degree from Smith College.

1949   Mitchell is struck by a car while crossing Peachtree Street in Atlanta on August 11. She dies in the hospital five days later and is buried in Atlanta's Oakland Cemetery.

1

Mode & Manners

Mitchell appeared in this photo which illustrated an unbylined
1923 *Journal Magazine* article, "Hats on Elevators? Yes! No!"

Atlanta Girl Sees Italian Revolution

—⟨∞⟩—

Mrs. Mary Hines Gunsaulus was in Rome when the Fascisti
took over the government. She tells of that,
of Paris fashions, and of poverty in Germany,
in the accompanying interview.

—⟨∞⟩—

R evolution in Italy. Fashions in Paris. Poverty in Germany. Mrs. Mary Hines Gunsaulus talked of these things at the home of her parents, Judge and Mrs. J. K. Hines, on Peachtree Road, where she is visiting after a three months' tour of Europe. Mrs. Gunsaulus was in Italy when the Fascisti overthrew the government.

"The Italians were so stunned by the suddenness of the Fascisti revolution that they didn't know what to think at first," she said, "but as life went on unchanged and their business and customs were not disturbed, they were disposed to look favorably on the Fascisti.

"No one seemed to be expecting the revolution; for in Italy, one does not feel the sinister undercurrent of discontent that is so evident in Germany. The Italian cities were as they have always been, dirty, contented, and picturesque; with little plumbing, no sidewalks, and with goats, chickens, and children playing in the streets.

"The day before the Fascisti seized the government, we were in Rome, and our guide was showing us the famous old palaces.

While we were viewing, from a respectful distance, the Palace of the Caesars (the police allow no one inside), our guide gave a shout of horror,

"'Look, in the Palace of the Caesars!'"

"There, in the forbidden courtyard, were four men in uniform, mounted on beautiful white horses, riding around defiantly. Finally, they waved their fists impudently and rode off. They were the vanguard of the Fascisti, I suppose, and they were 'daring' the police to arrest them. The next day, in Venice, we heard that the government had fallen into the hands of the 'Black Shirts' in a bloodless revolution. Italy, though startled at the suddenness of it all, is not greatly disturbed."

No Chance for Short Skirts

In telling of fashions in Paris, Mrs. Hines said, "I don't see any chance for our beloved short skirts to come back this season. Skirts are trailing the ground in Paris; long, tight skirts draped up on the sides and tight across the hips. Waists are still quite long and elaborately embroidered. Short sleeves seem to be coming into their own again, and with them, the French women wear a dozen bracelets on each arm. They say, 'I have pretty, plump arms,' and they fasten several bracelets above their elbows in an Oriental effect."

"Paris is very, very modest, this season," added Mrs. Gunsaulus. "The evening dresses are actually high-necked and have long trailing skirts! Even ears will be modest, this winter—they won't show. So many French women had bobbed their hair that a formal coiffeur is difficult. However, they have adopted the style of slicking back the hair on the top of the head, bringing it smoothly over the ears and fastening the psyche knot in the back with a Spanish comb. All Paris is flaunting combs—really gorgeous affairs. All are large, some of tortoise-shell; those for nightwear always glisten with iridescents."

Everything Cheap in Germany

In describing conditions in Germany, Mrs. Gunsaulus said, "The German system of finance is almost broken down. Show a German an American dollar and you can buy anything he has. The value of the German mark is based on the American dollar entirely. When the dollar goes up or down, prices all over Germany go up or down, accordingly. German paper money has no gold backing and the whole country is flooded with it. The amount of paper money one receives on exchanging American money is reminiscent of the last days of the Confederacy when one went shopping with a basket of money and returned with a handful of food.

"Everything is inconceivably cheap there—dresses, jewelry, in fact all the luxuries. No American woman could resist such bargains. Of course, they charged us three times as much as they did Germans, but even then, the prices were so absurdly low that no one would think of protesting at them.

"My first impression of Berlin was that everyone was spending money freely. The most famous street of the city, Unter der Linden, is lined with eating places, ranging from tiny cafes to palatial restaurants. You know the Germans eat enormously, usually six meals a day. Perhaps that's why they are so fat. But these restaurants are always crowded. They serve splendid, well-cooked food, and a dinner for two with four courses, costs only fifty or seventy-five cents.

"Berlin's five opera houses as well as the theaters are always packed, not so much by tourists as by Germans, spending their ever depreciating marks with feverish gaiety."

—*December 31, 1922*

Dancers Now Drown Out
Even the Cowbell

I n vain, the leader of the jazz band may burst blood vessels in his efforts to make himself heard above the din of the "Double Shuffle" and the "Fandango Stamp," the newest dances introduced to Atlanta's younger set. Formerly we had a vast respect for the amount of noise a jazz band could produce. Now we see it is utterly eclipsed.

The dances, this season, are going to be very Egyptian. Like the fashions, the current slang, and the popular songs, the Terpsichorean mode of the moment will reflect the widespread interest stirred by the opening of the tomb where "Tutankhamen, emperor of Egypt, King of Nubia and Syria, Lord of the Universe, Father of the Sun and Stars, Defender of the Faith" has slept undisturbed since 6000 B.C. or thereabouts.

Rudolph Valentino was the bright star on the horizon for a while and the "Vasilino" style of hair dressing, dancing, and Shiekish love-making had its day. Then the Chauve Souris displaced that fancy and now Tutankhamen is the rising star of the firmament. But it isn't to be an Oriental dancing craze—not in the usual, sinuous, snaky meaning of the Oriental dancing. Not at all! We are to imitate, if possible, in our dancing the angular postures of the figures depicted on the Obelisks and the hieroglyphic writings of the Egyptians. *A bas la shimmy! Fini jazz!*

One frequently wonders how the ancients managed to hold those poses long enough to be "sculped," but the still greater wonder of today is the fact that the young Moderns cannot only assume poses that would turn Tutankhamen green with envy, but can continue to repeat them at a high rate of speed for hours on a stretch.

For a while, it seemed that the gyrations of the toddle and the shimmy and Chicago would be their own cure and hopeful conservatives hailed the return of the waltz. Conservatives always cry for the waltz after any prolonged period of extravagant dancing, pathetic in their belief that the return of the waltz will mean hoopskirts, modesty, and old-fashioned gallantry. But alas for their hopes!

The Double Shuffle

The "Double Shuffle" and the "Fandango Stamp," the last analysis of the "Argentine Tango" craze inaugurated by Valentino, now endanger the shins and jeopardizes the ankles of our daughters. It was all very well for Valentino to stamp his feet and grind his heels viciously into the floor at each back-step. He was wearing spurs and they probably made a pleasant jingling noise. Then, too, Argentine damsels, accustomed to the Tango, are probably more agile in dodging these stamps and kicks.

American girls, used to milder dancing and gentler wooing, are likely to sustain injuries before mastering the intricacies of the "Fandango." To a casual observer, there seems no scheme to the dance. In fact, it appears to be more of a fight. The man clutches his seemingly unwilling partner, bends her back at an angle of forty-five degrees, leans forward like a hound in leash and away he goes in a series of jerks and stamps.

There is a crash of music, the saxophone squeals, and the trombones blare, then the young blades, with especially made wooden heels for stamping, shift back and begin to stamp.

Formerly, the noise would have been mistaken for a Horse Guard drill. So loud is it that it drowns out the cowbells of the orchestra. Everyone is "double-shuffling" and stamping and the hubbub is such that conversation, as well as music, is rendered useless.

Suddenly some psychic voice tells that the stamping time is over, and with long, stiff, angular steps, the man sets off across the floor, pushing his partner before him in a series of jerky strides that make her bobbed locks leap out behind spasmodically.

Good-bye, Baby Vamp

The Egyptian influence mingles with the Argentine. From the shuffling stamp emerge the pawing side-steps, so well-known, but this season much more emphasized and angular. For angles and not curves are the mode and will be till another fancy catches the public mind.

The Denishawns did this quite cleverly when they were in Atlanta a few weeks ago, but what the ball-room version of the new dances will be is another matter. If the Egyptian dancing really takes firm root, it means a radical change in the popularity of dancing partners. The blue-eyed baby vamp will have to give way to the long, lean, lanky girl, whose natural angularity has not been an asset in recent years.

Tut! Tut! Tutankhamen!
You had a lot o' fun!
For when it came to wives
You captured them,
You enraptured them
With Sheikish eyes.
Beside the pyramid
When you were feeling blue.
Egyptian maidens did
A dance or two.
You may be dead in 1923
But you had your fun in 6000 B.C.
Tut! Tut! Tutankhamen!

—February 18, 1923

Spring Styles in Slang Reach Atlanta

"What's wrong with this picture?" inquires the girl of 1923 in weary disgust when ennui is slowly consuming her. The flapper, long since passed into the limbo of dim memories, would have signified her boredom by drawling "I'm all un-strung."

Of course that expression is out of style just as are short waists and shorter skirts.

Atlanta has spring styles in slang, even as in hats, dresses, and lingerie, and the girl who doesn't keep up with the current style language is as hopelessly out of date as if she wore leg o' mutton sleeves with a sport suit.

Not content with having sent the maid of 1923 forth in vivid dresses adorned with romping hieroglyphics and playful pharaohs, Tutankhamen has even invaded slang.

"Sarcophagus," a word that would formerly have been a stumbling block to even the flapper's glib tongue, is now in common use. It is inelegant this spring to threaten, when roused to ire, to "wrap a scantling around the ear" of the offending party, or even "bounce a brick off their dome." This spring one "slips a sarcophagus" to one's enemy.

"Cake eater," "jelly bean," and even that classic phrase, "tea-hound," have been relegated to a back seat in favor of "mummy," while "King Tut" bids fair to eclipse Goldberg's famous title, "Steve Himself," when applied to a well-meaning man who is continually "putting his foot in it" through his own good intentions.

But, on the contrary, when "favorite mummy" is applied to a girl, it signifies highest approval.

Who can tell where the present Egyptian influence will lead? Perhaps in the future we will no longer exclaim "hot dog!" in moments of excitement, but "sacred Isis!"

"Sweetie" Changes to "Sheik"

No one has a "sweetie" these days, they have "sheiks." To have a "sheik" is a girl's highest ambition. But a "sheik" must not be a "Stacomb Sammy," nor must he have a propensity of "broadcasting," all of which means that he must not be a "slick-haired teahound who tells everything that he knows."

"Cuckoo" was a last winter's word, but from it has sprung the name "cuckoo's nest," which is very elastic and can mean any number of things, though usually it means a place where only "dumbbells" live.

An "oil can" and an "awful egg" used to denote the last word in feminine disapproval, but now "flat tire" rules supreme with "amoeba," culled from the pages of biology, running it a close second. (The biological definition of amoeba is the lowest form of animal life.) "Airedale" also comes in this class, as it refers to a hopelessly clumsy and homely man who possesses, despite these handicaps, an attractive manner.

"Dumb" and "dumbbell" are on the wane, but they have left in their places synonymous phrases of equal vividness: "Dizzy frog," "fluffy bean," "boo-cat," and "she leads out aces," from bridge.

"Laugh that off!" requests Miss 1923, as she relates some incident that particularly annoys her, or else, "Wouldn't that tweeze your eyebrows?"; "My flag fell on the poop deck"; or "Wouldn't that make you tear a toenail?"

"Young ineffectuals" have supplanted the slurring "highbrow" in the vocabulary of the younger set, in reference to the would-be intelligentsia, while "slipper flipper" designates the unregenerate materialist who occupies himself with dancing and scorns "serious thinkers."

"The Eel's Heels"

"Dirt dauber" once meant an industrious little insect that made its home from mud. It now means an equally industrious human with a genius for unearthing "dirt" (scandal) and "broadcasting" it.

Affection manifests itself in queer ways, to judge by the endearing terms exchanged by friends and lovers. "Mole," "wart," "worm" predominate, with "golliwog," "pie-eye," dewdrop," "moron," as other phrases of attachment.

Terms of approbation are few this spring, where in former years "peach," "lollapaloosa," "whiz," "chicken" were but a few of many that gladdened our hearts and enlarged out vocabulary. This season a beautiful girl is a "sunburst," "good news," or "cut glass."

One type of slang that has withstood the winter storms until spring (because it can be constantly changed to suit the author and affords such a wide field for originality) is the "leather lollipop" and "georgette poncho" brand. With it is its zoological co-partner, "the eel's heels," "the oyster's adenoids," and the long list of feline peculiarities, such as the "cat's meow," "pajamas," "elbows," "pants," "collar button," etc.

"That's el canary with me," seems quite cryptic on first sight, but when its predecessor, "that's Jake with me," is recalled, it becomes quite intelligible.

Among other verbal expressions are "two time," meaning "to deceive," and "siki" (psyche), to analyze.

It is a life work, keeping up-to-date on current slang, and those who can do this are, in their own parlance, "wise crackers."

—*April 22, 1923*

Who Owns The School Girl's Nose?

—⁓⁓—

High School Student in Arkansas, Who Appealed to State Supreme Court for Right to Wear Powder in School, Has Aroused the Question. Three Atlanta Principals State Their Views on Girls and Paint.

—⁓⁓—

Little grains of powder,
Little dabs of paint,
Make a homely little girl
Look like what she ain't!

W hether the school girls of Atlanta are to be permitted to look "like what they ain't," or whether they will be compelled to wear their own personal complexions— shiny noses and all—seems to be a matter of considerable controversy in certain quarters.

The question, locally, seems to be how old a girl should be before she starts painting and powdering, for the younger set as well as the older girls must have their lipstick and mascara. Only the young ladies should not start using these indispensable aids to beautify while they are still school girls, according to Atlanta authorities. Regulations on this subject are in force at Washington Seminary, Girls' High School, and North Avenue Presbyterian, the three largest girls' schools in Atlanta.

At Knobel, Arkansas, one girl carried her nose into the courts and insisted that the law should uphold her right to powder her nose as part of her inalienable right to the pursuit of happiness. Nothing of this sort has happened in Atlanta, but there is an ocean of difference between the viewpoints, on one hand, of Miss Jessie Muse, principal of Girls' High; Miss

Thyrza Askew, of North Avenue Presbyterian school; and Miss Emma Scott, of Washington Seminary; and of the girls themselves, on the other hand.

The Arkansas girl who recently made the fight for "school girl rights" was Miss Pearl Pugsley, of the Knobel, Arkansas, High School. Miss Pugsley was wont to take unto herself some of the little grains of powder and little daubs of paint, and by artistic application of the same add to her charms.

Anti-Lipstick Crusade

But the faculty of the high school held different views. They had inaugurated an "anti-lipstick" crusade, and they stood ready to enforce their restrictions. But, as will frequently happen, Miss Pugsley's nose became shiny and she proceeded to powder it.

The faculty proceeded to expel her.

Miss Pugsley, in righteous indignation and the family Ford, betook herself to the courts of law and justice—but "there ain't no powder justice," Miss Pugsley now thinks. The circuit court and the supreme court backed the school authorities in their right to make and enforce regulations concerning the conduct and complexions of the students.

"Personally, I don't care if my girls paint their noses green outside school," said Miss Emma Scott, principal of Washington Seminary. "What girls do outside of school is none of my business. All that concerns me is their conduct while under my jurisdiction.

"I specify in my catalogue that any girl who attends Washington seminary accepts my conditions and regulations when she enters the school. If the girls aren't willing to abide by my rules, they should go to other schools. Parents who aren't willing to make children obey our rules should not send their children here. And one of my rules is that girls cannot paint their faces.

"It is a personal matter with me—this face painting—and I think that I have a right to uphold my ideas of right on my own property.

"I will admit that some girls need touching up, or something, for Nature has not been equally kind in the distribution of complexions, but the very girls who need it most never seem to know how to put it on artistically! I often tell the girls that if they can put it on so cleverly that they can make me think that it's real—then I'll give them a prize."

Miss Scott laughed. "But the prize hasn't ever been won!"

What Painting Means

"Some girls come to school with cheeks of such colors as were never seen on land or sea and lips dripping vermillion. Then I make them wash their faces. If they persist in painting after I have warned them several times, I have to send them home.

"Why do I object to paint?

"For two reasons. Primarily, because of the origin of the habit. Paint was originally the badge of immorality. Then, older women who had passed the first glow of youth took it up, and then the girls. There is no reason why girls with fresh complexions and smooth skins should smear themselves up with paint.

"My second objection is that to paint means letting down the first subtle barrier of a girl's nature. Next come cigarettes, and then liquor.

"I don't like girls to paint and I feel, like the Knobel High School authorities, that I have a right to enforce my own ideas of right on my own property."

"I am opposed, heart and soul, to young girls painting their faces," declared Miss Jessie Muse, principal of the Girls' High School. "It betrays such bad taste and leads to equal bad taste in hair dressing and clothes. Few girls of high school age have very definite ideas on what looks well and it would be much safer if they confined themselves to simple things and no make-up.

"I have been very much interested in the lipstick case in Arkansas, and I quite agree with the decision of the supreme court. It seems to me that after school authorities have given due considerations to a subject, such as the use of cosmetics, their decisions should be upheld. Discipline and authority must always be upheld if any real aims are to be accomplished, for if authority is a thing to be easily put aside, it holds no weight.

"The question of cosmetics on young girls is one that lies very close to my heart, for I have so many, many girls at high school and I want to see them always do the things that will make them grow into fine women."

Mothers' Help Needed

"My girls are very sweet about complying with my feelings about painting," said Miss Thyrza Askew, principal of North Avenue Presbyterian School. "Of course, they laugh about it, I am sure, but they understand that I believe that girls of high school age are sweeter and more wholesome without rouge and powder, and they obey very well.

"Girls of the average high school age have no business painting their faces. Painting is neither a clean habit nor an attractive one. Painting the face tends to make young girls feel much older than they are and gives them desires and social aspirations beyond their years.

"Girls at prep schools are at a crucial age, when they need the utmost in training in quietness of deportment, dress, and manners. Rouge is so conspicuous, and it works against the efforts of teachers to instill the elements of dignity that we strive to inculcate in our girls.

"I believe that every principal of every girls' school earnestly desires the help of the mothers of the girls in their care. If the mothers would give their sympathy and understanding to the matter, there would be a nation-wide improvement. If the mothers and girls would just understand that we aren't objecting to paint for any petty reasons, but really because we thought it stood in the way of normal, wholesome girl life, they would co-operate."

What the Girls Say

Of course, in the matter of face paint for school girls, the girls themselves have the most to say. On the crowded school yards, at recess, with teeth sunk into hot dogs or sandwiches, they deliver themselves.

One pretty girl whose shiny nose proved that the anti-powder and anti-paint rules had been applied in her case, spoke her mind about the Arkansas ruling. "A girl's face is her own, and I think that she's got a perfect right to put anything on it that she wants to—including a nose ring!"

"Well, I don't know about that," remarked another, cautiously. "Goodness knows, some girls DO lay it on so thick that they look like old Chief Paint-in-the-Face themselves. The reason is that most girls look so obviously painted is that they don't know what shade of rouge to wear. Blondes put on lots of brunette rouge that makes them look dirty, and the brunettes floss out in blonde orange rouge that sticks out so that it could flag a train."

—April 29, 1923

Pep, Brains, and Clothes Win in Beauty Contests

(E)ach of the girls selected by their schoolmates as the most beautiful at three Atlanta schools have bobbed hair.

That fact may or may not be an indication that bobbed hair is "going out." It also may or may not indicate that the classic and Victorian standards of feminine beauty, face, and figure do not count for much when the schoolgirls select the most beautiful of their number.

Not that the three girls selected at Fulton High School, North Avenue Presbyterian, and Washington Seminary are not pretty! They are. But according to the statements of the girls who chose these three queens of beauty, personality counts for more than ability to measure up to whatever corresponds to Venus de Milo in the *jeune fille* size.

All three of these girls not only have the requisite personality, but also beauty of feature and complexion and all that can be desired in the way of wavy hair and dimples.

In the schoolgirl's mind, personality along with a reasonable amount of beauty is the first qualification in selecting the "most beautiful." The next qualification appears to be her clothes— the ability to wear them and the gift of being able to look well in good-looking clothes.

These impressions of the Atlanta schoolgirl's ideas concerning beauty were gathered from conversations with pupils of Fulton High, North Avenue Presbyterian, and Washington Seminary, where the "most beautiful girls" were chosen recently by vote of the student body.

Three Most Beautiful

The three who were selected are Miss Birdie Lichtenwalter, of Fulton High; Miss Marietta Norris, of Washington

Seminary; and Miss Edna Anderson, of North Avenue Presbyterian.

Miss Lichtenwalter is of medium height, slender, and of graceful carriage. She has large, liquid brown eyes with long dark lashes and a mass of bright bobbed chestnut hair.

Miss Edna Anderson, of Dawsonville, Georgia, is of a different type entirely. Hers is the Irish type of beauty, with dark bobbed hair, shot with bronze; deep blue, tranquil eyes fringed with long black lashes; and skin of the fairest white.

Miss Marietta Norris is tall and slim, with the gift of wearing the modern style of dress gracefully. Her hair is wavy and bobbed, of soft red brown color, and her eyes are merry and dark.

"In the matter of the 'type' of beauty I like best, I prefer perfect blondes," said Peggy Porter, of North Avenue Presbyterian School. "Blondes with real spun-gold hair and Delf-blue eyes. But there are so few of them that you hardly ever see that type.

"Of course, if the perfect blondes are perfect dumbbells, all their beautiful hair and fair skin doesn't make them attractive. There has to be something behind their blue eyes, or they might as well be cross-eyed for all the beauty they possess! A girl has to have brains to be really beautiful."

Elenor McGinty and Jane Small abandoned their Latin books to state their views on beauty, and their preferences show that times have certainly changed since grandma was a girl!

"People used to think that the slim, spiritual type of girl who swooned religiously whenever anybody said 'boo' was the real type of beauty," declared Elenor McGinty. "Some people still like the fragile, appealing type, but I think the modern girl with pretty bobbed hair and pep and ability to wear her clothes with real style has more beauty than the old-fashioned sort."

"Yes, that's quite true," said Jane Small. "I don't favor the Victorian damsel, either, but I don't think that the modern girl who is terribly brawny and freckled is pretty, if that is what you mean by modern. But the girl of today has a look of independence and style that, coupled with humor and pep, makes her beautiful to me. I haven't any particular preference as to the color of her hair and eyes as long as she has those attributes."

Clothes and Personality

Washington Seminary was relaxing from the throes of a French final examination, and the beautiful green lawn and walks were covered with pretty girls arm in arm, strolling home after the arduous three-hour session with irregular verbs.

They stopped to give their opinions on what constitutes beauty, and these opinions were quite well formed and definite as are most schoolgirl ideas in this day and time.

"Clothes," said Elenor Burns, "make more beauty than ox eyes and pink cheeks! Personally, I like the modern type, slim and straight, with bobbed hair, and an independent way of holding up her chin.

"Clothes do make the girl as much as they make the man— and a little bit more so than in the case of the man," said Idabelle Roberts. "But at the same time, without good features all the clothes in the world couldn't improve a girl's looks. I like regular features, clean-cut chin and nose, cool, serene blue eyes—I suppose you'd call that the classic type of beauty, wouldn't you?"

"There isn't any particular type of blonde or brunette I like best," smiled Edna Freeman. "I think people you like or love always seem beautiful to you!"

"Personality makes beauty, whether you have classical features or a pug nose and green eyes," declared Sophia Street. "My idea of beauty is that it isn't something of the exterior but it comes from within—from your brain or soul or wherever your personality is. A beautiful personality will make a beautiful face, because personality will cause the corners of a girl's mouth to turn up and her eyes to sparkle. No girl, however beautiful her blue eyes might be or how perfect her Cupid's bow mouth is, can be pretty if the mouth turns down and eyes are sullen."

"I think that the old standards of beauty are passing," said Catherine Howell. "Beauty used to be a matter of fair skin, large eyes, raven or gold hair—a rather set and stereotyped style of beauty.

"Now it's personality and style of dressing that make beauty. It takes sense to have personality and sense to dress well and in keeping with that personality! Therefore, I suppose my ideal of beauty is brain, for the brainy woman can make herself beautiful in a dozen ways, whereas the old style of beautiful girls always looked the same."

If Venus de Milo should enter any one of Atlanta's prep schools next September, she wouldn't stand a chance in the beauty contest because she isn't slim and couldn't, under any circumstances, wear "cute" clothes or have "cute" ways. As to the personality of the Venus who has stood for centuries as the criterion of all feminine beauty, very little is known, but it would seem that she possesses none of the requisites of beauty that Atlanta schoolgirls demand.

—May 27, 1923

What Keeps Women Young Now

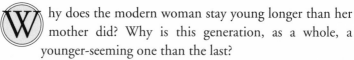 hy does the modern woman stay young longer than her mother did? Why is this generation, as a whole, a younger-seeming one than the last?

Some will argue that this is not the case, but a glance at the old red plush family album (if it has escaped destruction at the hands of the younger generation) will tell the truth of the matter.

Turn over a few pages—and there is Aunt Millie, only thirty

at the time but looking forty. Perhaps the intimidating pompadour and high-boned collar gave her that aged look. Why, Aunt Millie actually looks younger today than when the picture was taken, now that she has had her hair "permed" and her face "lifted."

The day of growing old gracefully had given way to the day when it is a disgrace to grow old without a struggle. Ninetenths of the growing old gracefully theory was compounded of sheer laziness and ignorance and one-tenth fear of ridicule at their struggle with the years.

There was a day—and not so long ago at that—when girls who had not married before reaching the great age of twenty realized that their matrimonial chances were over forever and resigned themselves to being a comfort to their families or teaching school.

There was a day, too—and it was not any more distant than the time when it was *comme il faut* to have red wallpaper in the dining room and conch shells on a whatnot—when all mothers, regardless of their age, looked "motherly," and all respectable matrons wore dark clothes after thirty. After forty, they wore stiff black taffeta. Fifty was the age for lace caps and oblivion.

In short, they grew old gracefully.

Ways of Staying Young

Today there are so many ways of staying attractively young that growing old, either gracefully or disgracefully, has lost its charms.

As long as beauty parlors keep their doors open, the fight against the encroachments of age will continue. Of course, it is a losing fight, for no mortal woman yet has ever beaten Time at his own game. But, at least, it postpones the inevitable day when wrinkles and a double chin betray a woman to be fortyfive, instead of—er—thirty-something!

Beauty specialists say that the reason the women of today keep young-looking until their children's children arise to confront them is that beauty parlors know more of massage and lotions and because more efficient creams and astringents have been compounded to carry on the undying battle with age.

Plastic surgery claims credit for the face-lifting process, which, though not perfected, accomplishes much toward eradicating the tell-tale sag of muscles under the chin.

Doctors triumphantly announce that their generation-old battle on the corset and other injurious feminine foibles has added years to youth.

And a psychologist—who always must be individual—says that the extension of the youth of the women of this generation is a matter of mind and of soul.

"Women of today have plenty to occupy their minds," said the psychological expert. "Formerly, they were required and allowed to do only things that, at best, took little constructive thought. Nursing babies, keeping house, cooking, gossiping were their chief occupations, and they avoided new ideas and intellectual things for fear of being considered 'forward' or a 'bluestocking'—the appellation applied to would-be highbrows in those days.

"As a result, their minds virtually atrophied and a stodginess of body reflected their stodginess of mind. A mind that has no new ideas inevitably shows itself on the face. At first, it is in a blank expression that in youth is frequently mistaken for pretty ingenuousness but which, as the years go on, is likely to degenerate into a fishy stare. Lack of expression in the eyes and the face of a woman over twenty-five makes her look older than any number of wrinkles on the face of a woman of forty who has many interests to claim her.

Better Than Cold Cream

"There are so many things that a woman can do today and so many encouragements offered that there is no reason why a woman should feel that her life is finished, just because she has married, raised a family, and married them off."

"Interest in life or a job, in books or things that go on in the world, clubs of many kinds, charity and settlement work that bring women to grips with Life—those are the things that keep the sparkle in the eye and the spring in the step far more than cold cream."

So says the psychologist, but the beauty experts indignantly defend their own.

"So few people—particularly men—know how much beauty parlors do in rebeautifying women!" declared one small bobbed-haired beauty expert, famous for her relaxing "facials."

"Women are younger to a greater age than ever before now, because they realize how much it means to them, not only to their own vanity but to their families and their employers. The least a woman can give those who love her is youth of face and of mind and of body.

"And beauty parlors aid them in doing this.

"Nowadays, there are so many more ways of smoothing out wrinkles than ever before. There are a thousand and one chemical astringents that draw up sagging muscles; there are clays of every color and thickness and strength for closing large pores that leaded rouge and improper cleansing have made in faces and noses.

"For oily skins that make a woman look greasy, old, and unkempt, there are astringents. For the scaly noses and cheeks, there are creams that cleanse and feed the skin back to smoothness.

Lines Massaged Away

"But these are what do most of the work," she smiled, stretching out a pair of small but muscular hands. "Women don't wait till they are old and wrinkled to have their faces massaged and smoothed of the tiny little lines that sooner or later become wrinkles. I have more girls as customers who are between the ages of fifteen and twenty-five than I do older women.

"These girls are sensible enough to come in and have the tiredness rubbed off of their faces while the muscles are still springy and firm. They do not wait till years of nerve strain and irritation have drawn a line between their eyes and at the corners. They immediately have the lines from nostril to mouth massaged away before years of being weary without facial relaxation has aged them.

"And permanents! Some like them—and some don't. It's all a matter of taste and type of hair. I do think sincerely, however, that more middle-aged women have been improved by permanent waves than by any other one thing. The old system of curling hair on hot irons was injurious, if continued too long, and besides it was so tiresome and inconvenient that many women preferred being straggly-haired to taking the trouble every day."

"Health is what makes the women of today superior to those of yesterday, not only in youthful appearance but every way," was the opinion of the doctor who, though middle-aged, has very modern ideas.

"Today women are more sensible about the clothes they wear. Oh, I know that moralists rave about the Girl of Today not wearing enough clothes, and say that bathing suits are a disgrace and her chiffon stockings and sleeveless dresses in midwinter are suicidal!

"But compare her with the woman of yesterday, and then you will understand how women with grown families manage to look slim and full of vitality instead of being washed out and forever ailing.

"The women of this and the last generation have been sensible in not wearing tight-laced corsets and clothes that fitted too closely. In addition, they have refused to coddle themselves or to believe that a breath of wind would blow them away!

"The women of today realize how much it means to remain young and how fairly easy it is if they start early in the game and take care of themselves."

—August 8, 1923

Boyish Bob Brings Back Corset

tylish stouts, women with figures, girls with long hair, and all female persons possessed of large feet and thick ankles, will groan aloud at the spring styles.

Piquant girls, with flat figures and "boyish bobbed" hair, will hail them with glad acclaim, for they are the very persons responsible for the spring styles.

Who would have thought that when the Chinese bob gave way to the "boyish bob" (or the "wet seal" bob as it is better known), that the styles of hats, coats, suits, and even shoes would have changed to keep the hair company? But such is the case, for the boyish bobbed coiffure has completely revolutionized the world of fashion—even to figures!

Corsets are coming back!

The starving corset makers are chanting paeans of thanks to the shingle-haired girls whose shorn appearance and boyish clothes have made corsets a necessity. The style in figures this season is no figure—just as the style in waistline is no waistline. To be chic and able to wear the swagger little suits, tiny cloche hats, and Puritan pumps, one must have a flat, boyish figure.

"And the only way to get the slim, uncorseted, boyish figure," announced a leading French designer, "is to wear a corset that will give it to you!"

Behold the Springtime Girl of 1924

She wears a "boyish bob," that is, her hair is a quarter of an inch long on the back of her head and three or four inches long in front. It is plastered down to her head, after the manner of a wet seal, with stickum swiped from her brother's bureau, giving her head a sleek, small boy appearance. A tiny cloche hat, small enough to preclude suspicion of either brains or hair, is tilted over one eye. The other eye is completely hidden.

Her silhouette is straight and boyish. Her severely cut tailleur is eight inches from the ground. Her short coat is straight in both back and front and almost squarely cut. The pockets of the coat, in which her hands are jammed, are large and well defined. Two buttons hold the coat in place. The lapels are notched in a thoroughly masculine style. A gaudy handkerchief peeks out of a breast pocket; across the flaming silk vest under her coat is draped a small watch chain, running from pocket to pocket; on her feet are colonial pumps, square-toed and possessed of enormous buckles; in her hand is a walking cane; her carriage is erect and swaggering (surely this can't be the girl who was the exponent of the debutante slouch three years ago)!

That is the spring girl of 1924. And the "boyish bob" started it all. Everything is boyish this season to match the sleek and bandolined hair of the girls. Unfortunately, Fate has not been kind enough to endow every woman with the pert face and flat figure requisite for the wearing of bobbed-tailed tailleurs and heavily beaded tunics—or Puritan pumps—so adorably clumsy on a tiny foot—and just clumsy on a large one!

Exactly what these women, who constitute about nine-tenths of the feminine world, will do about these styles, is a mystery, but they will probably manage to make out on the infinite numbers of variations of the boyish silhouette that fashion offers.

Futurist Prints

The boyish lines of the tailored suit, so essential to every woman's wardrobe this season, do not vary in their severity though the buttons, or the lack of buttons, and the length of the coat is subject to the whim of the wearer. The most popular model is the "bobbed-tailed" coats, square cut and scarcely more than a jacket worn with a tightly-fitting wrap around the skirt; others show the Chinese influence, still in vogue from last season, and reach below the knee, like Mandarin coats. All tailored coats, however, are cut on straight lines minus the barest hint of a waistline.

Beneath these swagger coats are vivid "wes'kits," imparting a still more mannish air. These little vests are of futurist printed silk, some cut so high that only the severe collar of the blouse is visible; others are of somber colors, more on the lines of a man's Tuxedo vest. These dark "wes'kits," however, are atoned for by the flaming "stock" collars and ties that wrap themselves snugly high about the wearer's neck and flaunt their loose ends in the breeze.

These stock collars and scarves are but another variation of the scarf which is more popular this season than ever before. The new scarves are longer and narrower, and the fringe is deeper, showing the Spanish influence. Scarves are now worn with every sort of costume from morning dresses to formal evening gown. Heretofore, the scarf was the property solely of the sport dress, but it has now invaded the field of afternoon and evening frocks in trappings of chiffon and georgette, instead of knitted silk and fuzzy wool.

Scarves for afternoon and evening dresses are of the filmiest of chiffon or georgette, embroidered or delicately fringed. Some are heavily beaded at the ends to give weight and color to the ephemeral appearing silken rags. There is no smarter accompaniment to the white sleeveless crêpe de Chine dresses that promises to be so popular than a brightly colored chiffon scarf to supply the relieving note of color.

The silk embroidered sweaters, hanging straight and unbelted below the hips, are also equipped with silk scarves to match. The fringe of the gracefully draped scarves is invaluable in relieving the severity of the unbroken line from the neck nearly to the knee.

"Mantilla" Hat

Before the opening of each spring season the feminine world is all agog to know what nation will cast its influence over the frocks of the coming season. In the past few years the Turkish, the Chaive Souris of the Russians, the King Tut of the Egyptians, the Mandarins of the Chinese have cast their colorful shadows over the crystal ball and then silently folded their tents and stolen away, leaving women to wonder whether the Hottentots or the Esquimaux would next send an ambassador to the court of Fashion.

However, all minds are relieved at the announcement that Russia, or rather Tartary, is back again and that Spain is sponsoring the fringed scarf, the lace "mantilla" hat and the embroidered shawl dress.

The shawl dress, Carmenesque in its vividness of flaming flowers embroidered on heavy crêpe de Chine, will be of especial interest to tall, slender women who can lend these dashing dresses the grace that their carelessly draped folds demand. So cleverly are these dresses contrived that they give the appearance of a long fringed shawl flung negligently about the body of the wearer.

The Tartar influence is felt more in the designs of printed silks than in the lines of frocks. Leon Bakst, designer of the costumes and scenery of the Russian ballet, has turned his versatile hand to the designing of printed silks—with the result that King Tut, his flaming chariots and warriors have beat an ignominious defeat.

A potent rival to the strictly tailored suit is the tailored morning dress, usually made of rep silk, alpaca, satin, moire, or plaid material. There are several versions. There is the straight, long, beltless tunic that comes to the bottom of the skirt. There is the straight dress with the circular movement at the very bottom of the skirt. There is the occasional model with an apron effect achieved by a pleated overskirt.

Extremes Frowned Down

White collars of all tailored types are seen on these dresses. Sleeves are long and tight with a tiny cuff or band of piqué to match the collars. Many of these models in alpaca and moire sound the boyish note by showing the tunic unbuttoned, seemingly from neck to waist, displaying beneath a surplice vest of white satin that is startling against the darkness of the tailored material.

Hats are small. Of course spring hats are always small, but the hats of the present season are unbelievably tiny. Sponsored, as they are, by the "boyish bob" hair, it is remarkable that any woman still possessing all the hair nature bestowed upon her can get her head into one of the tightly fitting cloches—or, having once gotten in, remain with any degree of comfort.

These little hats come low over the face, hiding most of the eyes and shadowing the nose so low that hardly a strand of hair is visible. For the most part, the tailored hats are devoid of trimming, save for a band of ribbon of the same shade as the hat. The afternoon hats are of the same shape, close fitting and down-turned, and nearly all trimmed with soft black lace that hangs still further over the face. One wonders how women are to see at all this spring.

An innovation in veil pins that is especially attractive on cloches is the narrow band of rhinestone, stretching in semi-circular form half around the brim of the hat and twinkling up from the soft folds of the black lace.

Fashion frowns on extremes in evening dresses and favors the simplicity of line so charming to behold and so difficult to wear with any degree of feminine satisfaction.

The evening dresses of the spring follow the same boyish lines of tailleurs and afternoon frocks. The evening silhouette remains predominantly narrow with no waistline or with a straight bodice which has sashlike drapery caught lightly at the waistline. These sheathlike dresses are modest of décolletage, higher in the front than the back and not exaggerated in either direction.

Fish Fin Effect

The straight-hanging, barbarically beaded tunic is still "good" for the spring, though rather in the nature of a survival than a new factor of the mode. These beaded dresses are of the most part sleeveless and beltless and of such fragile chiffon and georgette that one wonders how material so airy can support such a weight of colorful beads.

The lace evening dress is firmly established and has brought with it the airy ingenue dress of tulle. These dresses are in all light colors, though predominantly in whites and creams, so that they may be worn to charming advantage over slips of various colors. The embroidered net dresses, heavy with padded flowers in raised silk, set off to advantage by medallions and insertions of filet, are of especial interest, as they are designed for afternoon and informal semi-evening wear as well.

Chiffon, georgette, lace, tulle, and net seem the more fa-
vored of the season's material for formal evening wear, especially in all shades of rose, from pink to dahlia.

The types of afternoon frocks that promise to be seen everywhere are first, the solid white sleeveless crêpe de Chine, a relic
of the last season which has survived because of its appealing
simplicity—and second, the printed crêpe de Chine. Endless
enchanting designs are available in the latter. These afternoon
frocks are, for the greater part, one-piece models of simple and
slender line, in recognition of the strikingly decorative quality
of the futurist patterned fabric. The short sleeve is invariable.

—*March 23, 1924*

The Cat Has No Pajamas

Along With the "Eel's Heel," the Feline's Pajamas Have
Become One With Ninevah and Tyre. "Banana Oil" Is the
Newest Thing in Slang, Superseding "Apple Sauce" of Last
Year. "Cake Eater" Has Turned Into "Puncher."

Fashion is fickle in all things, from the position of waist
lines to the size of tips, but nowhere is She more
changeable than in slang expressions. Well-loved bits,
such as "skidoo" and "good night," date one at 1910 and 1917,
whereas the use of "peach" and "lollapaloosa" immediately rele-
gate the user to the Black Walnut era of American history.

In slang, as in dress and manner, one must be up to date and
not shame kind friends and loving relatives by using last year's
expressions among strangers who do not understand and love
you despite your clinging to old-fashioned mannerisms.

Perhaps the most notable of this year's changes is the superseding of "apple sauce" by "banana oil." "Apple sauce" has folded

its tent and silently stolen away into the limbo of lost slang, leaving the phrase of similar meaning but of more blasting force and virile nature to take its place in the great American vocabulary.

"Banana oil" is a phrase of derision, of unbelief. It challenges any statement from the permanency of prohibition to the hope of a hereafter. It slides glibly off the tongue and if given the proper intonation, "banana ROIL," is guaranteed to disconcert any voice of authority raised in protest against the younger generation.

Cat's Pajamas Are no More

The "wise cracker" has metamorphosed into the "salt shaker" and the "cake eater" into the "puncher." Likewise, the "cat's pajamas" and the "eel's heels" and the rest of the zoological ilk have gone the way of all slang, and the "fly paper spats" and the "fur-lined bath tubs" are one with Ninevah and Tyre.

"I'm sunk," or "that sinks me," has superseded "that defeats me," and "I'm laid out" has taken the place of "I've much too much." A girl "stands a man up" on a date, now, whereas she used to "throw him down."

To give an example of the constantly changing status of words and of slang, the following is a conversation between two girls concerning a party:

"I cantered over with my hommy and a couple of other punchers and their Sals but found the party was a flat tire from beginning to end. A puncture if ever I saw one. Not a drop of rat poison in the place. It was a parlor rodeo with only a few balloons and gobs of pilliwinks. There was one hoof an' mouther who was keen file, but I couldn't get my hooks into him and he cramped my style so that I couldn't strut my material for icicles. There were some red flannels chaperoning with their frozen-faced oaken buckets. I prettied up my smeller and up anchored and crawled through the keyhole and we went where we could break ankles in peace.

Father Bayed the Moon

"I got home at two o'clock and Father was up waiting for me and talked just like a costume picture. If I had been dressed up, drunk and highly perfumed, he would have had something to make a chautauqua over, but just getting home late is nothing to bay the moon about."

A translation of the above is as involved as that given by the "White Knight" to the bewildered "Alice" after she had read the poem he had composed:

'Twas brillig and the slithly towthes
Did jire and jimble in the wabe,
All mimsy were the barragoes
And the mome rath, out grabe.

In simple language, a flapper (now "Sal") was voicing disgust at having been roped in on a nice, pure party when she was expecting a jazzy one. She attended the party with her "hommy" (here current "sweetie," taken from *mon homme,* my man) and two young men who were designated last year as "cake eaters" or "drug-store cowboys" but are simply "punchers" in this season's argot. The two punchers had their own "Sals" with them.

The party did not live up to expectations. It was what would have been called "eggy" last year, or a "frost" the year before. It is a "puncture" now. There was no rat poison (whisky) at the party, as it was a "parlor rodeo" (a bridge party). There were only a few "balloons" (who were "speedy birds" a year ago) and many "pilliwinks." Pilliwinks were "sad birds" in former days, "eggs," or people of either sex who "hadn't went out much."

The "hoof an' mouther," or just plain "hoofer," referred to

with evident admiration, is no longer a dancer but a golfer, a term derived from the time-honored joke about all golfers suffering from the hoof and mouth disease, as they hoofed all day and mouthed all night. But the Sal was unable to "vamp" (now an obsolete term) the hoofer as her "hommy" was a "spare tire" about the matter. She had him "on her hip," which is about the same as having someone "on your hands" whom you cannot shake off.

The presence of the "red flannels" and their "oaken buckets" (middle-aged and disapproving chaperones and their husbands) so depressed the Sal that she decided to leave the "rodeo" and the "keen file hoofer" ("keen file" being a term of approbation borrowed from a West Point expression). So she "prettied up her smeller" (powdered her nose) and "up anchored" which is equivalent to "selling out." The Sal then went to a dance where she could dance in peace without the disapproving gaze of chaperones.

On arriving home at a late hour, her father voiced parental objections, in no weak tones ("talked like a costume picture"). The virtuous Sal, feeling that she had been unjustly lectured to, voiced the opinion that as she had come home sober, there was nothing for father to "take on about" ("do a Chautauqua.")

Flapperese is a language that would defy the best efforts of Egyptologists to translate or of Esperantoists to manufacture, yet it slides as glibly off the tongues of the flippant young as baby talk from a child.

—June 29, 1924

Gum Chewed at Both
Weddings and Funerals

T he universe, so scientists declare, is forever moving in cycles, and this includes all things from glacial ages to high waistlines. If one waits long enough, all things that have once enjoyed a vogue will return to their own again.

But no one ever expected good manners to come back into style. Good manners became obsolete in 1918. But good manners are the style once more.

Not the good manners of '18, to be sure, or the courtesy of the '90s, but a definite, standardized code of good manners has been established after a six-year "reign of terror." And this definite code is nothing new and revolutionary that the flappers will have to sit up late of nights studying. The manners of 1924 are nothing at all except the standardized bad manners of 1918— which have been in use so long that they have become accepted.

Where once the mark of a gentleman was his faintly deferential bearing to women and his courtesy, the distinguishing mark today is his insolence of air. To attain social prominence nowadays a young man must cultivate a studiedly insolent air, as insolent as that of a superior waiter who feels that his tip has not been large enough. The mark of a feminine so-called favorite is her ability always to interrupt conversations at interesting points with a remark on how bored she is.

Six years ago, such conduct would have been condemned, and those guilty would "not have been received"—dear old phrase! Nowadays, with bad manners wearing the habiliments of respectability, the insolence and the boredom are the expected thing.

True enough, in the process of standardization, the more glaring points of bad taste, so popular in 1919, have passed from usage. For instance, the hopelessly vulgar and the unintentionally rude no longer enjoy the prominence they once did. The studiedly ill-bred are the social lions and lionesses.

Older Generations Swooned

Six years ago, bad manners that are now standardized and accepted caused insulted fathers to request that certain young men never darken their doors again and mothers to talk at length and with pungency on how things were different when they were girls.

Six years is not a very long time as time goes. Six years ago, the war was ending, and men paid party calls and danced with unattractive visitors, didn't get too drunk in too public places, or tell other men what they really thought of their girls, and girls didn't chew gum at both weddings and funerals (but only at funerals), and young people always rose when elderly ladies entered rooms and men raised their hats when they met ladies and waited till lades spoke before they spoke and—but why enumerate? That was six years ago.

The older generation swooned at the lack of manners that characterized the youngsters and prophesied the utter collapse of the whole social system, based as it was on courtesy and a colossal fabric of lies. What was to become of society if everyone told the blatant truth, and rudeness was the open sesame to popularity?

But horrified as the elders of the tribe might be, they had to put up with the new rudeness. From 1918 to 1923, bad manners and lack of breeding ran rampant. The men who could stage epic drunks and direct orchestras with forks, or organize rowing crews on ballroom floors, were acclaimed social lights, as were the girls who shouted loudest about the most obvious things.

Hostesses Always Insulted

Hostesses expected to be insulted to their faces by invited guests and to be agreeable to numbers of uninvited ones. "Stags" never thought of dancing, but merely organized a Supreme Court in the middle of floors to pass, coolly, on the merits and demerits of the girls dancing by. In the cruel process of elimination, girls who were "wash-outs" but who, in prewar days, had enjoyed themselves, to a lesser degree, of course, than their more fortunate sisters, because of the prevailing customs of courtesy, were put out of the running. Only the girls who "knew their stuff" could pass the muster of the stag line, for it possessed as much of the quality of mercy as the judges of a Bolshevik court.

So the elders held up their hands and swooned, but after all, one cannot remain in a swoon over a long period of years, and hands become intolerably heavy after being raised in condemnation year in and year out.

So the parents capitulated, reluctantly enough, and in the process, the bad manners that had shocked them in 1919 became standardized. It is the unprecedented that shocks and after manners have been in vogue five years, they have been established traditions, and no matter how bad they were originally, they are acceptable later to the best people.

Six years ago, when a young man called on the damsel of his delight, he parked his car outside of her house, rang the bell, was admitted, took his seat in the parlor, and waited patiently till his "date" finished fixing her hair for the tenth time. Sometimes, the small brother or sister was sent in to "entertain" till the primping was finished. Sometimes, Father or Mother assumed the responsibility and inflicted political opinions and salad recipes on the polite but impatient visitor.

When the daughter of the house finally chose to make her entrance, it was the part of a gentleman to rise quickly with a smile and say, "No, I've just been here a moment. How sweet you look."

The Egg Arrives

Nowadays, the date rolls up in front of the house, stops the car and blows the horn. He makes no attempt at getting out. If the girl does not immediately respond, he keeps his hand on the horn, making the air hideous until the lady fair puts her head out of an upper window and shouts, "Cut it out, you egg! I'm coming."

It was the part of 1918 to leap from the car and assist a lady into her seat, closing the door easily. Nowadays, the date merely kicks open the door languidly and says, "What do you do with your time? You don't wear enough to take that long to dress."

Who pays party calls, nowadays? No one, of course. Hostesses do not expect it. They are grateful enough if invited guests actually put in their appearances on the night of the party and remain to the end, without making derogatory remarks upon the nature of the entertainment. Yet it was not so long ago that hostesses "talked about" young girls who did not pay calls and boys who failed to pay attention to unattractive visitors for whose special benefit they had been invited.

In 1918, hostesses did a favor when they invited guests to parties. The shoe is on the other foot now. Guests do hostesses a favor if they come to the party at all, or stay over a half an hour after having arrived. Hostesses no longer go into tantrums at "the ill-bred behavior of that young man who was escorting poor, dear Susan to the country club and left her flat after he had been stuck with her four dances." The affair is regrettable, of course, but then if Susan had . . . really nice girl would attend. Sweet-voiced girls sit in ringside seats and lustily encourage fighters to tear each other limb from limb.

No More Pistols at Sunrise

Not so long ago, it would have meant pistols and coffee at

sunrise for one young blade to tell another uncomplimentary things about his girlfriends. But the disconcerting frankness of comment, these days, on the merits of one's girlfriends has become accepted. If one's opinion has been solicited concerning a girl, one may say with perfect safety that she is dumb or an oil can or dances like a grain elevator or has a face that only a mother could love.

Chewing gum was the last word in bad taste in the not-so-long-ago. Chewing gum and an inordinate amount of cosmetics stamped a girl as vulgar. In 1924, debutantes in imported dresses chew their cuds at the most formal affairs. No one thinks it vulgar to see the pretty jaws of a whole receiving line at a debut party moving rhythmically. True, the modern make-up has toned down slightly from what it was four years ago. It is no longer quite *au fait* to appear in public painted like a Totem pole, but a healthy coat of rouge and a vivid lip stick are permissible, providing the wearer is not attempting to make the observer believe it is natural.

Six years ago, elderly ladies were held in esteem, or at least were accorded outward respect, no matter if they were confirmed reputation ruiners, acid of tongue, or feeble-minded of intellect. The mere fact that they were elderly made young girls rise pleasantly and remain standing when they entered a room, or stop and chat with them a moment when they lined the walls in the chaperone's corner at dances.

But now, the mere fact of a woman having grown old does not entitle her to respect in the eyes of the coming generation. Anyone, according to their viewpoint, can get old. Genuine accomplishment and worth alone will bring the post-flapper generation to its feet when a gray-haired woman enters. If she "knows her stuff" she will be given the respect due her. If she is simply an "old cat" or a "fat sister," in the common parlance, then the youngsters are likely to remain sprawled on their backbones in their chairs when she enters and greet her with a casual "'Lo."

If this be rudeness, make the most of it. At best it is a code of courtesy based solely on worth—on knowledge of "one's stuff." At worst, the standardized bad manners of 1924 make social opportunity a survival of the fittest in which those heretofore sheltered unfortunates who don't "know their stuff" are eliminated.

—August 17, 1924

What Makes the Pretty Girl Pretty?

What makes the pretty girl pretty, in 1925?

Ox eyes; an eighteen-inch waist with generous billowings both above and below; a tender, helpless, appealing smile; pale, translucent skin?

Oh, no!

Beauty in 1925 is not so much how you look as how you act. Beauty, according to the schoolgirls of Agnes Scott, North Avenue Presbyterian School, Washington Seminary, and Woodberry Hall—who have recently elected their prettiest girls—consists of:

➤ Nimble feet in sheer chiffon hose and high-heel French slippers.
➤ A fast and clever line of chatter about nothing at all.
➤ A hint of mystery coupled with apparent frankness.
➤ Stylish clothes fitted to a "trim, flat li'l figger."
➤ "A smile that won't come off."
AND—
(Breath easily, O Victorians!)
➤ Sweetness and modesty!

Ruth Miller, member of Washington Seminary Glee Club, contributed the last named requisite of beauty amid cries of acclamation and leers of disputation from her fellow Glee Club members.

"Sweetness, simplicity, and modesty make a girl just as pretty and attractive as they did a hundred years ago," she insisted. "I guess I ought to know. I've a brother and I have to listen to all his remarks about girls, and I know how much boys appreciate modesty."

Unanimous on Clothes

"Modesty may be an asset, all right," said Laura Candler, "if it comes under the general head of 'personality.' 'Personality' is beauty, wit and cleverness of line, pep—and clothes."

"Yes, clothes," chorused the Glee Club, agreeing unanimously for the first time.

"A girl can't be pretty without snappy clothes," declared Dorothy Bauman, of New Orleans. "That is, unless she is one of those beauties fated to be beautiful, even with cold cream on her face and a bath towel round her head. But there aren't enough of those to really count. Clothes make or break a girl. Clothes and the way a girl wears them."

"The way a girl wears her clothes is more beauty than the kind of clothes she wears—that's part of 'personality,'" argued Laura Candles, warming up on her subject.

"Animation is the secret of all beauty," declared Virginia Thurman. "Wear a smile that won't come off and always have something clever to say and cute ways to go with your line, and who's going to know or care whether you are beautiful or not?"

Neatness and Grace

"Neatness," ventured Sara Sanders, who was presiding as president of the Glee Club, "neatness is a very great help to beauty, and without it no girl can be really striking. It doesn't matter how stunning her eyes or stylish her clothes if her hair is tousled and rough and her skirt sags and her dress has spots on it and her heels run down, ever so little—then she can't be beautiful."

"Gracefulness of figure, especially in dancing, is beauty," said Margery Feagle. "Grace and poise can make anyone forget to notice if your eyes are a bit too small and your nose a trifle more upturned than can be politely called *retroussé*. But even if you have the eyes of Barbara LaMarr and the figure of Aileen Pringle, it won't do you any good if you have no poise and chew your fingernails and squirm your feet around."

"Poise and serenity," added Lois Dobson.

"A good all-round girl who is a good sport, who is always ready to do anything the crowd wants to do, and doesn't whine when she fails to get her own way is usually beautiful" was the opinion of Lucy Marion. "That kind of a girl, as a rule, is athletic and can swim and play a cracking good game of tennis and meet men on their own ground."

"Good grooming makes a beautiful woman," said Julia Ruth Turnbow, of Houston, Tex. "Good grooming means clean, smooth skin, well-tended hands and glossy hair, and the skillful, very careful use of cosmetics. Nothing so ruins a face as daubing too much paint on the cheeks and scarlet on the lips."

"Style, pep, and personality," summed up the opinion of Catherine Ginn, vice president of the Glee Club.

Handsome is as Handsome Does

And when they had rushed out of the room, laughing and talking, munching on recess sandwiches, it suddenly dawned on the interviewer that no one had mentioned faces, eyes, teeth, curls, complexions—all of which made up beauty in the old days.

Evidently, "handsome is as handsome does" was never truer than in 1925!

The girls of Woodberry Hall were very definite in their ideas of what constitutes feminine beauty.

"First of all, trim ankles, wicked dancing feet in sheer, chiffon stockings, and darling little slippers with little heels no thicker than your thumb," said Marion Morgan. "Nowadays, the first things people look at are your feet, and if they look cute enough they don't bother with your face!"

"A perfect 34," declared Peggy Greenwood. "A nice, little, trim, flat, boyish figger in tailored, well-fitting clothes can make a beautiful impression even if you haven't ox eyes and teeth like pearls."

"Intelligence enough to think up a dumb line of conversation so that boys will think themselves superior to you and love you for it," announced Virginia Boyer "That may or may not be beauty, but it passes for it on most occasions, especially where men are the judges."

"Clothes," said Betty Brown. "And cute ways, individual little tricks all your own that a man begins to look for and associate with your personality. And clothes that suit your ways."

A Good Line

"A good line," said Susan Livingston. "A line that isn't the same any two times and changes every five minutes—a line about nothing at all—a line that works in nicely with good dancing and loud music. And—"

"And twinkling eyes," interrupted Betty Stribling. "Not giggling eyes, but eyes that go with a poised face, that seem to be always twinkling as if you knew something awfully amusing that you MIGHT tell if sufficiently encouraged."

"Yes, that's good, and a part of being beautiful because it's a part of being mysterious and a hint of the mysterious is better than several pounds of intellectuality" was the sage opinion of Jane Clarke. "A man likes a good scout and a good sport and a playfellow, but he thinks there's nothing more beautiful than just a faint trace of something he can't quite understand."

"There's no such thing as looking beautiful in the same way all the time. Beauty consists of looking pretty but in a different way every time a man comes to see you," said Julia Clendenin.

"Pretty teeth," said Eleanor McHahon, "pretty teeth that show every time you smile make a beautiful face, because people begin to watch for your smile and say things just to make you laugh. But your teeth and smile don't do you any good if you smoke or cuss or use slang."

"Graceful, well-kept hands, expressively used," was Kate Rogers's opinion.

"Pep," said Auverne Harper, who was chosen the prettiest brunette at Woodberry, as Dorothy Mahoney was chosen prettiest blonde. "Without pep the most beautiful face soon gets passé-looking."

Pep. Personality. Chiffon sox. Flat figures. Dancing feet. "Lines." Modesty. . . . Everything except faces! The girls of today are in the same position of the sailor man in *Hula Lou,* who, after enumerating the charms of his Hawaiian girl, from her toes to her throat, finshed up that—

"I never even noticed her face!"

—*March 22, 1925*

All Dolled Up Like French Pastry

—◦◦◦—

That's One of the Newest Gems in Atlanta's 1925 Vocabulary of Slang. Others Are: "Well Meaning—Just Like Poison Ivy," "What's Your Wavelength, Dearie?" and "Why Cry Over Spilt Milk. Call in the Cat."

—◦◦◦—

W ould you know a "wet smack" if you met one?

And could you define, off hand, a "bush ape"?

If you decided "to wap," what would be your first steps in that direction?

It's no reflection not to know the meaning of these words. No one, except perhaps the brisk young people who coin them and whose main object in life is keeping up with the swiftly changing slang styles, could be expected to know that "cat nip" is no longer a dried weed that makes cats leap and prance, "brawl" no longer a fight in which knuckle-dusters and police billies figure prominently, and "fumbler" not a football term.

Styles in slang, like those in clothes and manners, change rapidly, and the winter season of 1925 ushers in some very interesting new slang words, phrases, and sentences.

A "wet smack" is an unfortunate person who in former times was easily recognized under the various names of a "total loss," a "flat tire," a "sad bird," a "washout," a "pill," or a "poor fish." A "wet smack," or one who is "all wet and a yard wide," implies a congenital condiditon. One is born a "wet smack"—as opposed to "bush apes," who usually acquire their characteristics later in life.

A "bush ape" is an undependable guy with a lot of nerve or brass. He is the kind who borrows your pearl shirt studs and forgets to return them. He is conveniently called to the telephone about the time the waiter approaches with the bill. It has been rumored that "bush apes" take girls on automobile rides

MARGARET MITCHELL: REPORTER

and not only permit, but insist, that they walk home. There are female "bush apes," of course, but the male of the species exceeds the female, three to one.

What's a "Wapper"?

"Wapper" is the noun of the new verb "to wap," meaning to reduce one's weight. "Wapping" includes diet and "daily dozens," as well as the tortures of Madame Takemoff's rubber reducing garments and the consumption of vinegar, lemon juice, etc., which plump damsels fondly believe will make them shed pounds as a snake shakes his skin. Fits of temper and temperament on the part of usually agreeable young women can easily be explained by the remark "Poor kid—she's on an awful wap, you know."

"Cat nip" is a crushing retort, designed to show incredulity. It is most effective when delivered with coolness and a touch of hauteur when someone is trying to palm off a line of obvious hokum as the truth. Formerly, "cat nip" was "banana oil," "boloney," "apple sauce," and, at a date, now shrouded in the mists of antiquity, "bull." A pleasant variant of the "cat nip" type of "come back" is to wait until a long and unconvincing speil has been handed out, and then remark, apropos of nothing at all, "And just then the shovel broke," or "Oysters don't get sunburn," or "Snakes wear no garters," or "Snow balls don't bounce," or any number of totally irrelevant statements. This brand of retort is most popular because, like the "eel's heels" and the "bee's knees" and the "cut-glass flyswatters" of other seasons, it allows a wide range for originality.

And "hopscotch"—no, it's not the game Mother used to play when she was a girl. Now it's usually a game that girls play on Mother. "Hopscotch" is a wide term, meaning variously to "get away with something," as, for instance, "I had Mother completely hopscotched. She never knew what time I got home from that dance." It may mean "playing around," as "I've ditched the Gamma Gamma Gamma tong and am hopscotching the Delta Delta Deltas." Sometimes it is an equivalent to having no excuse or "come back"—"I had no hopscotch when Bill saw me with Tom after I had told him I was sick in bed."

"Tearing Off Mushrooms"

As for "tong," mentioned in the paragraph above, it has completely lost its Oriental significance. The Hip Sings and the On Leongs would never recognize it. It means the particular "gang," "crowd," "frat," or "bunch" that one "hopscotchs."

And "mushrooms"—oh, yes, a light of recognition dawns in all eyes. They are the first cousins of toadstools and are very tasty when served up with steak and thick gravy.

Wrong again!

"Mushrooms" were once "wild oats," supposedly sown by every college boy before his senior year. Now he "picks" or "tears off mushrooms." This phrase does not carry all the weight of vice, wine, women, and song that lurked in "wild oats," but nearly approxiamtes it. However, the phrase "she knows her mushrooms," like "she knows her eggs" or "her onions," is one of commendation casting no slur on manners or morals, but merely expressing what was formerly meant by "she knows her stuff."

Mrs. Astor's overworked "plush horse" and the "sore thumb" of by-gone days are no longer called in when comparisons of sartorial glory are needed. Now it's "all dolled up like a French pastry."

Likewise, a new phrase is in vogue to describe the opposite condition. The 1925 model young lady, looking into the mirror and disappointed in what it shows her, no longer remarks that she looks "like Mrs. Devil," or "like an accident looking for some place to happen," or "the advance agent of a famine."

She graphically describes herself as looking "like Death's little playmate," and lets it go at that.

No Rival for "Sheik"

Strangely enough, the fall season has so far developed no new equivalent for "sheik," which admittedly has become somewhat threadbare from overuse. About the only variation is to nominate the sheik "Old Mahatma Ghandi himself," or "the local Abd-el-Krim," or some popular Oriental character.

Girls have ceased to be "janes," "flappers," "members," "ribs," "Shebas," etc. They are "shes." They may be "static shes" (formerly "dumbbells" or "dumb Doras"), "smooth shes" (who know their stuff), "wet shes" (utterly hopeless), but always "shes." There may be Banshes, too, for all we know, but, to date, nothing has been heard of them.

Among other additions and changes in the winter slang are "cookie pusher" and "divan demon," for "cake eater" and "lounge lizard" or "tea hound"; "fumbler" and "muffler," for inexpert "petters" or "neck artists"; "nifty" for "wise crack"; "blime" (word of two syllables with accent on the first) for "cuckoo"; "hoister," a word culled from the criminal world, for "gold digger"; "mullet" for "sap" or "boob"; "tight rope" for "pulling a bone" or "making a break"; "poison oak" for "chaperone"; "cokey" for feeling "dopey" or "pepless"; "cord" for "bunch" or "raft" (as a cord of college boys); "bicker" for "had a quarrel."

Two words that are not especially new but still retain their popularity are "fruit" and "brawl." "Old fruit," "my deah fruit" are synonymous with "old dear," "old top," etc., and "brawl" means a lively party. "To throw a brawl" is the usual form of expression, instead of "to give a party."

Phrases, some new and some not so new, that are popular with the younger set, include:

"Put that in your compact and puff it."

"Reline your brakes, my good man!"

"She's not in my orchard, old fruit!"

"What's your wave length, dearie?"

"Why cry over spilt milk? Call in the cat."

"So full of ideas there's an S. R. O. sign hung on his ear."

"He's the big-hearted butter-and-egg man from out West."

"He's no sheik—he's a mail order Mahomet."

"One of those bathroom baritones." (Evidently the eighteenth commandment abolished the "whisky tenor.")

"Not so dusty." ("Very good, indeed.")

"Pardon me, I forgot I wasn't at the Biltmore."

"He think's he's a why-girls-leave-homer."

"He's got a face like a bird bath."

"One foot in the grave and the other on a banana peel."

"Well meaning—just like poison ivy."

— October 27, 1925

2

The Debutante & the "New Woman"

Mitchell made her debut to Atlanta society but, as was trendy among her debutante friends, chose a day job over bridge days, and joined the staff of the *Atlanta Journal Magazine* soon after the end of the 1920–1921 debutante season. The staff of the magazine posed for this photo around editor Medora Field Perkerson (seated).

Society Girls Take Up Business

I f you were young and pretty and liked to sleep in the mornings till you just had time to motor to bridge luncheons fashionably late, would you like to tear yourself from your bed at seven o'clock and rush off to town on a street car, where an unfeeling typewriter engaged your attention instead of a hand of bridge—if you did not have to?

If you had pretty feet and chiffon-clad ankles made to stretch luxuriously in automobiles, would you deliberately imperil those dainty feet in crowded six P. M. street cars, where every "up to the front, please" surge would mash them?

And if your well-manicured hands were your abiding pride and joy, would you like to wear the skin off them, holding on to a strap in a "jolly trolley" that wasn't so jolly after a hard day's work in an office?

And lastly, if you had parents who were in the habit of being most liberal in the way of allowances and quite human even when you ran up bills that you knew you shouldn't have— would you forswear your allowance and work for soulless corporations who did not half appreciate how valuable you were to them?

Would you?

Many Atlanta girls, whose ideas of passing the time lay heretofore in terms of bridge parties, shopping, and golfing at country clubs are now doing these things. In fact, so many well-known Atlanta girls are working in offices, substituting in the public schools, doing designing, and running shops, that their less industrious friends are coming to the point of envy instead of pity.

Now, on every side you hear, "Really, my dear, I wish I did have something to do with my time. But I am so dumb. I can't do anything."

"I Seen Your Picture"

Venice Mayson, daughter of Mr. and Mrs. James L. Mayson, of 274 Ponce de Leon, who has the distinction of being one of Atlanta's best dancers, has been "substituting" for regular teachers in Atlanta public schools for the last two years.

"I will never forget my first class," she laughed. "It scared me so that my career as a teacher very nearly ended right there. It was a sixth grade, and when I walked in and faced those forty-five pairs of curious eyes, my knees simply knocked together! I managed to look properly stern until a boy in the back of the room piped up and said, 'Oh, Miss Mayson, I seen your picture in the paper!'

"'On, no, you didn't,' I contradicted, severely, 'And don't say seen!'

"But do you think that quieted him? No, indeed. He produced a greasy Sunday paper from his desk that did actually have my picture on it, and held it up triumphantly. His lunch had been wrapped in it! It ruined all my dignity, but I recovered somehow and have been teaching off and on for two years."

Ellen Wolff, daughter of Mrs. Bernard Wolff, of 37 Peachtree Place, is proprietor of her own business, The Little Book Shop, in Arcade. She is a small person with red gold hair and blue eyes that match the ruffled blue curtains over her own book shelves. She doesn't look at all aggressive or like a "go-getter," yet she is a very business-like young person as she sells copies of *Jurgen* to debutantes and reporters, and *Tarzan of the Apes* to ecstatic small boys.

Books and—Money

"There's nothing like making your own money," said she. "I believe that that is why most girls work, both those who have to work to eat and those who work to have something to do.

"I first worked in a New York library and then came south and worked at the Carnegie Library. Why? Because I always loved books and wanted to be near them. Another reason is that women ought to have something to do.

"I had always wanted my own little book shop, and now I have it and I'm quite happy. Marjory McLeod helps me out and we both like it very much. It's our business so we have some time off to ride horseback. I wouldn't want any job that took all my time so that I couldn't ride."

In the reception room of the Retail Credit Company, the original "voice with a smile" greets the visitor, and the pleasant impression is reinforced by a pair of humorous blue eyes and a pretty face framed with bobbed hair. The brass name plate on her desk announces that this is Miss Mary Bardwell.

"When I didn't go off to school," said Miss Bardwell, who is the daughter of Mr. and Mrs. R. N. Bardwell, of 141 Juniper Street, "I had a half year on my hands. I can't think of anything more boring than just sitting around waiting for the phone to ring, so I got ambitious and decided that the only thing to do was to get a job.

"Jane Sams (she's married now, you know) used to work here and she asked me if I didn't want to work at the Retail Credit. Oh, of course I was excited as could be, for that was just the type of work I wanted to do. I'm official information bureau now. I have to meet everyone who comes in and make it my business to remember their names when they call again and to see that they are pleased.

"I have been here a year and a half, and I would not be without a job for anything."

Idleness Worst Nightmare

"I loved Atlanta and I wanted to stay here when my family moved to Texas," declared Edna Chevanne, who possesses all the vivacity and brunette beauty that her French name implies. "I had decided to get a job anyway, and I wanted to work here. I had had enough playing around doing nothing at home, and it tired me out. Besides, when a girl works, she has just as much time to 'play' as before, and certainly can appreciate her fun more!

"So I stayed here with family friends and got a job in the classified department of a daily paper. I take ads and write them for people who don't know how, and give whatever information I can to people who come in."

Jane Cooper, daughter of Mr. and Mrs. John Cooper, of 67 Juniper Street, has on her slim shoulders the responsibility of Rich & Bros. Company's interior decorating department, but she seems quite undismayed by the thousand and one details of draperies, rugs, wallpaper, furniture, and even small ornaments that go into making an empty house with bare walls a home of beauty and cheer.

"Marion Goldsmith, who is now abroad, formerly had this job," she said. "Three years ago, while I was in the North Carolina mountains with nothing on my mind but golf, Marion asked me to come home and help her.

"I liked the idea. I wanted to work and particularly in such attractive surroundings and with people I liked. Now Marion has gone abroad and I have her position.

"I don't know what I did with my time before I came here. I can't imagine any worse nightmare than being without something to do. There is nothing better in the world for a woman than to have a job that engrosses her time and interest—something that she loves to do and doesn't ever get tired of."

"I was sick of playing around," confessed Rebecca Harrel,

daughter of Mrs. R. D. Hudson, of 60 East Twelfth Street. "That's the frank truth of why I decided to work. And if you get down to the truth of it, that's probably the reason most girls work who aren't forced to.

"Playing around and having a good time is lots of fun. Every girl deserves to have a good time. But when you don't do anything else, it gets boring, just as work would if you never played any.

"When I decided that the only thing that would interest me was a job, I got one. I'm the comptometer in the accounting department of the Western Electric Company. That name sounds very intimidating, so I never explain what it means, but it keeps me busy!"

Miss Estelle Lindsay, daughter of Mrs. M. A. Lindsey, 677 Ponce de Leon, holds a responsible position at the Seaboard Air Line railroad office, and her job has not interfered with a "good time" any more than the good time has interfered with her job.

"I wanted to work because . . . because I wanted to!" she explained. "That's not a very definite reason, but it is the realest reason I know. I wanted to work because I wanted something to do besides hold my hands."

—September 2, 1923

Do Husbands Object to Their Wives Voting?

Some Atlanta Matrons Give This as a Reason for Not Appearing at the Polls. A Few Won't Admit They are Over Twenty-one. But Investigation Proves that Women are More Interested in the Ballot than Ever Before.

"My husband won't let me vote."

That has a very medieval sound, reminiscent of the days when husbands could beat wives with the full sanction of the law. Yet, according to their own admission, that is one reason why many of Atlanta's young matrons do not cast their ballots.

Political indifference on their part runs all the way from actual deference to the wishes of their husbands and brothers to a distaste for admitting that they are over twenty-one!

To oppose these indifferent "potential voters," there is the League of Women Voters and large numbers of women outside of the league who are vitally interested in every election, no matter how small.

Has the thrill of voting grown stale, after the novelty of the first few years? Are women growing indifferent to politics, now that they have the legal right to take an equal part in them with men? Or is their interest in politics spreading rapidly?

Mrs. R. L. Turman, who for two years has been leader of the Women's Club class in citizenship and the chairman of the committee on efficiency in government of the League of Women Voters, and who has just completed a book entitled *Studies in Citizenship for Georgia Women,* is an authority on the trend of women's thoughts in politics.

"I think that there is considerable indifference among girls and younger women," she said, "but this is more of a help than a hindrance, because we do not want unintelligent and uninformed women voting.

College Girls Interested

"The young women who think are taking more interest in politics today than ever before. Particularly is this true of college girls. They are willing to study out the matter of national and municipal politics so that they can vote correctly. They are aware their ignorance, and try to educate themselves. Men do not seem to study. They are blissfully unaware of how much they don't know.

"A discouraging feature to most uninformed women who would like to vote is that when they ask their husbands questions, the husbands can't answer and laugh at them. A man had rather laugh and go on in ignorance than ask questions.

"I think the fact that women are reading books on politics and attending lectures and classes on government shows clearer than any one thing the interest they have in the ballot."

"Our husbands don't like for us to vote," said a young matron who is prominent in Atlanta society. "Of course, we could vote over their objections, but why quibble about such a small thing? Men seem to think that women voting is an insinuation that they aren't the head of the family, and men today are fighting the last stand of masculine superiority.

"Of course, it's very odd that husbands don't take a stand on the modern 'wild life' and on their wives losing money at bridge, for instance, and smoking cigarettes. But young husbands make no more than a passing protest against those things, whereas when it comes to voting, they talk about 'woman's place in the home' and 'duty to children' and all the other wornout platitudes."

Debutante's Opinion

"I have never gone in for voting," said the president of a well-known society charity organization, "and I think that I can speak for the others of our club. Most of us are young married women with babies, and we aren't interested in the ballot. It isn't that we object to women voting. In fact, I think if we all were registered and had voted a few times it would be entirely different."

One debutante said, "I never heard of any of the girls in our set mention voting. Of course, most of them are not twenty-one yet, and it isn't natural to suppose that eighteen and nine-teen-year-old girls would be straining at the leash, waiting to be twenty-one so that they could rush off and vote.

"I suppose that we are very indifferent—but there are so many other things to do that are more interesting than voting!"

"Perhaps I am old-fashioned," admitted one young "bud" of nineteen, "but I don't believe in telling my age. If a girl starts voting, soon people begin to say, 'Why, she's been voting for years and years!' She must be forty, at least!'"

"I have three brothers and a father," added another, "and I think that they are enough voters to have in one family. Besides, I don't know what it's all about and politics doesn't in-terest me."

"I am old-fashioned, too," said a third, "and I think it de-tracts from a girl's attractiveness to get wild-eyed about voting. Men haven't changed at all. They don't like women to vote."

Arrogance of Youth

"When I'm married and have got my husband where I want him so that it won't do him any good to howl when I say I'm going to cast my ballot, then perhaps I'll vote," declared a sub-deb, hardly over sixteen. "I don't think that most girls under twenty-one have sense enough to vote, much less to be interested in politics. After we are grown up and haven't anything else to do, then we'll be interested in voting!"

There speaks the arrogance of youth!

"There is less indifference among women voters now than there has ever been," said Mrs. Sanford Gay, president of the Atlanta League of Women Voters. "Of course, between elections, interest dies down a little, but with each approaching race the league begins to get inquiries about the candidates and the manner of voting.

"These inquiries come from women in all classes of life, from the society matron and her debutante daughters to factory workers. The indifference of women is dying out, just like the opposition on the part of men to their wives voting. However, if there is any one great reason why women don't come to elections, it is because they are discouraged and ridiculed at home by the men of their families.

"Of course, there is a type of women who are like some men. They simply don't care about voting. But whenever an issue arises that concerns them, or their children, or their property, or the candidate is a man they know, even the most disinterested ones vote. And once a woman has registered and voted, she keeps on voting."

"There are still some women who are indifferent about voting and have never cast a ballot," admitted Mrs. Alonzo Richardson, president of the Atlanta Women's Club. "The main reason for this is the indifference of the men voters in the woman's family.

What the Men Say

"After a woman has decided that she will vote in the next election, her idea is to ask someone about the candidates. But when she goes to her husband, or father, or brother and says, 'Dear, who is Mr. So-and-So?' and the man answers, indifferently, 'Oh, I don't know. I never vote, so I haven't any idea what it's about.' Then the ardor of the potential woman voter cools, for she feels that if voting isn't important enough to concern the lord and master of the house, it can't mean very much. And so she doesn't vote.

"Among young club women and college girls, there is plenty of interest in voting. They are usually a serious-minded type. Among the young girls who have the natural ideas of youth to be gay and have a good time, there is not much thought of politics. But when these same girls grow up, marry, and settle down, then they begin to attach the proper importance to the ballot.

"However, I am more encouraged by the interest women are taking in voting today than ever before."

—*November 11, 1923*

How It All Comes Out in the Wash

"I t'll all come out in the wash!" Every one has used that expression at some time, but how many have ever thought of exactly how things come out in the wash? How many have ever given a thought that the manifold sides of human nature are displayed more freely over a laundry counter than in surroundings more conducive to confidential revelations?

Laundries are not usually considered as scenes of drama and romance. Railway depots, public libraries, movies, police stations, all of these places are fraught with endless possibilities of human interest, agonized partings, tragedies, laughter, love.

But laundries—!

The only interesting things laundries bring to mind, usually, outside of their utilitarian purposes, are jokes, such as—

"No tickee, no washee!"

And—

"Mirandy, do you know of my wife's whereabouts?"

"Yas, suh, they's in the laundry."

But there is one person in Atlanta who declares that everything DOES come out in the wash, and that more drama, heart throbs and tragedy go on over a laundry counter than even in a public park on a moonlight night.

She is Miss Callie Erwin, of West End, and certainly she speaks with authority on the subject, for she has stood behind the counter of one Atlanta laundry for eighteen years.

Miss Erwin is forty (and proud of it)! Keen-eyed, brisk and efficient. She has a mental card index that enables her to connect names and faces correctly and to size up newcomers the instant they lean across her counter. She has a smile that is radiant with good humor and cheer and an interest in people that makes them suddenly decide to confide their secrets in her.

Knows Them All

She knows Atlanta's Four Hundred and Atlanta's down-and-outers.

She can tell at a glance that the tear-stained little shop girl who has spilled coffee on her best and only nice dress is "just petrified because my out-of-town fellow is coming tomorrow and I've ruined my only dress"—and she can run a practiced eye over the dress and render verdict as to whether the dress is beyond repair.

She knows that the petulant young woman who steps out of a limousine, carrying a beloved dress, is a debutante who has decided that she's "worn this dress three times and everybody knows it, and I want it dyed green."

If Miss Erwin looks at the hair, eyes, and complexion of the deb and thinks that green would be unbecoming, she frankly says so. If the deb insists on green, Miss Erwin refuses.

"If you have that dyed green and it looks badly, you will say, 'Miss Erwin did a bad job; that why it don't look good.' And you'll never come back to see me again." And usually the debutante agrees. Miss Erwin has no hesitancy about telling gray-haired society matrons that they shouldn't have their dresses dyed dull brown or sand, because it will make them look drab. She stands firm when sallow ladies insist on having their dresses dyed purple or mauve.

"Of course, it's their dresses," observes Miss Erwin frankly. "But I am not going to be responsible for having customers looking badly. It's bad business."

When the rush of business dies down and she has stopped her constant—"No, this is ruined; you'll have to dye it." "Good morning, how is your little girl's cold now?" "How are you? Did your daughter like the shade of dress you picked out for her?" "Don't sit on that radiator, son. We don't want any cooked little boys around here,"—Miss Erwin will pat her smooth, brown hair, readjust her crisply starched waist, and talk of the people who come to her across the counter.

"Every laundry has packages of unclaimed clothing," says Miss Erwin. "We do not sell our unclaimed packages, but give them to needy people. I always keep a set of clothing on hand—collar, shirt, and underwear—in case of emergency. One of my 'emergencies' was the most pathetic case I ever saw in all the time I worked here." Her keen gray eyes suddenly blurred up with tears that threatened to fog her glasses.

The Man from Prison

"One cold day an old man of about seventy sidled in here and stood by the radiator to warm himself. He was almost in rags—the upper part of his body nearly bare, for his shirt hung in ribbons. With him was a thin, flop-eared hound dog with big, splay feet and an apologetic air. The old man was so pitiful looking that I called him over to the counter and talked to him for about an hour.

"He had just been released from prison in Mississippi, where he had been serving a life sentence for a murder he had not committed. The deathbed confession of the real murderer had set him free after twenty years of imprisonment.

"He shivered and talked and the old hound, of which he was very solicitous, shivered beside him.

"'Where are you going now?' I asked him."

"'Wal, ma'am,' said he (he had a north Georgia mountaineer accent), 'I lives up in the mount'ins and I'm walkin' home. Me and my houn' walked all the way from Mississippi. We'll git home some time or other. I want to go back to the mount'ins —jes' to see if that's anybody thar that I knows.'"

"He was such a pathetic old man and his beloved old hound was so pathetic, too! So I gave him a suit of clean clothes and a meal ticket to the Salvation Army to speed him on his way.

"No use giving money," she broke off with a return to her brisk manner.

"They always spend it on whisky. I give meal tickets instead. So the old man went away.

"But he came back three weeks later on a rainy night, and dragged in to warm by the radiator. He was dirty and tired and even the houn' looked plumb tuckered out."

"'Lady,' he said 'I dun been home. And thar wasn't nobody thar that knew me or had ever heard of me.'

"And I don't mind telling you," admitted Miss Erwin, tears rising at the memory, "that I stood here and cried while the old dog thumped his tail on the floor sympathetically!"

"I asked him, 'What are you going to do now?'

"And he said, 'Lady, I don't know any place that's home except the jail, an' so I'm goin' back to Mississippi an' see if they'll take me back in prison. But I ain't going unless they'll take in my houn' dog, too,' he declared very fiercely.

"'I didn't have nobody to talk to 'bout it 'cept you, ma'am, so I come on back here to tell you.'

"I gave him another clean shirt and sent him on his way back to Mississippi with his houn' dog trailing after him.

"Now, a surprising thing about people who come in here begging for clothing is that very, very few are women," said Miss Erwin, switching briskly from the subject of the pathetic old man. "It makes me proud of my sex to say that most women, no matter how low they've fallen, would rather starve than beg. They've more backbone than men. Of course, many DO come here, asking for help, but they always want to do work for it or sell you chewing gum or pencils or shoe lacings. Women have too much pride to beg.

"Men are different. Men always have the courage of their collars and they feel that if they have on a clean collar and shirt they can get jobs. So they have no hesitancy about begging. Life is a bit unfair to women that way," said Miss Erwin, philosophically. "A man can sleep behind a garbage can in an alley and come here in the morning and beg a clean shirt and collar, land a job and be self-respecting. But a woman can't. Once a woman has slept in a barrel in an alley and begged for clothes, she's gone. Women's pride and self-respect are built on different foundations from men's.

"I have been here so long that many of my customers are just like friends, and I know most of their family histories. What interests me most is observing how people come up in the world. I can tell it by their clothes that come to the laundry as well as by their faces. For instance, we have many colored customers. Some years ago they used to come in and bring a few sorry looking clothes. Then the clothes began to get more numerous, and I noticed that with the advent of better clothes, colored folk always get straight hair and carry themselves better.

"Something of this sort happens with our foreigners. Foreigners, unable to speak a word of English, will bring their laundry to me. Perhaps the clothes are curious to our eyes—or at least foreign looking. Soon I begin to notice that the clothes change to American types. Then, the foreigners' children, who have been put in school and can speak English, bring in the laundry for their parents, and I can see the gradual change in the whole family. Oh, it all comes out in the wash!"

—*April 13, 1924*

Jobs Before Marriage
For High School Girls

"Having a job before you are married is just as good sense as carrying 'mad money' when you are out with a date you don't know very well," announced a demure small girl in the back row of the Girls' High School study hall in response to the question as to why all the senior class intended working for at least a year before they married.

"If you don't like the man or the way he acts you can always use your 'mad money' to take a street car home. That's the same way with a girl who has worked and been independent before she married. She can always fall back on her job if her husband is an egg."

Then the small demure person, feeling that she had doubtless expressed herself too unequivocally for a demure person, sat down in confusion amid the giggles of her classmates.

"But," stammered the interviewer, "Joseph Hergesheimer, the novelist, says that women shouldn't work—that it spoils their charm. He says that women should stay at home and cultivate charm. What about it?"

The senior class was too well bred to shout "Bunk!" at the top of their voices, but they smoothed their shingled bobs and looked superior. Evidently they were sure that their charms would outlast their jobs or that Joseph knew nothing whatever about the subject.

Nurses to Undertakers

If an Irreconcilable of the Old Regime had suggested to the graduating class that teaching a little French, music, and china painting was the utmost a genteel young lady could do in the matter of attaining independence, the seniors would have batted their eager eyes politely and shouted, "Old stuff!" in chorus. For the "after Graduation" ambitions of the Girls' High seniors range from operating rooms and (it is rumored) undertakers to banking and invention.

Teaching, however, led all the ambitions. The question of "How many seniors want to teach school?" brought up a waving of many hands and the impatient scuffling of feet anxious to have the floor.

"I want to go to Agnes Scott first and then teach afterward," said Louise Gerauldaux, who gained the floor first. "It is the contact with human nature I want—and you can certainly get it teaching children! I'd like to do social service work on the side."

"I want to do social service work, too, in connection with my teaching," said Jessie Hyatt, "but I am going to train at the State Normal, first."

"I don't want to teach," came the shy voice of Ida May Goldstein, from the very last row, "but social service work appeals to me very much and I think that would be the happiest work of all—helping other people."

"Especially little children," said Martha Riley. "I'd like to do social service work among children more than grown people because they seem so much more helpless. I'd rather work around—or in conjunction with—a hospital."

Reporters and an Actress

"I want to work with children but I'd rather teach kindergarten," said Alice Johnson.

Bena Archer and Marcel Johnson, who are going to attend State Normal, declared that kindergarten would be much more interesting than either social service or teaching older children. Jane Callahan and Frances West, whose ambitions lay along the same lines, nodded vigorously. Amid respectful glances, Ruth Hemingway arose to announce that she was going to "specialize in 'Math'" at Agnes Scott and teach it later in some school.

Anna Knight admitted that she was swayed between two desires, one to do newspaper work and the other, social service. "And nothing but time will tell which I want to do most or can do best."

"Oh, I want to do newspaper work, too," cried Frances Hargis. "I'm going to take a course in journalism at Emory next year and write—oh—write anything I can—newspaper stuff or short stories—"

"I want to be a reporter," interrupted Sara Glass, encouraged by her classmate's confession of journalistic ambitions. "The other girls want to do social service and teaching to 'learn human nature,' and I want to do reporting for the same reason. You can see every kind of person in the world if you are a reporter."

When the students of human nature had had their say, there arose a commotion in the middle aisle and whispers of "Go on, Sara! Get up," and a pretty girl stood in the aisle and flung back her red gold hair, half defiantly.

"I want to be an actress," she announced, boldly, and then, hastily, as an afterthought, "only my family would never let me, I know. But that's what I want to be. So if I can't be an actress, I'm going to specialize in dramatic art and do—oh, platform elocution and all that!" and she sank to her seat amid giggles and a faint pattering of applause.

Painting, Decorating, and Architecture

Sara White was the only one of the seniors who would admit to an inner urge toward the stage, but the artistic desires of the rest of the class had a wide range.

Edna Volberg, brown-eyed and soft-voiced who won the Magna Cum Laude a few weeks ago, had leanings toward writing, but—

"It's painting I want to do most. Portraits, all kinds of them. Portraits of little children with personality—and old people with character."

"Lamp shades!" cried a pretty brunette waving her hand and arising at the nod of the teacher. "I'm Hazel Neal. I'm interested in interior decoration but most of all—silk lamp shades. I like to design and make them. My sister, who is connected with the lamp department of a big department store here, has told me all about making them. There's an art to it—getting shades that blend and shapes that suit different rooms. It's fascinating."

"Put us down for interior decorating, too," said Anne Choate and Ellas Sue Head while Katherine Koontz, who was going to Hollins for a year before specializing in interior decorating, said that she wanted to "Make houses beautiful."

"I don't want to make houses beautiful—I want to make beautiful houses," declared Dorothy Methvin. "I'm going to study architecture."

"A woman architect told me that there was a great need for more women in the architectural game," added Louise Madden. "She said that women knew how to design houses better than men because women were in their houses more than men. So I decided to study and be an architect."

"I'm not going away to school to specialize," said Hortence Cook, "I'm going to stay here in Atlanta and take a librarian course."

Librarians and Inventors

"I can't think of anything better than spending my life sur-rounded by books," declared Elizabeth Hyatt, "so I am going to take the librarian's course, too."

"Being surrounded by books is all very nice," contended Dorothy Spratt, "but I'd rather be surrounded by beautiful ma-terial—silks and satins and laces. I want to design clothes. Not stiff tailored things, but fluky, filmy, clingy things," and she spread wide her hands in pantomime of bouffant skirts and trailing draperies.

"Designing is all right," admitted the girls who were bent on entering the business world, "but routine office work is better."

"I'm going to study banking," said Charlotte Hailey, while Viola Towery and Doris Wallace, whose next destinations were business colleges, said they had not exactly decided what line of work they would take up, but that they were sure it would be office work because it was so much more interesting to "work with people." Genelle Cartledge's ambition was to be a private secretary.

Sara Williamson had an ambition unique in a schoolgirl. She wanted to "work with her hands."

"I want to invent something. Of course, that takes head work as well as hand work, but I like to monkey with machin-ery and hammers and nails and things like that, and see what I can make out of them."

Elinor Speer, a quiet, brown eyed girl on the front row of the class, spoke up:

A Surgeon

"I want to do something with my hands, too," she said, "but it isn't to use a hammer. I'm going to specialize in playing the pipe organ."

"I'm going to specialize in music, too, at Bessie Tift," said Elsie Davis. "I'm going to teach it afterward."

"We are going to teach music, too," declared Alice Hunter and Alice Gayle.

"Seems as if teaching is popular here," laughed Mildred Kelly. "Elizabeth Hollinsworth and Lucille Cassell, who is basketball captain, and I are going to study to be gymnastic instructors."

For a moment there was silence in the room and prodding whispers arose:

"G'wan and tell the truth about what you want to be—or I'll tell it," and Sara Gardner arose hastily and admitted to a longing to be a doctor.

"A surgeon," she insisted, and the room was again swept with a gale of giggles that worried the embryonic doctor not at all. "I'm not the only one here who wants to be a doctor—Mary Frances Wiggins wants to study surgery and Frances Malone wants to be an operating room nurse. Edwina Malcombe is absolutely sure that she's going to take a nurse's course and specialize in anaesthetics."

"I'll help you doctors out," said Frances Elliott, "for I am specializing in chemistry and expect to do laboratory work. I'm going to do chemical research work, but I'll fill your prescriptions for you whenever I'm not too busy."

"Don't any of you want to stay at home and be a comfort to your families?" questioned the interviewer, somewhat taken back by the vast array of ambitions spread out before her eyes.

There was an embarrassed silence.

"Hasn't anybody here a hope chest? Doesn't any one of you want to get married?"

"Not right away," announced Elizabeth Hynde, amid gleeful laughs from the rest of the room. It was then that the demure little thing in the back row made the remark about jobs, "mad money," and marriage.

"I think," hesitated Ruth Hemmingway," that as our families have done so much for us it is time for us to show them how much we appreciate their goodness by becoming independent."

"Then it is independence that makes all of you want jobs?"

At that a tumult arose in which the words, "Self-expression!" "Independence!" and "Paycheck!" were loudest—and then, the same demure young thing in the back row piped up:

"Self-expression, nothing! Jobs are just marking time till you get married!"

—April 27, 1924

Pulling Teeth in a Harem

When a Hindu lady has a toothache, she usually continues to have it and bears it with all the fortitude she can muster until merciful Providence stops the aching, according to young Mrs. Carlton Kelly, who is visiting her parents, Mr. and Mrs. A.H. Milner, at their home at 194 Atwood Avenue, after a six-year residence in Calcutta, India.

Mr. Kelly, who practices dentistry in Calcutta, has a clientele largely of men, says Mrs. Kelly, because in India no stranger is ever allowed to look upon a woman's unveiled face. Only the husband may do that. On one occasion, however, Dr. Kelly was called in to ease the aching tooth of a harem beauty and she was the wife of a very high-caste and well-educated Hindu. It is interesting to imagine the trepidation and excitement that went on in the Hindu household before the visit of the dentist. A strange man was to invade the precincts of the harem and see the wife without her veil!

"The poor woman must have had a terrible toothache to have permitted it," laughed Mrs. Kelly, when telling of her husband's experience, "for Hindu women feel about the same without their veils as we would feel without any clothes at all. My husband said that he could feel intensely curious eyes on him from behind curtains and doors from the moment he entered the circular court where his patient was, until the time he left. The lady of the toothache was terribly embarrassed and attempted to keep her veil on while he was working on her teeth, and as that was impossible, she contented herself by holding it over the top part of her face and covering her head."

Killed First Tiger

No doubt Mr. Kelly's visit to the harem provided conversation for the inmates for months thereafter. All visiting ladies from other harems were doubtless told the story in detail and listened breathlessly, punctuating the narrative with "Well, I declare," or whatever the Hindu equivalent is.

Mrs. Kelly spoke interestingly and with authority of India for she does not see it with cold, Occidental eyes, picking flaws in the custom of the country and comparing it unfavorably with America. After a six-year residence in Calcutta, she has come to feel that India is home, and she loves it and misses it.

She has not spent all of her time playing bridge with the "American colony" in Calcutta to the exclusion of all things Indian. She talks most interestingly of the political unrest in India, the Ghandi "non-co-operation" movement and its dissolution when Ghandi experienced a change of heart toward the British government due to the excellent treatment he had while suffering from appendicitis in an English prison; she knows of the 4,000 different castes of India, the intricate religious forms, and the hundreds of gods; she has witnessed Hindu funerals and marriages and Hindu "miracles" and is able to see the Eastern viewpoint with a sympathetic eye.

Mrs. Kelly has been hunting with her husband upon many occasions, and, just before leaving India for the States, was with him in the jungle when he shot his first tiger. Her eyes flowed as she described her sensations when crouched in a tree with her husband while the native "beaters" and the entire population of a neighboring village "who trailed along curiously to see whether or not we would be eaten," drove the tiger toward them.

In fact, Mrs. Kelly has seen and done most of those things of which Kipling wrote in his many Indian tales, and she agrees with him that:

"If you've heard the East a-calling
You won't never heed naught else."

However, it is concerning the women of the East that Mrs. Kelly speaks with most feeling.

Need Women Doctors

"The greatest need in India today is for women doctors, dentists, and teachers, for, of course, the Hindus will not permit, except in rare cases, a man to look upon their women, much less doctor them. The women would prefer to die in their harems rather than have a strange man see them. Women doctors could do a great work in the Orient where the feminine population is always guarded and watched over and veiled.

"High caste Hindu ladies never appear on the street at all except on the special 'shopping days' that the stores have occasionally for the harems. Upon these 'ladies' days,' the Hindu women arrive in carriages, with curtains drawn, at the shops; the entrances to the stores are curtained, and so they pass inside without being seen. To further conceal themselves, they wear long white sheets that come from the top of their heads down over their faces and entirely to their feet. There are two eyeholes cut for them to see through, but over these eyeholes are gauze mosquito netting.

"Inside the shops, there are only women to display the goods to them; they choose what they desire, get back into their closed carriages, and are driven home to their harems. No strange man ever looks upon their faces.

"Naturally the flapper movement has had little effect upon the Hindu women.

"Thanks to the millions of dollars that the American missions have poured into schools and hospitals in India, the high-caste women are slowly becoming educated. But it will take years and years for Occidental customs really to take effect upon India. A few women have abandoned the veil, but that act, in itself, makes them social outcasts. A few women have gone to schools and colleges, but they learn Western ways slowly, and when they return to their homes, they revert to their old customs. In the home of many wealthy Hindus, there are quarters for European guests, furnished tastefully in European style. But the Hindus in their own quarters will sleep on piles of cushions and eat their curry and rice with their fingers.

Modern Apartments

"My friends in Atlanta seem to think that my husband and I live in a steaming jungle, in a bamboo hut set up on long poles with snakes hanging from the thatched roof and tigers snarling in nearby trees. I wish they could see my new apartment!

"Oh, yes, there are many modern apartments in Calcutta. The one in which we live is a huge stone building. The rooms are as big as the whole of an ordinary American apartment and the ceilings twice as high. That is done to make the rooms cooler. The floors are of marble and the walls stone and there is a swinging fan on every ceiling to keep the cool air circulating.

"Every one who keeps house has eight or ten servants, because no servant ever does more than one job. The cook cooks, the butler buttles, the yardman looks after the yard. They would be breaking caste should they ever do anything except their own especial task. And when they are not occupied, they all lie down on the back porch and go to sleep.

"In the heat of the day, all India goes to sleep. The white

people never go out at noon. They darken their houses and sleep. The natives, however, lie down in the bazaars and streets and sleep peacefully in the heat which is now around 115 degrees.

"Really," broke off Mrs. Kelly, "I haven't been warm since I left Calcutta. I find Atlanta most chilly!

"People who have visited India and the East for only a short time seem to find it strange that I love it so. 'Don't you burn up with the heat?' they ask, and 'It's such a dirty place and there is so much disease. I think that the spell of the East is all bunk.'

"They think that way because they have not stayed long enough to love India and her customs and her dirt and color.

Human Sacrifice

"People in the East look down on Orientals. People who pay only short visits and do not stay long enough to really know the country usually conceive a distate for it. They have no respect for the Indians nor India, nor do they realize the latter were an old, old race even before America was thought of.

"Tourists usually laugh at the customs and beliefs of the East, especially the things that we call 'occult' and supernatural. They say 'Bunk.' But these things are not bunk. There are Hindu priests who can materialize ropes out of thin air, hanging from space to the ground, and make a man appear magically from nowhere, run swiftly up the rope, and disappear into nothing. They can make great trees grow from tiny seeds and disappear suddenly at a wave of their hands.

"But these things are not supernatural. The priests have perfected, through countless generations, the art of so dominating the wills and imaginations of those around them that they can force them to belive they see things that do not exist outside of the minds of the priests themselves.

"The most startling example of this kind that I know of," continued Mrs. Kelly, "happened to a group of soldiers who had been detailed to go into the hills after a priest who was guilty of offering up a human sacrifice. They trailed him for days and finally surrounded him in the hut of an old man who was famed for his proficiency in 'magic.'

"Beyond a doubt, the priest was concealed in the hut and there was no way for him to get out. But the officer in charge did not take any chances. He stationed some men at the bottom of the hill near the hut and some all around the house. A few he sent inside to make the capture.

"The old man who owned the hut had been sitting in front of the door all during the proceedings, in a sort of trance. Just as the soldiers entered the door to take their prisoner, he roused himself and threw a handful of powder on a small fire that was burning near him. A burst of blue smoke rose and a small dog walked out of the door, ran between the captain's legs and out into the jungle.

"The soldiers ran out of the hut, in chagrin, declaring that the place was empty, and at the same time, shouts arose from the men stationed at the bottom of the hill.

"They cried, 'Catch him, you fools! There he goes! He crawled out between the Captain's legs!'"

Mrs. Kelly smiled as she finished her tale.

"That story is true and many others I could tell that are much more incredible.

"Many white people hate India because they can find there only smells and heat and fatalism. They are so blinded by these things that the Spell of the East is lost to them. They are most unfortunate, for they miss the color and the glamor and the age-old mystery that no Occidental can ever quite fathom or ever quite tire of."

Mr. and Mrs. Kelly have planned to return to Calcutta in October, where they will remain until they pay their next visit to Atlanta in two years.

—*June 22, 1924*

In & Out of Wedlock

Mitchell and Berrien "Red" Upshaw married on September 2, 1922.
John Marsh (far left), later her second husband, served as best man.

"No Dumbbells Wanted,"
Say Atlanta Debs

"'I deal Men' are as obsolete as—bustles! Ages ago, when it was the style for girls to be languid and swoony, every girl dreamed about her 'ideal,' or the time when her 'knight would come riding.' Ideals always had wavy hair and soulful eyes and the girls didn't ever seem to gift their knights with brains. But nowadays, girls insist that men have sense, and not be just good-looking dumbbells."

Elizabeth Owens was speaking. She was one of seven of this season's debutantes that I interviewed on the subject of men.

"Do you prefer wealth, good looks, or brains?" I asked.

And the answer was: Dumbbells, beware! Sighing Valentinos with melting eyes—and vacuums behind them, take care! The femininity of 1923 demands more of you than that you be ornamental.

"I don't like dumbbells, either," said Elizabeth Buchannan, "but Heaven defend me from these Intellectuals! Their main idea seems to be to make you feel as stupid as possible!"

What then, exactly, do the girls of this generation believe to be the "pearl beyond price?" There doesn't seem to be any standardized, conventional "ideal man" in the minds of the girl of 1923. Each of them has her own, very firm conviction as to what constitutes an eligible.

Valentino vs. Meighan

"When it comes to differentiating between the types you like best," continued Elizabeth Owens, "it's rather hard. As far as appearances are concerned, I frankly prefer a man of the Rudolph Valentino type to the Thomas Meighan* sort. But looks don't matter so much after all. What does matter is whether or not he can talk and be jolly and clever. I think that most of girls may have a preconceived notion of what their fate is going to be like—but most likely, when he does come along, he won't be at all as she imagined."

"I don't think that a man has to be wallowing in money to be eligible," continued Elizabeth Buchannan. "But it is my frank opinion that few girls really enjoy marrying a man and then starving with him, no matter how much she loves him! So, of course, a man ought to have some money!

"But I like a man who has lots of pep, zip, and go about him. I loathe being bored. I prefer a man who always has something funny or clever to say. Then you won't ever get tired of him, whereas, I imagine a man who was 'beautiful and dumb,' or still worse, terribly highbrow would drive anybody to despair."

"Perhaps I'm a little old fashioned," ventured Julia Memminger, who has a shy, appealing way, "but I like men who are sweet and considerate and thoughtful. You remember that cute line from the play where the little 'baby talk lady' said, 'Oh, I jus' wuve him 'cause he is tho big an' stwong but oh, tho gentle and tho good to me!' I like big, athletic men and I just can't stand flip tea-hounds. Of course, they are cute and all that, but they just don't last long."

Hates Conceited Men

"I like real, honest-to-goodness He-Men, too," acknowledged Sara Orme. "And if there's one type of man that I hate, it is the conceited type! Men have got so spoiled these days that some of them are unbelievably conceited and they are usually the ones who aren't worth shooting. Real men are not in the least bit stuck up, and that is the type I like best.

"I don't think it matters much whether the man of one's choice is ravingly good-looking or not, but what does matter is whether he has brains."

Sue Brow Sterne puckered her pretty brows as she gave her attention to the engrossing subject.

"I don't think any girl would like to marry a man who was ugly enough to stop a train, but then looks, like money, are not absolutely essential to a happy marriage," she said, "Give me a brainy man any day to a good-looking, even a wealthy simpleton! If a man has brains he can do anthing. There are no limits to his attainments. I can't see what a girl would get out of marrying just a handsome man, yet loads of girls insist on good looks as the first requisite in the man of their choice. Besides, if the man is so very good-looking, he is always thinking of his own looks and never of his wife's!

"Give me a sensible man, any day!"

Corneille Torrance said that most people believe debutantes would not consider a man unless he had lots of money, but this is all wrong.

"Of course, movies and novels always picture Debs as being fortune-hunters, but the Deb of today is just like any other girl in that what she wants is a real man," she declared. "Movie actors are nice to admire from afar, and wonderful-looking athletes are thrilling, but I want an all-round man who has lots of sense, so that I can be proud of him. I think there's nothing a girl hates worse than being out with a man she's ashamed of.

A Deep Man

"Nothing makes a man so attractive as the fact that he has some 'depth' to him. Lots of men have a 'cute' line of chatter.

But when a man is deep, his character and strength stand out all over him and you just can't help liking and being proud of him."

May Emery was quite firm in her conviction that personality was the trait most to be desired in a man.

"I like a good-looking man just as well as any girl does," she said. "But there is nothing so attractive as a man with a fascinating personality. Money is a nice thing to have, and so is a face like an Apollo Belvedere, but a man with a clever personality is just like a sparkly diamond, he is always flashing and brilliant no matter what light he is in.

"I think if I had to choose between an attractive young man with brains and not much money, and a man whose father was willing to give us lots of money so that he wouldn't have to work, why, I'd take the clever young chap any day. There is lots more genuine satisfaction, I imagine, in starting at the bottom with a really brainy young man and helping him work up to the top than in getting bored with a man who just hung around and never did anything to make you respect him.

"I can't say exactly what type of temperament I like best. Some girls love 'cave-man stuff' and others want to be made love to a la Valentino. Now, I can't say so much for the cave man variety, but then again, I am always wary of these terribly quiet men! At least with a cave man you DO know what to expect, but with one of these quiet, silent men you can't ever tell what he is going to do. One thing you can be pretty sure of is that it's going to be what you least expect, and though it's nice to be surprised every now and then, for a steady diet, I like a man with sense, one you can always count on."

"No dumbbells wanted," say Atlanta Debs.

—*January 28, 1923*

Star of action films and Westerns, Thomas Meighan was know for his blue eyed, all-American good looks.

Just Like a Woman; Ditto for Men

Patience is a virtue,
Find it if you can.
Seldom in a woman,
And never in a man.

W hich is a very ancient truism, but unlike most truisms, this one happens to be true, for the rhyme is very old and has been told an infinite number of times, and, where there is much smoke, there is some fire.

Obviously then, this quality of patience, which has been considered always an attribute of the sex masculine, is really less a part of that sex than it is of the less strenuous one.

Besides all of which it has always been obvious, even to the most casual observer, that the antics of men as a whole seem to have less bearing on what they pretend to be than their actions. There are dozens of things which prove this beyond all peradventure.

Who can explain why a man, in the processes of being shaved and massaged at the barber shop, will insist on sitting in the front chair, facing the wide plate glass window where all who pass can see him belathered and uncollared? When a woman goes into a beauty shop, all is secretive, from the little enameled closets in which each woman is beautified, to the intense quiet preserved during these rites. Few women will even allow their best friends to accompany them to beauty parlors, whereas a man flaunts his unaesthetic and half-shaved face to the world.

Men and House Cleaning

There never breathed a woman who would not rise up and call her husband blessed if at fall and spring, he wrapped a towel around his head and cleaned the house from cellar to attic. She would go around boasting of his cleanliness among her envious and less fortunate friends. But, to make a man swear to leave a loving wife and a good home, it is only necessary for him to glimpse a mop and broom and see the furniture removed from its familiar resting place. Yet, if only a cobweb is sighted in a distant corner or the window clouded from dust, he cries aloud that he is living in indescribable squalor.

Then, too, men display the inconsistencies of their sex when they approach the most serious perhaps of all their undertakings, for there has never yet been wooed a daughter of Eve in exactly the right way. Almost inevitably, that particular bit of sunshine which should be beaten over the head with a very large club is meekly approached with candy, flowers, books, and inanities. Whereas her equally lovable sister, who craves just these things and the utmost in chivalric wooing, is faced most often by some earnest caveman who firmly believes that his are the only methods which lead, with any degree of certainty, to the altar.

Women, of course, do make errors in the bait they toss men. But their well-known intuition usually brings them swiftly face to face with their mistake and they subtly remedy it. But a man can never be convinced that the course he had chosen, no matter how ridiculous it may be, can lead other than to his lady's heart.

However much milady may grieve over her inability to find a particularly fascinating jabot, meant to set off a certain coat, she is usually philosophic about the loss and puts on another which may or may not look as well. To her it is simply lost. A woman would never summon in the household and call on Heaven to bear witness that the male contingent of her family has entered into a foul conspiracy to hide all her underwear and socks, as men are wont to do on similar occasions.

Primping

One of the favorite peculiarities of the betrousered part of humanity is his criticism of the amount of time women spend on "primping." Doubtless women do put in some quarter of their waking hours before a mirror, but the end usually justifies the means in that they step forth well-groomed and smooth of locks. Amusingly enough, there is the same critical male who spends no less than twenty minutes before his mirror "slicking" his hair with various unguents and guaranteed "stickums" and then jerking a cap down to his eyes and ruining it all.

Doubtless women are curious creatures, at least they have been so touted from time immemorial. Yet women seldom allow their curiosity to make them foolish. Recently, there was displayed in a florist's window, at Valentine time, a box bearing the cryptic sign, "For Men Only." Was there a heart beating beneath a vest that did not bump faster with curiosity and yearn to peep surreptitiously, even though he well knew that the box probably contained only the admonition of "not to forget to send Valentine violets to your sweetheart?" Despite the fact of the crowds that assembled to watch and roar at the curious men who peeped, curiosity prevailed over vanity and every man looked, grinned sheepishly, and ran off.

Men are endowed with ostrich-like attributes which Providence spared women. A man firmly believes that if he does not want to yield up his seat on the streetcar to some feminine straphangers, he has only to ensconce himself behind his newspaper and he will disappear magically from sight. If a woman has some unpleasant duty to perform, she does not duck out of sight and believe that if she cannot see, she cannot be seen. She glares straight into the face of the unpleasantness and usually routs it.

Loud are the cries of protest that women talk eternally of their children and their many cunning little ways. But what man has not waxed grieved when his listeners fell into merciful sleep over his glowing description of how he negotiated a very difficult fourteenth hole in par by sinking a mashie niblick pitch six yards off from the green?

And, too, the man who most criticizes his very attractive wife for wearing, at the breakfast table, an entirely charming (if he but knew it) Japanese kimono, is always the first one when he is elected generalissimo of his particular lodge, to take the most childish pride in appearing at the head of the parade dressed in a costume which would bring joy to the heart of some African aborigine.

Wherefore and because of these things, it is unquestionably evident that in the matters of peculiarities and inconsistencies, man yields the palm to none. Man can never yield the palm to woman.

—March 11, 1923

The article above ran alongside and under the same headline as a piece by Bert Collier. While Mitchell's piece discusses a poster beside a box of Valentine candy, Collier's piece discourses on a poster placed by the Georgia Railway & Power Company in its streetcars which read "When you move up front you keep your seat longer—Women will not move up front." The subhead for the pieces reads, "The two posters are made the subject here of a discussion of peculiarities, male and female, from both the masculine and the feminine viewpoint."

Football Players Make the Best Husbands

"I think that football players make the best husbands," said Mrs. Dewey Scarboro, bride of six months—and she ought to know.

For not only did she marry a Tech football player, but her two sisters, formerly Ruth and Loretta Jackson, daughters of Mr. and Mrs. J. M. Jackson, of Decatur, also married Tech stars of the gridiron and are now Mrs. "Daddy" Amis and Mrs. "Big Six" Carpenter, respectively.

To make matters more amazing, they all married within six months—Mrs. Scarboro in January, Mrs. Carpenter in May, and Mrs. Amis in June. The bereft Jackson family had barely caught its breath at the sudden marriage of their young nineteen-year-old daughter to Dewey Scarboro of football fame, when the other two daughters announced their intention of forsaking the Tech set, of which they had been reigning belles, to become the lifelong belles of Messrs. Carpenter and Amis.

Mrs. Scarboro is small even to tininess, slim and bobbed-haired with ingenuous blue eyes and a soft little voice that fits her face and personality.

"I say that football players make the best husbands—though of course, I've never tried any other kind of husband. You can always be sure that you've married a real man if you marry a man who has played through several seasons of football, because if he wasn't a real man, he would have never stood the test.

"I had seen Dewey playing football lots of times before I finally met him—and it never occurred to me that he was the man I was going to marry. But you never can tell how things are going to turn out," she smiled wisely.

Each Brought a Husband

"The oddest thing about the whole affair," continued Mrs. Scarboro, "is the way we all met the boys. One night, 'Pup' McWhorter brought out 'Big Six' Carpenter for a double date with Ruth and Loretta. The next week, 'Six' brought out 'Daddy' Amis to see Ruth while he had a date with Loretta. And two days later, 'Dad' came out with another boy who was none other than Dewey.

"Ruth said, 'Come on down and have a date with him. I have a date with Mr. Amis'—so, I came on down and met Dewey. Each one of the boys brought us a husband!

"No, I can't say that any little voice whispered 'Here's your future husband' when I first saw Dewey, but I did like him ever so much.

"And then we went on that camp!"

Little Mrs. Scarboro beamed in reminiscence.

"I guess that's where the romance really started. 'Six' Carpenter wasn't there, as he was in Chicago, but the rest of us went. Father owns a beautiful tract of land out on the Briar Cliff Road, and twelve of us camped there in tents. There were Loretta and Ruth, Maude Butler, Una Powers, Lucia McDavid; and the boys were 'Dad' and Dewey, Bob Pritchitt, Lote Webb, Gene Martinier, and Fred Caunders. Mother and Father went with us, as well as Mrs. W. J. Griffith.

"There is nothing like camp life to get people acquainted with each other, is there? We lived in tents and cooked on the oil stove and swam and drove the automobile. We even took along the cat and the cow and pony!

"That was where I fell in love with Dewey," confessed the bride, unembarrassed, "and where Ruth and 'Dad' first started 'going together.' My engagement wasn't ever announced, but after the camp Dewey and I didn't go with anybody else, so I guess it was rather obvious.

Glad Football is Over

"Dewey and I had planned a big wedding, such as my sisters had, but we grew tired of waiting. So one day Dewey called me up and said, 'Let's get married today' and I said, 'Alright.'

"So we got married that night."

Just the bare details of a happening, but how fraught with romance! Questions elicited no more details. The small bride merely smiled and said that they didn't want to wait any longer and that she didn't mind missing the "big wedding" to which most girls look forward.

"Ruth and Loretta wanted to have a double wedding," she added, "but they never could get together on what kind of a wedding to have! Ruth wanted a church wedding and Loretta a home wedding. So each one had her own, in her own way. Loretta was married at home on the last day of May, and Ruth and 'Dad' had a church wedding at the Decatur Presbyterian Church on June 7th.

"They are both on their honeymoons now—Ruth in California and Loretta in Florida. When they come back, Ruth is going to build in Decatur next door to Mother, and Loretta is going to have an apartment in Atlanta like Dewey and I.

"Of course, it's mighty hard on Mother. Imagine having three daughters that you fondly hoped you were going to keep with you for a little while after they grew up—daughters who would marry off over a period of several years—and then to have them all rush off within two or three months of each other! Dewey and I would go out to see her very often to keep her from being lonesome.

"I'm glad Dewey isn't playing football anymore! And I think my sisters feel the same way. Dewey graduated from Tech last year, and so did 'Daddy,' while 'Six' was in the class of '17, so their football days are over. I used to get so scared when Dewey would go charging around over the field, for I just knew that he'd get killed! I met him in June of one year, and he played all through the next season so I had plenty of time in which to get scared.

"But he came out all right and we got married. I think that there's no doubt that Ruth and Loretta and I will highly recommend football players for husbands, particularly if they were Tech boys!"

—June 24, 1923

Divorces for Canaries

—⁓⁓—

Romances and Divorces Among Canaries Are Frequent,
Finds Mrs. Edward Smering, Atlanta's Canary Expert.
Even Co-respondents Are Found in the Canary World.
Mrs. Smering Declares That Her Fluffy Yellow Pets Are
Capable of Thoughts and Mental Processes as Complete as
Those of Human Beings, and That Their Small Hearts
Can Feel Both Love and Hate.

—⁓⁓—

"**B**irds in their little nests agree," runs the legend in the copy books that first-graders so painfully inscribe on scratch pads. And—

"Birds in their little nests agree," say mothers, reprovingly, when the young son of the family is prevented from braining his small sister with a meat ax.

But birds in their little nests don't agree. Like many other hoary-headed myths that are foisted on a credulous public, the belief that birds in their little nests were models of domestic bliss and worthy of emulation in human nests is firmly implanted.

But Mrs. Edward Smering, of 18 Matthewson Place, who has

made an exhaustive study of canaries and other birds, and who is the South's leading authority on bird breeding and doctoring, says that there is as much tragedy and divorce, as much love and self-sacrifice, in canary circles as there is in human ones.

Mrs. Smering knows her birds from the tips of their horny toes to the tips of their yellow heads. She not only raises canaries for the market and runs a bird hospital, but she even teaches her baby birds to sing. This is accomplished by hanging a "trainer" bird outside of the darkened cages of the youngsters or by playing flute-like selections on the small pipe organ that Mr. Smering has constructed for this very purpose.

Mrs. Smering not only knows the physical make-up of her feathered family, but she knows all the mental processes that go on behind the tiny bright eyes and the tragedies that take place in the cages that are home to canaries.

Good and Bad Canaries

As she approached the rows of cages that house the small songsters, they all hopped to the bars and chirped affectionately. Even the sick birds with their hunched shoulders and bedraggled feathers drew closer and poked small bills through the wire, as Mrs. Smering whistled softly to them.

There is no fear in their small hearts, for they know that she is their best friend, and when she puts a finger into the cages, they eagerly hop up on it and warble.

"Birds are very much like human beings," said Mrs. Smering, holding a yellow singer close to her lips so that it could kiss her with its small bill. "There are good canaries and bad ones and steadfast ones and fickle ones.

"For instance, sometimes a male and a female will be keeping house very happily and respectably and beginning to raise a family. Then the little wife will hear some other canary who sings better than her husband. His song is sweeter, and after she has listened for a day or two, she begins to get restless and discontented with her husband. Then there is nothing to do but move her from her cage and transfer her to the cage of the sweeter singer!

"One of my favorite birds was a small hen named Green River. She was a tiny, home-loving little person, very much like many sweet homebodies in real life. But her mate was just naturally a grouch—just like some men! He made himself very objectionable. Green River wanted to raise a family, but her mate's main idea in life seemed to be keeping her off the eggs.

"He wouldn't feed her when she sat on the nest, as a good mate should, and he wouldn't even sit on the eggs to keep them warm when she would hop down to eat.

The Neglected Wife

"Poor little Green River had a hard time hatching her eggs, because her objectionable husband was doing all he could to make life miserable. A good mate takes turns with the hen in keeping the eggs warm, while she hops about and gets food and exercise. He brings her choice pieces of lettuce that I put in the cage and sings his sweetest songs to keep her contented while she is on the nest.

"But Green River's mate did nothing of the sort. In fact, he worried her so much that I had to take him out of the cage. Canaries have separations and divorces, too! Green River had five little birds to take care of—five little babies with the most enormous mouths to be filled, and five little bodies to be covered at night.

"Little Green River acted just like a plucky little woman whose husband had deserted her. She worked morning and night keeping the hungry mouths of her five children filled till she wore herself down—for the care of the nest is the work of both the father bird and the mother too.

"One day I found that the smallest of the birds had disappeared. I couldn't imagine where it could have gone until the next morning, when I saw the little bird trying to bury her next smallest under the nest! Instinct told her that she couldn't take care of them all by herself, and so she was sacrificing the weakest babies so that the stronger might live!

"After that I helped her feed her family, pushing the food gently down their yellow throats with a feeder. She was the most appreciative little feathered bit! And she raised the rest of her children into a fine family of singers.

"I find that if the father bird is taken away or dies, the mother will raise the family, no matter what the struggle. But if it is the mother who is taken, the father never looks after the nest or raises the family. He always goes away and takes up with another hen, which is true in nine cases out of ten in human beings.

Canaries' Studio

"Birds have their love affairs and their heartbreaks, as people do, and their divorces and reconciliations. People can learn many things from birds—particularly children. Personally, I advocate a pet canary for all homes where there are children, for the study of birds is fascinating and instructive and teaches the helplessness of youth and of dumb things, and the sublimity of loving kindness."

In the basement of Mrs. Smering's home, she has fitted up one room for "lung" exercises for her baby birds. In this room is a tree, bare of limbs, extending from the floor to the ceiling, on which the birds can perch. The air is full of sweet twitters as the dozens of colored birds hop and fly about, trying both their wings and their voices.

When the singing lessons are in progress, Mrs. Smering darkens the room, and hangs a "trainer" canary outside the screen door. This bird, an expensive "roller" singer, so named because of the rolling trill of unfaltering notes that pours forth from his bill, sings his best to the listening youngsters. When he is removed, the young birds try to imitate his song, and, by practice, they gain perfection.

In the treatment of sick birds of all varieties, from mockers to parrots, Mrs. Smering is an authority. She has a bird hospital that is every whit as complete as a human one, for each bird has its room and chart, and its temperature is taken and recorded at specified intervals.

"There are only two causes of all bird illnesses," said Mrs. Smering. "One is through improper feeding and the other is by taking cold.

"Most people are not good diagnosticians and give their sick birds all manner of medicines to help the little fellows. Most of these remedies are no good at all. About the best medicine for a sick bird is ten drops of good whisky to five drops of castor oil administered a drop every hour."

—October 9, 1923

Wives Wanted by World's Greatest Freaks

How do they get that way?

Are they born freaks or do they acquire freakdom— these queer people of the Southeastern Fair over whom Atlanta was marvelling a week ago?

How did the snake charmers and the fire-eaters, the glass-dancer and the sword-swallower, the whatzit and the lion-faced man, get started in their professions?

Beneath the exteriors that the world calls "freakish" because they are different from the majority, what are the giants and the midgets like? Are they freakish alike of body and of mind? Or do they live simple, normal lives despite their abnormalities?

Sometimes freaks are born, sometimes they acquire freakdom through an accident, and sometimes they achieve it by constant practice. But one and all, when the spielers of the midway have shouted their last ballyhoo of the day, they become as other people closing up shop after a day's work, and they are just as willing to talk of their lives and their freakishness as business men are to "talk shop." Their conversation proves that freaks are an intelligent type of people despite their outward peculiarities. They are freaks, they know it, and are proud of the fact.

Lionel, the Lion-Faced man, enjoys the distinction of being unique, even in the world of freaks. His face, head, and even chest and shoulders are covered with long, tawny hair which gives him the leonine appearance from which he derives his name.

Although his entire face, with the exception of his eyes, is covered with hair, the blue eyes look out kindly and with intelligence from their hirsute fringe. Lionel was born covered with hair and as his father, an animal trainer, had been killed by lions, previous to his birth, his tawny hide was ascribed to prenatal influence. As the theory of prenatal influence was exploded some years ago, scientists can only deduce that he is the victim of atavism and is a throw back to some hairy ancestor.

May Marry Soon

Lionel is soft-spoken and well-mannered as becomes a gentleman of some wealth and education.

"I studied to be a dentist," he said, "but I gave it up because I knew that no one would let me work on them. I could make nothing at all in dentistry, whereas I can make any amount in a show because I am the only one of my kind." He shook his head a trifle sadly, but with dignity.

"No, I am not married, but I may be soon," he continued. "She lives in Chattanooga," and under the hairy covering, one felt that he was smiling. "I have a castle in Poland and two au-tomobiles—if I can get some girl to take me. Many of the freaks in the shows are married and are very happy—perhaps I shall be, too, some time. Who knows?"

"Orienta," snake charmer extraordinary, sat on her platform between acts with her slim ankles crossed, reading a copy of "Snappy Stories." Around her leg was coiled a torpid-looking snake that opened sleepy eyes and licked out a forked tongue as strangers approached. Orienta was young and pretty, and her black bobbed hair gave her the look of one of John Held's chic and flapperish "Belles," instead of an intrepid handler of poi-sonous reptiles.

"I wasn't born without fear of snakes," she admitted, putting down her magazine and unwrapping the snake from her ankle. "I think that fear of snakes is born in everyone. But I married the manager of this show and became accustomed to having them around. One day one of the charmers made me take up a snake and put it around my neck. Like most people, I loathed the thought of touching a reptile because I believed it would be cold and slimy. But snakes aren't slimy—they really are the cleanest of creatures. After once handling them, I was no longer afraid," and she caressed the languid-appearing serpent affec-tionately before gently placing it on the floor. It licked out its tongue in response to the pat and, gliding to her ankle, recoiled itself there comfortably.

Never Could Get a Wife

John Creech, who is eight feet, five inches tall, cannot sit on an ordinary chair because his knees will rub his ears. He says his height, his extreme thinness (for he weighs only 141 pounds), and his cadaverous appearance spoiled his matrimo-nial chances.

"Never could get a woman who would take me," he drawled from the heights with a twinkle in his eye. "Being tall has its disadvantages even if it is a good paying proposition. I wasn't born in the show business, as are so many people here. I was a country boy," and he laughed. "And I lived out on the Red River in Arkansas. When I started growing, I simply didn't stop, and though I eat five meals a day, I don't ever seem to be able to get fat.

"I went into the show business when the Red River over-flowed and ruined my farm and 'busted' me. It's a good life and I like it better than farming. Folks who are called 'freaks' aren't very different in the way they think and feel from folks who aren't freaks. They just look different."

Dare Devil Zelmas, the champion glass dancer and walker of the world, sat on a bench beside the box of sharp broken glass in which he dances with his bare feet, and carefully cared for his "stock in trade," as he terms his remarkable feet. Zelmas, who is English by birth, is a thin and pleasant-faced man, but jerky and nervous of talk—as anyone would naturally be who makes a living dancing in broken glass and climbing up and down ladders made of razor-sharp swords and saws.

"I jumped into the show business both literally and figura-tively," he said, massaging his delicate-looking feet, which de-spite his glass dancing habits show not a scratch. "When I was a little boy, I hated to wear shoes and was always getting spanked for running barefooted. Even now, I would go barefooted if it were the style, for though I can walk on razor blades without getting cut, shoes are absolute torture.

"One day, when I was eight years old, I was playing 'Follow the leader' and was leading a dozen children around through a building that was going up near my home. I jumped two sto-ries in my bare feet and landed on a pile of cut up rock—and didn't get a scratch! Mother was so thankful and surprised that she didn't even spank me. My jump caused so much comment that the show people heard of it and made me an offer.

Romantic Love Affair

"I've been in the profession for twenty-three years now. I am married—quite a romantic affair. I met her in Rio de Janeiro. My wife is an Italian singer, and she is in the profession, too. Her act is both a singing and a memory test," he continued proudly. "She has a wonderful memory, and anyone in the audience has only to name an aria from any opera and she can sing it immediately. We met in South America and were married there—and since then we have traveled the world together. We own a hotel in Chicago, and she is there now looking after it while I am on the road. Each year I say to her, 'This will be my last year in the game,' but each year there is too good an offer to be refused, so back on the road I go."

The glass dancer looked wistful and slipped his feet into the bedroom slippers that he wears between acts. "I want to spend the rest of my life in peace. Although I never cut myself, even when I jump ten feet into glass, still my feet are so sensitive that I feel it, and it gradually gets on my nerves, particularly if I have to give many performances a day."

"Yes, it is the too many performances that worry me, too," admitted Lorello, the man with the revolving neck who, like an owl, can twist his head all the way around and backward as easily as he can forward. "When I was in vaudeville, I did my trick three times a day, but in a side show one does these things too frequently. Each time I do my trick, my heart stops beating when I have turned my head just so far. And when I turn it farther, my heart beats again. Too often, I do it."

Lorello, who is German by birth, is a dark-haired, tragic-eyed man who talks English slowly and with a strong accent. His "act," of being able to twist his neck all the way around in a way that would certainly both strangle and break the vertebra of a normal person, is enough to make the hearts of the beholders stand still as well as the heart of the performer.

"When I was young, eighteen, by accident I found that my neck would twist like other people's would not," he continued. "After that, it was practice that made me able to do it so well. Everything, it comes by practice. When I could twist it all the way, I went in the show. I have a friend with the circus," he said brightening, "who can swallow any kind of sword, and now he is practicing swallowing an electric light bulb. It looks very funny to see him in the dark with the light shining through him," he smiled gently. "That came through practice. It is a good trick; but me, I prefer my own neck," he said proudly.

—October 21, 1923

Do Working Girls Make the Best Wives?

"Do married men make the best husbands?" runs the immortal question, and "What kind of women make the best wives?" is one coupled with it.

Do girls who have been reared with all the luxuries a fond father could bestow make better wives than girls who have known what it means to toil over a typewriter, or coach children through the Three Rs, or teach dancing or singing, or write advertisements?

Does the girl who has worked make a poor wife because she has become too practical, too masculine in her outlook, and too independent of men? Atlanta girls who are working say "no" with emphasis.

It is "smart" to work now. In Atlanta, it is even difficult for a hostess to gather together enough girls to have a four-table morning bridge party. And as for making good wives, the girls declare that far from ruining them as homemakers, a job before marriage is the best insurance of a happy married life. Girls who have worked realize the man's side of marriage as well as the woman's, and are more apt to make a real partner in the modern "fifty-fifty" marriage.

"Marrying a girl who has worked is a very different matter from what it would have been some years ago," laughed Miss Martha Stephenson, daughter of F. L. Stephenson, of Oakdale Drive, who graduated from Linmoore Hall this June and is "just dying to get a job."

Husband or Job?

"In the dark ages before 1914, when it became fashionable for women to work," she said, "men on matrimony bent used to count their pennies and sigh and think themselves very heroic to make sacrifices for the girl they loved." But it is different now. Usually a working girl gives up much more when she marries than her husband does. It is she who does some tall thinking about whether her life-mate is worth giving up a good salary for pretty clothes whenever she wants them, expensive perfume, and all the other privileges of a paycheck.

Miss Ruth Yarbrough, who is the daughter of Mrs. L. W. Yarbrough, of 323 Piedmont Avenue, had held a responsible position for some time at the Capitol in the Public Service Commission office. Slim and blonde, Miss Yarbrough has the charm and poise of one accustomed to drawing rooms as well as the tact requisite to a business woman.

"While I love my own work and wouldn't be without it, I don't advocate every girl working before she marries," said Miss Yarbrough slowly, as if considering the question from two sides. "I don't think that any girl should work except for two reasons, the first being that she has to work, and the second that she has an overweening desire or talent to do some one thing. I don't believe in girls getting jobs just because they have tried everything else and are bored. Such girls are mischief-makers.

"There is no doubt, however, that a girl who has worked makes a better wife than one who has not seen life from the masculine viewpoint of an eight-hour day. Then she can understand how a man feels when he comes home hot and fagged and sullen and just wants to flop down in a chair, and not talk or play bridge or run over to see the neighbors!

"A woman who has worked knows how it feels to come in tired, and she isn't so likely to nag her husband because he doesn't want to go to a dance or a movie after he has had a hard day. She knows the value and the necessity of rest and sleep after work.

"Of course, there's the other side, you know," she continued. "Although ex-working girls make the best wives, working undoubtedly does make a woman more independent and unfeminine and frequently keeps a girl from marrying at all. She get so accustomed to having her own money and things her own way that she keeps putting off getting married till she doesn't have any desire to."

Should Wives Work?

Miss Edna Horine, daughter of Mr. and Mrs. E. M. Horine, of 80 East Fourteenth Street, who has been teaching dancing in Atlanta for the last two years, is opening a school in Miami in October, where every type of dancing, from aesthetic to novelty dances, will be taught. Miss Horine, a piquant little blonde who is herself sufficient advertisement of the benefits derived from dancing, declares that she thinks all girls should not only work before they get married, but afterwards, too, if it is at all practicable.

"Of course, when there are children, it is out of the question for a wife to work," she said, "but it seems to me that a young married woman with no children would be so bored with life that she would welcome a job!

"I think every girl should know how to do some sort of work and do it well, whether she ever intends to marry or not. Work particularly helps a girl who intends to marry later. It teaches her the value of a dollar. She knows how hard money comes.

"A girl who has worked and has known what it means to give up parties and dates and keep long hours is not so likely to fling away thoughtlessly every cent her husband makes. She has learned consideration and has seen life from the man's viewpoint, and she isn't a poor sport when things go wrong. You see, she understands and doesn't pout about not having things her way."

Of like mind is Miss Christine McGhee, daughter of Mrs. Carlton Green, Piedmont Court Apartments. Miss McGhee, who studied voice both in New York and abroad, is now teaching it in Atlanta. As can be judged by her name, she has eyes of Irish blue that twinkle even in her most demure moods.

"The trouble with most modern marriages is that women expect too much from the young men they marry. They expect to have as much as their fathers gave them, and, of course, except in the case where a girl marries a man who has inherited wealth or is old enough to have made his pile, that is impossible. Yet the girls expect it, and most of them are disappointed if they don't get all they want.

"Martyr Before Her Bridge Club"

"When a young husband goes broke and his wife is one of those girls who never worked and didn't think it 'nice to work,' just hear her howl if she has to work! Or if she doesn't howl, how she enjoys posing as a martyr before her bridge club!

"American women are spoiled. They have their feet on the necks of the American men and intend to keep them there. When I was abroad, I noticed that the French women were always partners in their husbands' businesses, or at least knew all that the business was all about and were shrewd and practical in viewpoint.

While Miss Anna Harriet Shewmake, daughter of Mr. and Mrs. Claude Shewmake, of 606 West Peachtree Street, still has one more year at Mary Baldwin College before she can actually take a job, she has very definite ideas about women working before they marry.

"You know Emerson? I mean Ralph Waldo, himself? Well one of his remarks, that is a special pet of mine, is "Know thyself." No girl ought to marry before she knows herself and her capabilities and her limitations, and there is no better way to learn than by working.

"Thank goodness I'm not old fashioned about girls working," she continued. "Even if I do like Emerson, I believe that the world would be a lot better off and men and women would be much more satisfied and more understanding of each other if all girls worked before they married."

Miss Dorothy Talmadge, daughter of Mrs. Myrtle Talmadge, Park Lane, who has recently returned from New York, where she was employed in interior decorating, bases her theories on a very practical idea.

"Don't you know a lot of women who would starve to death if their husbands died and they didn't have any relatives to support them?" she asked. "Well, if those women had ever learned to do anything before they married, they would not be in such a plight. Even the very best of husbands die, sometimes, you know, and few men leave enough money to take care of a woman for the rest of her natural life. It is very bitter for a woman to have to go back to her family to be supported after her late lamented husband's life insurance has given out."

Miss Dorothy Hale, daughter of Mr. and Mrs. D. P. Hale, of 112 Hurt Street, is so diminutive that she is scarcely larger than the child pupils she teaches to dance. But though petite in stature and appealing of face, Miss Hale is as earnest about her work as though she were a statesman of responsibility or an engineer tunneling a mountain.

"I wouldn't be without my work for anything," she declared. "And I think that every girl who has ever worked feels the same way about it. Some men are so silly about not wanting women to work. They say that it ruins a woman's femininity and makes her mannish and all such foolishness. If men only realized that work makes a girl more considerate of the man she marries, they would have laws passed to make all girls work till they got married!

"Lots of times men criticize girls for being so thoughtless and inconsiderate of their husbands, but how is a girl going to know what a man rubs up against every day in his work unless she has had a taste of the same thing?"

—*July 13, 1924*

College Girls Tell How Men Should Propose

"When your father proposed to me," says Mamma, with that far-away look she reserves for such purposes, "he had been coming to see me for three years, but, of course, I never dreamed that he cared anything about me!"

"Your father was every inch a gentleman, and so he first asked my father if he could 'pay his addresses' to me, and when father said yes, your dear father came to me, as I sat on the sofa, in the parlor, and—well, he didn't exactly kneel down," confesses Mamma, with blushes, "but he thrilled me to death. He said, 'Miss Jones, may I call you by your first name?'"

"How sheikish!" murmurs the irreverent daughter of 1924.

"Then," continues Mamma, complacently, "he said that he wasn't worthy of an angel like me and quoted just reams of the most divine poetry and asked, 'Dare I hope that you will be the guiding star of my life, henceforth?'

"After I had told him that it was so sudden and that I'd have to have a month or so to think it over, we were engaged and in a year we were married."

As Mamma finishes her narrative of the kinds of proposals that thrilled girls in her day, daughter has a mental picture of a young lady of the early nineties, encased in a skin-tight basque, heaving breathlessly from combined emotion and lacings, as she sat upright on a horsehair sofa, all thrilled because a be-whiskered gallant in shepherd plaid pants was being so auda-cious as to call her by her first name.

"What an Egg!"

"Heavens, Mamma," says the daughter of 1924, "what an egg Father must have been! Poetry? I suppose he said that your teeth were like stars because they came out every night! I'd like to see a man spout poetry to ME when he's asking me to starve for life with him! As long as a man is able to say the right words, I don't care if they are 'Kid, I like your style. Let's get spliced!'"

That seems to be the idea of most modern girls about pro-posals. In days gone by, proposals were the high point of a girl's life, and if the time, scenery, and circumstances of her "ultimate surrender" were not appropriate the girls always cherished a se-cret grievance against her husband because his proposal had not been romantic. Sofas in front of fires, benches in moonlight, canoes at twilight, rose arbors at midday—all of these locales were popular in mother's day as were the appropriate language that went with the scenery.

Amorous young men had "lines" then, as well as now, though they were not so designated. That was the era that fostered such proposals as began, "I have led a terrible life—I am not worthy of you, but you alone can lead me upward to better things," and "For years I have worshiped you from afar—" and "You shall be the queen of my castle—" and endless pretty speeches that today are called "guff" by practical-minded girls.

Nowadays, to judge by the remarks of some twenty college girls, on the subject of their ideal proposal, young women are not so interested in how the right man proposes, as long as he does propose.

"The result's the thing," say Agnes Scott girls, and according to them, the proposal itself is a casual affair. However, they will admit, under pressure, that there still remains in the feminine heart a hankering after a romantic proposal—although poetry and "dear-I-am-not-worthy-of-you" do not figure in them at all.

No Proposals by Mail

One and all, however, they were unanimous in that no proposals should ever be accepted if made by mail!

"Goodness! If a man waited that long, I'd propose myself. I believe in Leap Year style. Of course, I'd ease the poor man along gently till he was unsuspicious of what my intentions were, and then I'd pop the question so fast that he would have no chance to turn me down!

(But after one look at the diablerie in the pretty blue eyes there is no believing that she would ever have to do any proposing!)

"I want something different when my big moment comes," said Georgia Mae Little, of Atlanta. "Seems to me that the novels and movies have exhausted all the romantic settings for proposals. I want to be proposed to by a man with a good 'line.' (I don't care what kind of line it is as long as it's a good one.) And I want it to happen on the Greyhound! Imagine the thrill of having him pop the question just at the top of one of those long dizzy drops into a dark tunnel!"

"Yes, but think how you'd give the whole thing away when you came out of the tunnel with your hat on the back of your head and your hair net in shreds!" coolly reminded Rosamonde Neisler, of Atlanta. "For my part, I want to have my proposal happen in the moonlight, in a high wall at the end of an avenue of sycamores."

"So you could push him over backwards if you didn't like his line of chatter, I suppose," interposed Georgia Mae Little. Rosamonde, however, continued serenely:

Lace Paper Bouquet

"I want the man who proposes to me to treat me like a human being—not a Dresden china shepherdess. I want it to be a fifty-fifty proposition, and I don't care for any pedestal stuff.

"And he'd better not do it in the morning! Any man who would ask a girl to marry him in the morning has no idea of the fitness of things. And I don't want the man to be so scared that I wasn't going to take him that he would be all upset about it."

"Yet, of all flat tires there's nothing worse than a man who is sure that you are going to accept him!" declared Polly Stone, of Atlanta. "That ruins a proposal. For my part, I like an old-fashioned touch to a 'will-you-be-mine?' I want a regular hand on heart and lace paper bouquet proposal because that would be romantic. What's thrilling about someone saying, 'Sister, ain't that hot? What do you say, we two can eat as cheap as one.'"

Out of the back of the crowd came an anonymous voice:

"Girls, maybe you think I'm mercenary, but I think if a man long-distanced me from Frisco or New York so that it costs fifty-eight dollars, I'd accept him right away, because I know that his heart and his pocketbook were in the right place! That would be my idea of an ideal proposal, and if I didn't happen to want to accept him, I could hang up on him and act as if central had cut me off!"

No Sheik Stuff

"I don't want any 'sheik' proposal, but outside of that type it makes no difference how he does, as long as he gets the fatal words, 'Will you marry me?' out of his mouth," said Mary Ben Wright, of Atlanta. "I don't want a caveman proposal, but, of course, a girl likes to feel that a man could be masterful. It makes it so thrilling! I don't want him to say much. I'd rather his actions spoke for him."

"All I ask is that the man who proposes to me be original in the line he hands out," was the plea of Isabelle Clarke, of Atlanta. "Men seem to cling to the same old lines and the same old methods. It would be refreshing if he would get new ways of saying sweet nothings. Why, you can simply catalogue the methods of proposals and know that you are getting proposal number six or seven or nine!

"As long as he was original and was truthful that would be all I'd ask. I wouldn't want a man who'd lie to me and say, 'Life with me will be a path of roses and I'll run ahead of you and pick out all the thorns!' I want the truth."

"I'm modern," said Billie Cowan, of Conyers, Ga. "I want an up-to-date proposal in the front seat of a high-powered auto and a foxtrot proposal at that. I want it to be peppy. If I knew anyone who had an airplane, I'd prefer a man to pop the question up in the air!"

"I'm a conservative," said Dina Thornton, of Elberton. "While I could dispense with much of the slushy sentiment of the Victorian era, and use a lot of the pep of 1924, I'd prefer a good combination; for instance, a touch of sentiment backed up with humor and pep."

Marion Cawthorne, of De Funiak, Fla., said that any hint of domesticity in a proposal would ruin it for her.

"I can't abide poetry in love making and I think it is terrible that every man always starts with your eyes when he begins to 'speak softly,' but on the other hand, I don't want anyone to say, "Dearie, what about cooking my dinners and mending my socks for the rest of your life?' I'm not that anxious for the truth."

—March 23, 1924

Georgia Bids Good-bye to Elopements

Alas for romance! It has been struck a body blow by the unfeeling Georgia legislature. Eloping has been legislated almost out of existence in this state by the new law requiring five days' posting of applications for marriage licenses.

No longer can the lover kidnap his sweetheart from under her family's vigilant eyes, crank up his trusty Ford, and begin a mad race for the nearest minister. No longer will the irate father, breathing vengeance, give pursuit in the family Lincoln, only to arrive too late to stop the ceremony. The new law has eliminated the hasty marriage and leisurely repentance (with which most people could dispense), but it is with reluctance that Georgia gives up the stock characters of elopements, the excited but determined lovers, the hysterical mother of the bride, the enraged father, the benign minister.

With the passing of elopements from Georgia, the newspapers have lost one of their best features, for, next to murders, elopements are most popular reading with the reading public. When the well-known headlines appear, "Elopers Elude Parents," or "Parents Forgive Eloping Couple," certain readers settle back with smiles, sympathetic, sentimental, or grim, to learn how the bride climbed down the ladder from her window, and how the groom narrowly escaped a load of buckshot at the hands of his future father-in-law. They breathe a sigh of relief that the loving hearts were at last united in the parlor of a sleepy minister.

The practical-minded legislature has cut down on the public diet of romance. With the working out of the new law, the secret marriage, the marriage while intoxicated, the marriage on impulse, and the cave-man wedding will all go the way of the elopement. The secret marriage becomes automatically an impossibility, for there is nothing less secret than the bulletin board in the ordinary's office where the applications for licenses are posted.

No longer will it be possible for a young girl to "be swept off her feet" by a determined lover who comes a-wooing, armed with a license procured unknown by his lady fair. This practice in bygone days seldom failed to make the girl "sign on the dotted line" if the groom followed up the presentation of the license with cave-man stuff and carried her off to the minister before her head stopped whirling.

There is little chance of success for this system now, depending as it did on an audacious unexpectedness for its strength. Under the present law, a girl would be well aware of the intentions of the would-be groom after his application had been posted five days and other young men, under the impression that they, too, were engaged to her, had called on the ordinary, only to discover the truth.

The five days that must elapse between the first burning desire to get married and the ceremony will probably be a blessing to impulsive youngsters whose ardor very likely cool if given time to think over minor details such as finances, jobs, the inability of the bride to cook or the groom to keep his temper.

Not only are Georgia lovers faced with the fact that there is no place for them to elope to, unless they travel all the way to Florida or South Carolina (where marriage is easy to get into but impossible to get out of), but eloping couples from other states where marriage laws are stringent find themselves as much at a loss as Georgians.

For many years Georgia has been used as the Gretna Green of other states. Alabama requires a physical examination entailing several days delay before a license will be granted, and Alabama elopers also have been in the habit of crossing the Georgia line to be married.

When the new Georgia law went into effect, many couples from Tennessee and Alabama who had crossed into the Georgia border towns to be married were filled with consternation at discovering that they had taken all their trouble in vain. They found that Berth M. Clay's novel, "Parted at the Altar," had a personal significance that was not at all pleasant, and in many cases the pursuing parents were enabled, by the delay, to recapture their daughters.

In Atlanta, for the most part, the shouting and the tumult occasioned by the new law has died and the bridegrooms and the brides departed. However, there are still frantic young men who tear their hair in the ordinary's office because they did not realize that the day upon which the application is made does not count as one of the five days, and as a result many marriages with dates set for five days after the application have been held up another additional day, to the intense annoyance of all concerned.

The "emergency cases" where the ordinary, at his discretion, issues licenses to take effect immediately, are sometimes very amusing. The parents of the contracting parties must appear to give their approval, and in the cases of middle-aged and thoroughly responsible brides and grooms, the appearance of an aged white-whiskered father or a small, faded mother gives a comic air to the proceedings.

—September 14, 1924

Marriage Licences that Are Never Used

The old-fashioned girl collected hope chests and pined herself into a decline when fate intervened so that she never could use them. The modern girl collects marriage licenses that she doesn't use, and instead of pining away from broken heart, usually congratulates herself on her lucky escape and numbers them among her trophies of the chase.

There are many girls in Atlanta who have hidden away in locked boxes and in the bottoms of bureau drawers licenses that bear their names and those of men who certainly are not their husbands—licenses that were not used for any number of feminine reasons.

Judge Thomas Jeffries, ordinary of Fulton County, says that there is no way of estimating the number of licenses that are unused because "successes advertise themselves but people try to cover up failures." However, some unused licenses have been turned back to the ordinary's office, usually with the idea of having the price refunded.

"One night," said Claude Mason, clerk of the ordinary's court, "a tall, gangling countryman who had just purchased a license that morning rambled in and stood uncertainly in the door. He was dressed in his Sunday best and in his button hole, in lieu of a boutonniere, was thrust the frilled tissue paper end of the wrapping of a molasses candy kiss. Finally I enticed him over to the counter and asked him what he wanted.

"'She's done backed out,' he said, and reaching in his pocket, he pulled out the license and threw it down on the counter. 'I want my money back. This piece o' paper ain't no good to me.'

"A Bull-Headed Girl"

"I explained that we didn't refund money on unused licenses and tried to give him a little Dorothy Dixish advice. I said,

'When your girl said *yes* the first time, you couldn't marry her because you didn't have the license, and so she got out of the notion. Now, you just take this license back and carry it around with you till the time she gets back in the notion again, and then you can run her right on up to the preacher's before she gets time to change her mind.

"'You don't know that bull-headed gal like I do,' he said, sadly. 'She don't never get back into a notion once she's out of it,' but he picked up the license and went on out. I've often wondered if her notion to marry him ever came back."

"Lots of people want their money back when they don't use the license," said Judge Jeffries, "but I never gave it back except in one case. One man who was evidently in very poor circumstances brought back his unused license and begged for his money. His was a very sad case—his bride had died on their wedding day. He evidently needed every cent he could get, so I returned the money.

Cold Feet

"One young man," continued the dispenser of licenses, "came in and asked to be issued a marriage license. After I had made it out and he had paid for it, he pulled another license out of his pocket and said, 'Will this previous one taken out for my fiancee make mine illegal?'

"I looked at it and found that it was made out for his girl and another man.

"'You see, I cut him out,' he explained, 'and so she gave this to me.'

"I told him to tear it up, that the other man never would have any further use for it.

"Many people who have made application for licenses since the new law went into effect have never come for their licenses. As to why they don't show up, I don't know. Get cold feet, I suppose."

There is one Atlanta girl, since married and living in New York, who will always think of Judge Jeffries in the light of a kindly and rescuing angel. She was possessed of a red-haired "beau" of untiring persistence whom she had no intention of marrying. Her father threatened to disown her should she even contemplate matrimony with him, and her real fiancé grew green with jealousy whenever his rival's name was mentioned.

But the red-haired lover took out a license on New Year's Eve, knowing that he would see the girl at a masquerade given at Marietta, Ga. that night. He inveigled her into his car with another couple, between dances, and drove her to the door of one of the Marietta ministers, and drawing up in front of the house he displayed the license and said masterfully, "Now, no more foolishness!"

Appealed to Judge Jeffries

After an hour of anger and pleading and threatening, they returned to the dance, the lover chagrined, the girl hysterical, the license having changed hands. The next morning a tearful young lady was waiting in front of the courthouse before any officials arrived. When Judge Jeffries put in appearance, she told him her troubles, explaining that her father was a lawyer and might be in the courthouse and see the stub of the license—"And he'd never believe me," she finished. Of course she didn't want to tempt Judge Jeffries into doing something illegal in destroying the incriminating stub but—

However, there was no law compelling the ordinary to keep the stubs, and so the judge destroyed hers and restored her peace of mind.

"I had an awful time explaining a license and a wedding ring that I bought for myself during the war," confessed a former debutante who has since married and is now the proud mother of a little daughter. "I was very young when the war broke out, but I thought I was so old, and I was desperately anxious to send boys away with a smile and to go to dances at Camp Gordon and wear crossed guns like the older girls.

"But mother wouldn't let me. She said I was 'uniform crazy,' and sent me to school in New York. Of course every girl who ever went to a boarding school has had a secret love or a tragedy in her life, because that's all that made the blamed places endurable. Of course, I didn't have any black past or romance—(no school girl ever has one)—but I made up one just like the rest of the girls.

"I spent the last of my allowance before going north in buying a wide gold wedding ring (I yearned for platinum but it cost too much) and took out a license. Maybe I wasn't scared when I did it! Course, I made up a man's name—a lieutenant. I wouldn't have ever gotten the idea except for a movie Madge Kennedy was playing in where the girl did the same thing.

Mother Had a Fit

"I took it off to school and told about how we were to have been married but he was ordered off—used to wear the ugly old ring on a dirty ribbon around my neck. It went over big. And then I killed him off in the Argonne and was a young heroine till the end of the semester. I was so brave it hurt.

"But when I went home mother went through my trunk to mend my clothes, and found the ring and the license, and just had a fit. She showed it to father and sister and you'd have thought I had been caught in murder. When I told them the truth, they wouldn't believe me, and when I told them lies they hit the ceiling. They watched me like a hawk for months, thinking I was going to run off and elope with my fictitious lieutenant when he came back from France. I never hated any man so much in my life as I did that one I made up. He kept me from going to so many dances and having so much fun.

Mother still believes that I'm holding out on her—even after all these years."

"A couple of unused licenses cost me a perfectly good fiancé," admitted another young matron, who made her debut some few years ago. "I was engaged to a real sweet boy, one of the serious kind who believed everything you told him, and I was really thinking about marrying him at some time or other. Just like every other girl, I had lied to him and sworn I had never been engaged before or even in love, and of course I had! It would be dreadful to be twenty and never have been engaged!

"I had the licenses that boys had taken out for me and never used because I got cold feet and wanted to be married in white satin and a veil instead of eloping in a coat suit. I kept them in a drawer in my old secretary along with some real hot love letters. I learned my lesson about keeping letters and incriminating documents right then!

"But I had kept those licenses because all the girls in my crowd were making a collection of them—(it was lots more fun than collecting frat pins). It didn't bother me when my serious-minded friend showed up one day with a brand-new license and a request that I elope with him. Of course, I talked him out of it and took away the license and that made three! There was only one other girl in the crowd who had four and I wanted to break her record. I put the license in the drawer of the secretary, locked it and hid the key under the overstuffed cushion on the sofa.

A Prying Fiancé

"And then I got appendicitis. It was acute and they thought I was going to die, and I was so sick I didn't care whether I died or not. But my fiancé wouldn't even come to see me. It nearly broke my heart, till I got well enough to take an interest in the interns. When I was getting well, he came around to see me, and he was so mad that his hair was on end. Seems like the poor egg had been afraid I'd die and that the family would find the license and wonder about it so he had taken it upon himself to go in the secretary and destroy the license. And, lo and behold, he found two others made out by boys he simply couldn't stand. Of course, it served him right for being so prying, and it made me so mad that I didn't mind him calling me all kinds of things before he shook me."

"Of course, I married a lot sweeter man, so I'm glad it all happened, but all the same—"

"Oh, yes, I had a license that was never used," admitted one young matron who had been married for four years, and to the same man who took the license out. "I had been engaged secretly for some months while Edwin was a senior in college. Father didn't approve of him because he was so young and still in school and played on the football team. Father never believed that anything good could come from a boy who played football.

"I used to cry my pillow wet lots of times wondering how it was all going to come out! Lots of times when I went over to the university to dances, he'd try to persuade me to marry him secretly, but somehow I had sense enough not to. Then, one day, he came to town, took out the license, hired the biggest limousine in town (it looked for all the world like a funeral carriage), rolled 'round to my house and said masterfully that we were going to get married.

"Oh, I was thrilled about it, all right, for about five minutes, and then I got some sense and refused and took the license away from him. (I was afraid he'd take it back to Athens with him and his roommate would see it and then it would be all over the university.) He went off in the funeral wagon in an awful huff and swore he'd never speak to me again. And I cried—and cried—till that night when I got a special and some violets from him!

"I put the license away and forgot about it till we really decided to get married, with consent of parents. And then I couldn't find it anywhere. So we took out another one and got married. And at the wedding supper, when everybody was reading foolish telegrams, father got up and produced the old license (it was rather dirty by that time), read it and chuckled and—and the date. He had had it all the time!"

—*March 15, 1925*

Athens, Georgia, referred to in the article above, is the home of the University of Georgia.

Shot Three Times, Missed Him— Divorced

Last straws.

The little things that break the backs of camels and the yoke of matrimony! The repetition of an irritating phrase, "If you don't like my peaches don't shake my tree," has done more toward precipitating divorce proceedings than delicate attentions with flatirons. Also, husbands who pull vines down on porches every night are more to be hated than those who black eyes for love's sweet sake. At least, as testimonies given in divorce cases in Atlanta courts seem to indicate.

One wife put up with her husband's habit of taking her money until he "flung a party" and failed to include her among the guests. Another finally became wearied of her spouse's remarks that he was going to blow her brains out; while one Atlanta husband testified that the straw that broke his endurance was when his wife shot at him three times—and missed!

Loss of temper, to judge by most cases in the Atlanta courts, is the prime cause of many separations and of many erratic actions. Temper that leads to sullenness is a great factor in "last straws" that precipitate divorces.

It would seem that a woman would like nothing better than to have the floor entirely to herself when she was expressing her opinions of her life mate, but to judge by the number of petitions filed on grounds of "husbands refusing to speak" to wives, such is not the case.

"My husband used to come home at night and take off his hat in silence and not even kiss me," said one wife. "Whether the supper was good or bad he wouldn't say anything. He'd just set and wouldn't say a word no matter what I said to him. He wouldn't speak if I cried or if I fussed. He didn't speak to me for two whole weeks and at last I couldn't stand it any longer. The only word I got out of him was when I told him I was going to get a divorce.

"Then he said, 'Good.'"

Threw Bed Clothes on the Floor

There are few women who will not agree that the worst possible cruelty that can be inflicted on a woman is not to answer back when she is "spoiling for a fight."

"My husband used to get in a pet about little things," testified a small blond woman, "and he'd come home from work so mad I could not get a civil word out of him. I put up with it till he started pulling off all the bed clothes every time he lost his temper. He'd get mad as sin, snatch all the bed covers off, throw them in the middle of the floor, and sit on them. And he'd sit there all night so that I couldn't sleep."

"My husband used to snatch all the vines off the porch," stated another woman impressively, and the jury looked puzzled.

"Snatch off the vines?" questioned the judge, bewildered.

"I had planted vines by the porch of our bungalow," explained the injured party, "and trained them up on strings to grow over the porch. They were the only thing that made the house pretty and homelike, and he knew I set a store by them. And every time he'd get mad he'd tear out on the porch and snatch at the vines and break the strings and throw them all on the ground. One night after he'd been out there a-snatching, I just decided that I'd stood enough. So I took my hat and went home to my folks. That don't seem like much, your honor, but. . ."

"It's the little things that count after all, gentlemen," observed the judge, who knew from long experience in divorce courts that women cannot stand having the "pretty fixings" of their homes systematically wrecked!

The Dentist's Wife

Jealousy leads to many impulsive deeds as the divorce records show, particularly in the wives of professional men, such as doctors and dentists, who come in contact with many women in a professional capacity. The wife of one dentist, according to his testimony, used to call him every hour to make sure that he was still in his office.

"She would always manage to call just when I was filling a patient's tooth," testified the dentist, "or when I was treating an abscess, and if I didn't come to the phone, she'd cry and take on about it that night, saying that I hadn't been in my office but had my office nurse posted to say I was busy. Then she took to coming down to the office and sitting there most of the day and glaring at nice-looking patients. She even insisted that I keep my office door open so she could watch me.

"As a result, my practice suffered and I worried myself nigh to death."

The experience of a doctor was similar. His wife not only

insisted on sitting in his outer office, but insulting his office nurse and insisting that he get a male assistant.

A pretty manicurist, whose wages were the chief support of the family, applied for divorce on the grounds that her husband was so jealous that the thought of her touching other men's hands even with nail buffers and files "gave him fits."

"He said he knew I wasn't true to him if I held other men's hands. He even came down to the place where I worked and sat there looking black and nasty till my boss told me I'd lose my job if I didn't make him stop."

Trailed by Detectives

Too numerous to mention are the divorce cases where jealous husbands or wives testify to discovering that their mates had employed private detectives to trail them. Frequently, it has been proven that each party had the other under surveillance by detectives. This fact was brought out in the testimony of one indignant wife who evidently did not believe that what was sauce for the gander was also sauce for the goose. When invited in dulcet tones by her lawyer to tell the jury the wrongs suffered at the hands of her husband, her words tumbled out, head over heels.

"He was so jealous—he didn't trust me at all. He was suspicious of every move I made, and my life was miserable. It just ruined my health. Why, he even put a detective on my trail!"

"How did you discover this?" questioned the judge.

"Why, the private detective I had watching my husband told me about it," explained the self-righteous lady.

One of the most interesting and most pathetic cases was that of a young woman, holding the hand of a handsome little red-haired boy, who testified that she had lived in perfect happiness with her husband until one day when she chanced to open a letter addressed to him from a legal firm. It was then she discovered for the first time that he had been previously married and was, at the time, applying for a divorce from wife No. 1.

"He said he thought that she was dead," explained the young mother, "and when he found out that she wasn't, he thought he could file suit and get a divorce from her and that I would never know."

A pretty woman, accompanied by a young and pretty daughter, had little difficulty when she told the jury that she had not minded her husband's habitually drunken state nor the profanity he showered upon her, but that she could stand no more when he informed her that she was "old and ugly and he was tired of her."

"That's not only cruelty—that's brutality," said the presiding judge.

Missed Him Three Times

Under the head of severe mental anguish came two suits involving the threatened use of firearms. In the case of the first, a young woman testified that her husband had never struck her, cursed her, or in any way abused her, but that he had a bad habit of taking out his pistol, oiling and polishing it all night as he sat on the edge of the bed, while she peered at him over the edge of the coverlet. At the same time, he would remark over and over that some night he was going to blow her head off.

"It gave me nervous prostration," she finished.

"No wonder," said the judge, sympathetically.

In the second case, the testimony of an aggrieved husband disproved the theory that an angry or frightened woman can always shoot a man squarely in the stomach, no matter how poor her marksmanship ordinarily.

"My wife lost her temper one night because I wouldn't take her to a dance, and she pulled my pistol from the top drawer and shot at me three times. She missed me all three times, and it made her so mad that she threw the gun at me and started screaming. She made so much racket that we got put out of our apartment. The embarrassment of that was almost as bad as being shot at."

"My wife refused to have any children," said a mild-voiced, middle-aged man. "I love children and she hated them. Except for this we were quite happy. But she was always running around to parties—and I didn't like to go out much—and as a result I stayed at home and was lonely. I wanted a child, but she said no, it would take up too much of her time looking after it."

"My wife used to stay out till all hours, and I wouldn't know where she was," was the plaint of another occupant of the witness box. "And when I'd say, 'You must stop doing this; you must stay at home,' she'd always answer, 'If you don't like my peaches, don't shake my tree.' Your honor, I stood for her saying that for two years, and one night she said it once too often!"

"My husband was awfully extravagant, and used to throw away all his wages on parties," testified one young wife, "till at last he told me I'd have to go to work. I didn't mind that so much, though it nearly killed my family, but he took to taking my money every week. I never got a cent, even to buy new hats with. He used to fling parties with my money—and never once invited me to one!"

—*February 8, 1925*

4

Personality Sketches

Hollywood heartthrob Rudolph Valentino and Mitchell chatted on the
roof of the Georgian Terrace Hotel for a 1923 interview

Plant Wizard Does Miracles Here

There's a man out Peachtree road who can give a strawberry plant a "shot in the arm" and make it feel so good that it doesn't care a whoop for freezing weather. He has a bunch of these immoderately bold plants with big, red, juicy strawberries on them, growing out in the open air, right now—not in a hothouse or under glass—but in the chill of this January weather.

And winter-bearing strawberries are not the only strange things that this plant magician has produced. He has pried into Nature's innermost secrets, so that he is able to make ordinary plants and trees do extraordinary things.

With a doctor's hypodermic needle, he injects a mysterious solution into a plant that makes it forget all the traditions of its ancestry. Sensitive plants, like the strawberry, he can render totally indifferent to cold weather and make them ever-blooming and bearing. Plants that naturally grow to a great size, he dwarfs to pigmies, and vice versa.

It's all so unreal that it's hard to believe until you've seen his collection of weird plants.

Chestnuts Big as Lemons

Here's a chestnut tree, full grown, but dwarfed to the height of eight feet, yet bearing chestnuts nearly as big as lemons. And there is a magnolia, in full-foliage, its usual glossy, green leaves now a bright gold with a tiny border of green on the edges. Here are some dwarf fruit trees, which, having bloomed in September, are now crowded with tiny apples and pears.

"Grafting" plants for the creation of a new species is not what this man does. By his injected solution, he is able to produce hybrid plants, as for instance, his cypress.

This diminutive tree was originally a cypress and is still a cypress, but now has the additional feature of being a spruce, a cedar, and an arbor vitae, as well as a cypress. For the magic solution injected has caused the separate natures of the four trees to be blended into one—a queer sort of tree, which has four kinds of foliage appearing on it at once, indiscriminately and with no apparent system at all.

Over there is a Japonica, which looks as if it belonged in *Alice in Wonderland* or in a fever dream. Remember how Alice was always eating and drinking things that either made her too large or too small? That's what happened to this Japonica, in the strange garden on Peachtree road.

By nature, a Japonica is tall and graceful, with narrow leaves shooting out at intervals from the joints, only one on each side. This flower is still a Japonica, but its own mother wouldn't know it. Instead of being slim, graceful, and sparing of leaves, it is thick of stem, short, and adipose, and where only two leaves grow at a joint, some twelve or fourteen fat leaves crowd each other for existence on the stem. The Japonica has had a "shot in the arm."

Specialist in "Sports"

All this sounds like the ravings of a disordered imagination. But these strange plants are actually growing right here in Fulton County, and the magician who produced them is a native Georgian.

His name is Iverson D. Hudgins, and he is an employee of

Ashford Park Nurseries, a man who has learned secrets of plant growth and propagation which are perhaps known to no other human being, certainly no other occidental.

By trade, he is a nurseryman, and he does a day's work at Ashford Park Nurseries, on Peachtree Road, out beyond Oglethorpe University. By nature and profession, he is a scientist in botany, one who has gone deeply into plant lore and acquired original knowledge of the life processes of flowers, fruits, and trees. Like many another scientist, he has been contented to acquire this knowledge simply for the sake of acquiring it and he has not attempted to benefit by it. In fact, he is so thoroughly indifferent to the practical side of his scientific discoveries that his work is practically unknown even here in his home city of Atlanta.

Mr. Hudgins is a specialist in "sports." The origin and causes of "sports" have heretofore defied the analysis of scientists, but he knows why they happen and what produces them. A "sport" is the scientific name for a freak in the botanical world.

It is a specimen that defies all rules of its family for no apparent reasons. An enormously large chestnut tree, of the same variety as much smaller trees, would be a "sport."

"Thyroid" Solutions for Plants

Mr. Hudgins' theory of the causes of "sports" is that insects, carrying pollen and plant protoplasm from plants of a relative species, inject this substance, by biting, into other plants, thereby causing them to react in peculiar ways.

Taking this theory as a basis, Mr. Hudgins has spent years of investigation. Many years ago, an American brought back from India the information that the marvelous "magic" tricks of the eastern fakirs were not tricks at all, but realities. The trick of making beans and mangoes grow before one's eyes was actually done. The Indians had discovered that a certain insect, while laying its eggs in the bark of trees, injects an acidulous fluid to protect the eggs. By using this fluid in a solution of plant protoplasm, they were able to produce unnaturally rapid growth and size in plants.

Scientists for years have been experimenting on human beings with Thyroid solution, in attempts to discover a solution that will make human growth controllable. They have been unsuccessful. Mr. Hudgins has made this discovery for the plant world.

His experiments and discoveries are still more remarkable in light of the fact that he has not the use of one arm and one eye, due to burns received in early childhood. Yet despite these handicaps, he has pursued his scientific investigations with unswerving zeal.

Knows 8,000 Botanical Names

He is a small man with a kindly face, a white mustache, and a shock of white Paderewski-like hair on which a battered derby was tilted. A shirt open at the collar, a sailor's peajacket, and a pair of muddy, kneeless trousers completed his costume. But from the lips of this muddly little man issued faultless English and a bewildering flow of Latin names of his beloved plants. Questions brought out the fact that he had taught chemistry, botany, and allied sciences for eighteen years at Gainesville, Georgia. During this period he dabbled in floristry, but, finally, the call of the vegetable kingdom was too strong for him, and giving up teaching, he has devoted his life to experiments.

There are over eight thousand botanical names that he can call off-hand and talk volubly on each one. He has an artist's and a scientist's pride in his ever-bearing strawberries and dwarf chestnuts, and talks of them eagerly and with affection.

When he wishes to change the color or nature of a plant, he simply takes a hypodermic needle, fills it with chlorophyll, the scientific name for vegetable coloring matter; protoplasm; and this mysterious "India solution;" and injects it into a study of a plant.

In this way he has produced variegated magnolias and also a box hedge which is bright pink, almost red, instead of [its] natural color of green. Some of the things that he has produced are freaks and nothing more. Others, he believes, will be valued additions to the plant life of America.

"From my experiments, I believe we will be able eventually to produce plants like the strawberry that will bear all the year round," Mr. Hudgins said. "I have already produced a hardy variety which is able to live through an Atlanta winter, and I hope to develop it still further. With the aid of this 'India Solution,' there will be no limits to the progress that science can make in our horticultural industry."

Mr. Hudgins was born in Hall County and comes of a family of florists and botanists. He has lived in Georgia all his life and his has been an inconspicuous place, but in future years science may accord him his rightful place of honor as one who has made valuable contributions to the world's knowledge.

—January 7, 1923

I can't stand perfumes.

—⟋⟋⟍—

I believe another war is to be fought soon and that weapons will be used in it such as men have never before dreamed of—high explosives that will lift entire towns off the map, bombing planes that will carry huge crews, and gas—the most damnable thing God ever allowed to be invented.

—⟋⟋⟍—

I believe my greatest invention is not an explosive, but a book—*The Science of Poetry*.

—⟋⟋⟍—

I know Gutzon Borglum will succeed in printing a photograph of his war memorial across the face of Stone Mountain.

—⟋⟋⟍—

These are excerpts from the accompanying interview with Hudson Maxim, famous inventor, secured for the *Journal's Sunday Magazine* while Mr. Maxim was in Atlanta recently to attend the National Conference for Boll Weevil Control.

Maxim Talks of Perfume, War, and Poetry

Mrs. Maxim, tiny and sweet-faced, was holding Hudson Maxim's bare feet on her lap, drawing on his socks, in their room at the Piedmont Hotel, where the interviewer entered, somewhat abashed.

"Oh, don't mind this," roared the inventor, affably, waving one bare foot cordially toward a chair, "I'm used to being interviewed while dressing. I've been interviewed in nearly every stage of negligee except the bathtub."

He plunged back into the deep chair in his characteristic posture, his neck on the back of the chair, his body sprawled out. Great is the power of genius—it can afford to be natural! Mrs. Maxim continued to pull on her husband's socks, unconcerned.

Hudson Maxim tugged at his white beard and smiled—a sturdy old man with magnificent leonine head topped by a mass of unruly white curls, a personality as well as a celebrity. Seventy years old, but vigorous and hard-muscled, his dynamic force radiates from his piercing brown eyes and in every sudden movement of his body. The telephone was jangling every other minute and secretaries running in and out. Mr. Maxim was plainly restless and rolled and twisted in his chair, jerking his foot back and forth out of his wife's grasp. However, she remained serene and smiling, gripping his ankle firmly.

"I'm glad you didn't wear any perfume," declared he, sniffing at the interviewer. "I can't stand perfume." (The interviewer had been carefully warned before hand.) "It isn't just an obsession or my imagination. Perfume really has a bad effect on me. I am supersensitive to smells.

"The sense of smell in animals is more strongly developed than sight. As you know, a dog will run by a rabbit that he is trailing, for he will be following the smell.

"But with men, the sense of sight is stronger. I suppose my sense of smell is as highly developed as an animal's, but at any rate, my nose is supersensitive and the smell of perfume makes me sick. It gives me a violent pain here," and he clutched at the back of his head and made a ferocious face.

"I cannot stand the smell of perfume and I don't see why I should try. So I don't. Once I went to the theater with Lovely (Mrs. Maxim) when I had such a bad cold that I couldn't smell anything. Yet before I had been there five minutes, I developed a terrible headache, exactly the kind I always get when I smell perfume, yet I could not smell a thing. We had to leave and Lovely said that a woman a few rows below us was simply soaked in perfume.

Another War Soon

"I have found that men who make dirigible balloons suffer in the same way. They have to paint the outside of the gas bag with strong chemicals, and constant contact with the odors makes them unbelievably sensitive, particularly to perfume.

"I was the same way with tobacco. I never smoked, myself, and always avoided people who did smoke. But one unlucky day, in London, an officer invited me to dinner at the Army-Navy Club. The place simply reeked with smoke. I—I endured it," he said, grimly. "That is, I didn't rush out of the club, cursing at the top of my voice, as I was inclined. But I was sick for three weeks and my face turned to purple. Did something to my liver—don't know what, but it was aplenty!"

Hudson Maxim, world's greatest inventor of high explosives and smokeless powder was, with Theodore Roosevelt, America's strongest "preparedness" advocate. It was he who wrote *Defenseless America* in 1914, from which the photoplay *The Battle Cry of Peace,* was made. In those days he was advocating preparedness in the contingency of war.

Now, he does not talk of preparedness, but of the fearful weapons that will be used in the next war.

"Of course, there will be another war soon," he said. "Perhaps America will not be drawn into it. But the European situation is very shaky now and real war seems imminent any moment. Germany has the greatest resource in all the world—the German Wife!

"In twenty years the German wife will have so throughly re-populated Germany that the losses in the last war will not be remembered. Then we will hear from Germany for certain!

"There will certainly be war in Europe before long, but the biggest war the world will ever see is yet to come. It will not be between the forces of the White and Yellow races, but between the clear-thinking, sane people of the world and the insane, rabid forces that are always working for the destruction of Civilization!"

Evidently, Mr. Maxim feels very strongly on this subject, for he sat up and pounded vigorously on the table and then writhed himself back into his comfortable slump.

"In the next war there will be weapons never even thought of before. High explosives that will lift entire towns off the map—bombing planes that will carry huge crews—and worst of all, the gas, the most damnable thing God ever allowed to be invented! The United States government has, at present, a formula for a poison gas that is the most destructive thing the world has ever known.

"This accursed gas is peculiarly penetrating and no gas masks can withstand it. It simply goes straight to the lungs. A damnable thing, truly!"

His greatest Inventions

When questioned concerning some of his own inventions, he waved them aside with a lordly sweep and leaping out of his chair, suddenly snatched a thick red book off the table. "This is the best thing that I ever did!" he acknowledged proudly, *The Science of Poetry*. Before I wrote this no one knew that poetry was an exact science, or if they knew it, they did not know all about it. This book is far, far better than anything I have ever done, better than any of my other inventions. Didn't know I wrote poetry, I suppose? Well, I do!"

"Who do you think is the greatest poet?"

"Hudson Maxim!" came the instant, solemn reply.

"And the next?"

"My wife," with a fond glance at Lovely, who, having finally succeeded in putting on his socks, was quietly embroidering in a corner.

Then he roared with jovial laughter, the hearty laugh of a

man of forty, and, with his usual unexpectedness, leaped up and went to the telephone, where he called Gutzon Borglum, the noted sculptor.

"He's a good friend of mine," Mr. Maxim explained, "and he is taking me out to see Stone Mountain today, where he is going to carve that monument to the Confederacy."

While he conversed, Mrs. Maxim, gentle little Englishwoman, well deserving of the name Lovely, serenely sewed on in spite of the noise and confusion.

She is the "balance wheel" of his life, and he frankly admits that Lovely is the "most wonderful thing Almighty God ever happened to create." Married over twenty-five years ago, they are inseparable, even in his laboratories, where she helps him with his experiments, for he lost one of his hands in a terrific explosion some years ago.

Almost boyish, despite his seventy years, given to sudden impulses, unexpected cholers, and lightening bursts of enthusiasms, "Lovely" is the only one who has any subduing effect on him.

"I can't imagine anyone making Huddie do anything he didn't want to do, but then, he's quite—tractable!" and she smiled.

The little shack at Stone Mountain that houses the projection lamp to be used by Mr. Borglum was the scene of the meeting of the three geniuses, Hudson Maxim, Gutzon Borglum, and Edwin Porter—Maxim, whose name is synonymous with high explosives, Borglum, famed for his sculptures, and Porter, inventor of the wonderful lamp to be used in projection of the colossal figures of the Confederate leaders on the side of the mountain in the size and proportion in which they are to be carved there.

The seventy-year-old inventor stood at the foot of the mountain with the wind waving his white curls, and flung his arms out in a mute gesture as he groped for words to express the thoughts that his first sight of the mountain brought him.

"Great Caesar's ghost!" he finally shouted.

"This is going to be one of the Seven Wonders of the World," he cried, "I wonder if Atlanta people realize it yet? Thousands of people from all over the globe will come here to see this carving when it is finished. Just imagine that grand old man, Lee, in eighty-foot figure, leading all the generals of the Lost Cause across that stone face! Why, Gutson, it's stupendous!"

Man Who Made First Movie

Standing near the excited and voluable Maxim was Edwin Porter, whose invention of the lamp makes Borglum's work possible. Porter, president of the Precision Machine Company, of New York, was in Atlanta on his first visit to view his invention for the first time since it has been set up. A very modest and self-effacing man is Edwin Porter, despite the fact that he has contrived this remarkable machine, the first of its kind ever made. He has also to his credit that he worked with Edison for ten years and assisted in the invention of the moving picture machine.

Diligent questioning brought out the fact that Mr. Porter had made the first moving picture.

"It was called *The Life of an American Fireman*," confessed he. "Prior to that time the moving pictures had been just short 'flickers' of marching soldiers or men running. The public, delighted with the novelty of it all at first, rapidly tired of it. I got the idea of a play and everyone laughed at me.

"But then I made *The Fireman,* and strangely enough, it 'took!' I made other short pictures, and then they became the rage. In the first company, I worked with Miss Pickford and a few others who are famous now. Then I helped organize 'The Famous Players' and took abroad a company to make *Queen Elizabeth* with Sara Bernhardt. It was considered quite an undertaking in those days to take a company abroad, and as for making a picture with the 'Diving Sara,' everyone was quite overcome!

"Most people seem to think that the moving picture is a comparatively recent development. I have been working on moving pictures and projecting machines for nearly thirty years. I was with Mr. Edison for ten years aiding in the development of such machines. It was back in 1896 that the first machine was perfected, but very few people realize it was that long ago.

"Since the invention of the 'movies,' I have given my time to the study of projecting machines. Mr. Borglum told me of the difficulties he was undergoing in trying to get an outline of his sculpture on the face of Stone Mountain, so I turned to and fixed up this lamp for him.

"Without the strong lamps that were perfected during the war, this lamp would have never been possible. The lamps used on the front in wartime and also to aid anti-aircraft guns in picking out planes at night were very strong, in fact, some of the beams would carry twenty miles. I have utilized this type of lamp in my gigantic magic lantern, and I don't believe Mr. Borglum will have any difficulty in projecting his picture 600 feet."

—*March 4, 1923*

Heroine of Seige of Urfa Is in Atlanta

tlanta today has a heroine who rivals Molly Pitcher, Betty Zane, and all the other great heroines of American history. Her name is Mary Caroline Holmes, and she was in charge of the Near East Relief Unit at Urfa, in Arabia, during the sixty-three days the Turks were besieging the city. Over this period of time, she had only horse meat to eat, and on one occasion she saved her unit from massacre be telling the Turkish general "where he got off."

In 1920, Miss Holmes was put in charge of the relief unit at

Urfa, a city of 80,000 inhabitants, situated 1,000 miles inland from Constantinople. Her "job" placed on her shoulders responsibilities that few men would care to assume, for it included the care of 1,000 little children, orphaned by the war; 1,500 women and girls who had been rescued from the Turks; a large industrial plant where work was given to 2,500 refugees; and a hospital.

It was after the British troops evacuated Urfa, leaving a French garrison in possession, that the Turks attacked the town. Still greater proof of the high esteem and respect in which this American woman was held is the fact that Turks and the French used her as an intermediary during the siege.

Bearding the Turk

"While the siege was in progress, shells fell around the hospital and even in it, killing some of the wounded," said Miss Holmes. "I went out and told the Turkish general that he simply must not fire on the hospital."

The mental picture of this intrepid little American woman bearding "the Terrible Turk" in his den was irresistible.

"He told me to evacuate the wounded from the hospital, for he was going to blow it up. I told him that he wouldn't do anything of the kind, because we nursed Turks as well as French and Armenians, and that no country even thought of firing on a hospital. There was not another shot fired, even in the neighborhood of the hospital, after that.

"The siege of Urfa lasted sixty-three days and the sufferings were terrible. The food supply got lower and lower till finally we didn't know where our next meal was coming from—or if there was going to be any next meal. The women and babies died by the scores, and the poor wounded in the hospital suffered terribly. I had as many to look after—an orphanage full of little children, an industrial plant, and a rescue home—and I had to feed them somehow.

"Finally, we came down to horse meat. Wait till you have eaten horse meat! It made me sick to taste it—sicker still to feed it to my little ones. But horse meat was far better than donkey, and toward the last, we were pathetically grateful for donkey.

"All during this time, I was the means of communication between the French and the Turks. I have lived in the Orient for thirty years and speak Turkish as well as Arabian and French. I have a very extraordinary pack of letters I received from the Turkish generals and high officials urging me to influence the French to surrender. I dare say they are the most unique collection on earth in that they show so clearly the Turkish viewpoint and how hopeless it is for the Occidental and the Oriental ever to reach a plane of common understanding.

Massacre of the French

"At last the French evacuated Urfa," Miss Holmes added, her face saddening. "They were starving, poor men, and the fight was useless. They signed articles of evacuation with the Turks that guaranteed them all the honors of war, their weapons, and private possessions. They marched out of Urfa with flags flying and heads up proudly.

"How we hated to see them go! When you've been though such an experience with men they seem tied to you by stronger ties than friendship. They suspected no treachery. We certainly did not. But eight miles out of Urfa, they were surrounded and cut to pieces."

Her blue eyes glinted coldly.

"All our friends were killed. The French commander was killed and his head carried though the streets of Urfa on a pole. The heads of the various officers kicked through the streets and the bazars—the heads of our friends!

"The Turks took over the town, of course, and shortly afterwards the Turkish general sent me word that he was going to shell and burn the Armenian quarter. Our relief unit was on the outskirts of the city, with the Armenian quarter between us and Urfa. I said to him, 'You shall not do this thing,' and after we talked a long time, he promised he would not."

No amount of questioning could elicit the exact method whereby she convinced the Turk of the error of his ways, for on personal matters Miss Holmes is very reticent.

"Then, the general begged me to come down into the town where he could protect me and my co-workers better," she laughed sarcastically. "I told him, no indeed, that I was going to stand on my exterritorial rights under an American flag I'd made and that no Turk could put foot on the Relief grounds without my permission. Protect me! That's a good joke."

Croix de Guerre Given Her

At this moment the wind blew back Miss Holmes' coat and betrayed a small red and white service bar with a gold palm attachment to it.

"Where did you get that Croix de Guerre?" she was asked.

She laughed, somewhat embarrassed.

"I was never so surprised in my life as at that decoration!" she answered. "It was given me after I left Urfa and went to Beirut. I was on my way back to America and stopped there for a while as a guest of the French government. Of course, there were many functions and parties that I attended, but on the last night of my stay the largest reception of all was given.

"I was talking to General Gouraud on nothing in particular when he suddenly asked, 'Have you received the Croix de Guerre yet, Miss. Holmes?'

"'Who? ME?' I answered, so surprised I could hardly talk.

"'Yes, you,' he said, putting out his hand to his aide, who handed him the citation. Then, everybody stopped talking and in the silence he read it and then pinned the cross on my dress.

I simply couldn't say anything I was so confused. No, he didn't kiss me on both cheeks," she laughed, "but he did kiss my hand! He was a very dear man."

—March 25, 1923

Bridesmaid of Eighty-Seven Recalls Mittie Roosevelt's Wedding

"Mittie Bulloch didn't starve her wedding guests to death when she was married here in Roswell at Bulloch Hall to President Roosevelt's father," declared Mrs. William Baker, the only surviving bridesmaid at that wedding. "I daresay people thought a good deal more of eating then than they do now, for at present-day weddings you never get anything to eat at all. Mittie's wedding was one of the prettiest I ever saw."

Mrs. Baker lives at Roswell, twenty miles from Atlanta, in historical Barrington Hall, which is only a few hundred yards from Bulloch Hall, girlhood home of Mittie Bulloch. Both dwellings are of colonial style of architecture, with white columns and wide porticos. Barrington Hall is an enormous white house, built by Mrs. Barker's father, Mr. Barrington King, in the late eighteen-thirties, when the Indians still fished in the nearby river and roamed through Barrington Kings's land.

The tall white columns glimpsed through the dark green of cedar foliage, the wide veranda encircling the house, the stately silence engendered by the century-old oaks, evoke memories of Thomas Nelson Page's *On Virginia.* The atmosphere of dignity, ease, and courtesy that was the soul of the Old South breathes from this old mansion, as it stands at the end of a long walk, bordered by old-fashioned flowers.

Mrs. Baker is a little lady, with a surprisingly unwrinkled face for one who has seen eighty-seven years pass, and black hair as yet but faintly tinged with silver. Surprising, too, is the energy with which she delivers herself on the customs and times that Roswell once saw, but which have now passed into the land of memory.

Mittie Bulloch's Best Friend

Living alone in the huge old hall except for her granddaughter, Miss Evelyn Simpson, Mrs. Baker is picturesque in the extreme. With dark hair parted in the middle and drawn smoothly back above the ears and a narrow black velvet ribbon holding it in place, she seems to have stepped out of one of the old daguerreotypes that hang on her walls.

She was the best friend of President Roosevelt's mother, Mittie Bulloch, and one of the bridesmaids who waved goodbye to the happy bride as the latter left Roswell for her New York home in the year 1854.

"Weddings were great affairs then," said Mrs. Baker. "People came from miles around and stayed for days. There were only six or seven families in Roswell at the time when Mittie Bulloch married here—it was just a small colony—but friends came from every direction in their carriages and wagons to help this entertainment and to see the fun.

"Weddings were different then from what they are now. The bride and groom didn't rush off right after the ceremony. They stayed at home sometimes for a week or two, and everybody gave them parties. There were parties every night, with plenty of good things to eat and lots of servants to serve it. Oh, those were the good days," laughed Mrs. Baker. "The cooks knew how to prepare things, and I believe that people liked to eat better than they do now. At any rate, they paid more attention to the way the food was cooked and served.

"Of course, Mittie Bulloch's wedding was a very fine affair, and for days beforehand, all of the girls visited each other to have 'icing parties.' That was the way we iced our cakes," explained

Mrs. Baker. "All of the girls got together and iced cakes at each other's houses.

Ice Brought From Savannah

"The wedding was at night, and everything was very sweet for the ceremony. The dining room at Bulloch Hall was decorated with flowers and vines, but of course not so elaborately as houses are decorated now. Mittie wore a long veil that became her beautifully, and we bridesmaids wore white muslin dresses made with full skirts and tight basque waists.

"We carried flowers, too, and came down the wide step of Bulloch Hall with the trailing clusters in our arms. The ceremony took place in the dining room, and we grouped ourselves just at the folding doors. Everything was beautiful.

"When the wedding was over, everybody had crowded around, congratulating the Roosevelts and kissing them and shaking hands. You could even see the servants peeping out of the back hall and beaming round corners.

"There were long mahogany tables covered with refreshments. On one table there were all kinds of baked and roasted meats, some steaming hot, others cold. On another table were cakes of every conceivable kind with the bride's cake, large and white and frosted in delicate designs, rising from the center.

"We had had ice brought all the way from Savannah to make the ice cream, and no one there was more astonished at it than Mr. Roosevelt's parents. It was their first trip South, and, like most Northern people of that time, they were very ignorant about the South. Goodness only knows what they expected us to be like, but they were amazed and pleased by the elegance of everything." Mrs. Baker smiled complacently and spread her freshly starched dress about her.

"We sat at little tables and the servants served us. There is no such service now, because then there were so many servants to do things and so much time to train them.

"After the wedding there were parties for some days, and then Mr. Roosevelt took Mittie away to New York. Everybody packed up and went home, for it was all over and we were all very tired."

Mrs. Baker smiled again and patted the black velvet blue ribbon that bound her still dark hair, her gesture having a charming air of grace that brought up a mental picture of what a pretty bridesmaid she must have been.

The President's Visits

She smiled as if in memory of some event that had pleased her—and sighed as she looked through the window toward the hill where Bulloch Hall rears its stately columns.

The smile was for the joy of that far-off day, perhaps; the sigh for the fact that out of all that gay bridal party, who clustered on the steps of Bulloch Hall in the long ago time, she was the only one left.

Of all the galaxy of belles and beauties who "iced" cakes and sewed dainty garments for the bride of Bulloch Hall, she, a tiny old lady, in the huge house of echoing halls, was the last bridesmaid.

"Mittie came back to visit several times," continued Mrs. Baker. "She always loved the South, though her husband was strongly abolitionist in sympathies. A very nice man he was, to be sure," she nodded her head. "But he was firm against slavery.

"Poor Mittie died young, you know, and I never saw President Roosevelt until the time he visited Roswell after his big African trip. He had heard so much about the town that he was anxious to see it.

"As his mother's old friend, I invited him and his party to breakfast with me, but it seemed that that was an unprecedented thing, so he ate in his private car that morning. The man who was his secretary—or at any rate, arranged his engagements—did not want him to come out to my house for some reason.

"This secretary sent word to me that I could see the President at the reception at the church." Here Mrs. Baker drew herself up and folded her hands firmly in her lap. "I sent word," she continued, in positive accents, "that if President Roosevelt did not care enough to come see his mother's old friend, I certainly would not go to see him."

"That very day I had a lovely visit from the President and his wife," she continued, with triumph and dignity struggling in her voice. "I met them at the door myself and said, 'Good morning, Mr. President,' and showed them in, instead of sending the maid.

"President Roosevelt was a wonderful man—a great man, I should say—and his wife was every bit as lovely as he was. He came in here," she swept her hand about the room in which she was sitting, "and we all talked very pleasantly. I told him of his mother and her girlhood and her marriage, and he sat and listened. He liked the South, he wasn't like his father in that matter. I told him all about his mother's romance, too."

Mittie's Love Letters

It seems that the father of the President met Mittie Bulloch when on his first visit to Roswell and fell in love with her at once. He was nineteen and Mittie only fifteen. But fifteen was a great age in those days, for many girls married at sixteen and seventeen, and anyone who passed twenty-one in single blessedness was looked upon as a hopeless old maid.

When Mittie visited her sister in Philadelphia, Theodore fell still more in love with her, and finally gained her consent to be his bride. His second visit to Roswell was the occasion of their marriage.

Letters that were exchanged between the lovers during the

period of waiting between the Philadelphia visit and the wedding are now in the possession of President Roosevelt's sister, Mrs. Robinson, and they cast a light on the lovers of that day which proves that they are no different from the lovers of 1923.

The following are two of Mittie's letters to her fiancé:

ROSWELL, July 26, 1853.

Thee, Dearest Thee—

I promised to tell you if I cried when you left. I determined not to do so if possible, but when the dreadful feeling came over me that you were indeed gone away, I could not help my tears from springing, and had to rush away to be alone with myself.

Everything, now, seems to be associated with you. Even when I run up the stairs to my room, I feel as if you were near and turn to kiss my hand to you. I feel, dear Thee, as if you were a part of my existence and that I can only live in your being, for now I am confident of my own deep love. When I went in to lunch, today, I felt very sad, for there was no one to whom I could make the request to 'move just a quarter of an inch further away': but how foolish I am—you will be tired of this rhapsody. Tom King has just been here to persuade us to join the Brush Mountain picnic tomorrow. We had refused, but we are reconsidering.

July 27.

We have just returned after having a most delightful time. It was almost impossible for our horses to keep a foothold, the mountain was so steep, but we were fully repaid by the beautiful extended view from the top.

When we descended, at the bottom, the gentlemen had spread planks, and carriage cushions were arranged for us to rest on, and at about four o'clock we had our dinner. Sandwiches, chicken wings, bread, and cheese disappeared miraculously.

Tom had a fire built and we had nice hot tea, and about six o'clock we commenced our return. I had promised to ride back with Henry Stiles, and I did so though you cannot imagine the picturesque effect our riding party had— not having any habit, I fixed a bright red shawl as a skirt, and a long red scarf on my head turban fashion with the long ends streaming. Lizzie Smith and Anna dressed the same way, and we were all perfectly wild with spirits and created quite an excitement in Roswell by our gay cavalcade.

But all the same I was joked all day by everybody, who said that they could see that my eyes were swollen and I had been crying.

Bulloch Hall, the old mansion in which Mittie Bulloch passed her girlhood and in which she married, stands on a sloping hill overlooking a beautiful little valley. The Hall is now owned by Mrs. J. B. Wing, of Atlanta, who uses it as a summer house.

Like Barrington Hall, it is of Southern colonial style with a wide portico, supported by graceful columns that tower high to meet the roof. The rooms of the Hall are unbelievably large in the light of comparison with the band-box rooms of modern apartments, and, in particular, the room in which the marriage of Theodore Roosevelt Sr. and Mittie Bulloch took place is airy and commodious. It is now used as a dining room by Mr. and Mrs. John Powell, of Roswell, who occupy the Hall during the winter and spring months.

Another Claim to Fame

But the mother of a President is not the only claim to fame that Roswell can boast. The Rev. Francis Goulding, the author of *The Young Marooners* and the inventor of the sewing machine, lived at Roswell, and his old home, Goulding House, still stands there.

In one of the disused cemeteries, behind a church, is an old grave with an insignificant headstone, on which is carved *The Reverend Francis R.,* and on the little foot stone, *Goulding.* Another cemetery, that long years ago passed into disuse, is on a wooded hill above the river where the roar of the falls comes clearly.

In this little lot, where marble pillars are discolored with moss, and the honey-suckle and blackberries run wild over the bricked-up graves, lie the remains of Roswell's first settlers. Here on granite slabs may be read dates of 1839, 1845, and old names of Bulloch, Dunwoody, and King.

One monument that has survived the test of time and rears its moss-covered marble head among the choking underbrush is that of Roswell King, the founder of the little colony of Roswell.

This little "shoe-string" town, running for three miles along either side of the road, from the covered bridge at the river to the slopes above the town, has seen the Cherokees a great nation, has withstood Sherman and his army, has known war and peace and romance, and remains a quiet old town, looking out at the world with dignity from behind its long avenues of cedar trees.

—June 10, 1923

Valentino Declares He Isn't A Sheik

Rodolph Valentino casts his fascination over femininity of every class. It doesn't matter much whether they are shop girls or society ladies. A glance from his dark eyes gives them a thrill, and the privilege of standing next to him is apparently something to be fought for.

The morning after his appearance at the Auditorium he was being interviewed and photographed and gazed upon adoringly at the Georgian Terrace.

Valentino!

A name to conjure with! Visions of white-clad sheiks, fascinating caballeros from the Argentine, slim toreadors, floated before my eyes. But when he turned to bow and grip my hand in a grasp that made my rings cut into my fingers, I suffered a distinct shock.

Dressed in a fuzzy tan golf suit, with tan sox to match and well-worn brown brogues, he seemed shorter and stockier than when on the film. He seemed older-and just a bit tired.

His face was swarthy, so brown that his white teeth flashed in startling contrast to his skin; his eyes—tired, bored, but courteous.

I suppose I ought to be terribly thrilled. I can't say that I am, in spite of the fact that Rodolph gave me an experience that half of the girls of Atlanta would have given the bobbed hair off their heads to have had.

How I Entered

He was on the graveled roof of the Terrace when I arrived to interview him. The only entrance to the roof lay through a low window that dropped four feet down. I crawled through and landed in a heap.

He was talking of his dislike for the play *The Sheik* when I came up to him, breathless and embarrassed, to be introduced.

"I am pleas' to meet you," and oh! his voice! That was wherein his chief charm lay. Low and husky with a soft, sibilant accent that is unbelievably easy to listen to, it held me with its well-bred, almost monotone intonation.

"That *Sheik*-pah-no! A mess! Who ever say an Arab act so except in a Coney Island sideshow? 'Julio'-he was bettair for I was 'Julio' in the *Four Horsemen. Blood and Sand,* I liked very much, but the others, no! Messes." (The last emphatically.)

He paused in this discourse, while the photographers "show[ed]" him in every conceivable pose and from every angle, and then continued to answer questions put to him concerning his phenomenal popularity with the ladies.

"But there are as many men that come to see as the ladies," protested he, waving a cigarette. "Why will you say the ladies like me so? I have not seen it. It is mistak'."

(At this moment there were gasps of admiration from a crowd of ladies, ranging from sixteen years old to white-haired ones, who were clustered about the window through which I had made my difficult entrance.)

The photographers were still "shooting," when Valentino's anxious secretary crawled half through the window and entreatingly implored the star to recall his eleven o'clock engagement. Shrugging his shoulders slightly, Valentino walked across the roof to the window, whereat the awe-struck knot of admirers fell back.

Thrill of a Lifetime

Trotting beside him, chattering away a mile a minute to conceal the thrilled condition of my cosmos, I reached the window and stopped, for the window was four feet from the floor and I am exactly four feet eleven.

And then—*then*—came the thrill of a lifetime—the great event which the 10,000 flappers referred to before would have parted their hair to have experienced!

"Allow me," breathed a husky voice in my ear and as masterfully as ever he sheiked Agnes Ayres, he picked me up in his arms and lifted me through the window!

As he stood there, with me in his arms, one young girl gasped, "Oh, the lucky little devil!" and then he deposited me on the floor. I scrambled to my feet, all aglow, wondering whether I had better register deep emotion, thrills, or say, "Sir, how dare you!" I ended by registering a world-beating blush, dropping my vanity case, pulling the hem out of the back of my dress with my heel as I bent to retrieve it, and bumping heads with Valentino!

Rodolph Valentino bent over my nerveless hand, and with matchless grace, whispered these words:

"I'm glad to have met you!"

—*July 1, 1923*

The now seemingly unusual spelling of Valentino's stage name, based on his real name of Rodolpho, was standard at the time of Mitchell's writing. The Georgian Terrace, today a condominium tower and hotel, was built on Atlanta's Peachtree Street in 1911 as Atlanta's "first million-dollar hotel." Clark Gable and Vivien Leigh later stayed at the hotel after the première of Gone With the Wind. *Agnes Ayres was Valentino's co-star in his most famous film,* The Sheik.

Former Policewoman, Held in Shooting, Needs the Help She Gave to so Many Girls

——◈◈◈——

Never imagined it would come home to her, Mrs. Evans sobs on couch at headquarters

——◈◈◈——

"I have been through tragedies like this so often with so many other poor girls when I was a policewoman," said Mrs. Windsor Evans, who is being held at the police station in connection with the shooting of her husband Tuesday night, "but I never thought that I would ever have to go through it myself."

Mrs. Evans was wearing the same navy blue dotted swiss dress that she wore when the tragedy occurred—a rumpled, lace-trimmed dress, stained with her husband's blood. She is a young woman, very pretty and girlish-looking, despite the fact that she has been married ten years and has two little girls, Martha and Marion. She lay on the couch in the matron's office at the police station and dabbled at her tear-swollen eyes with a sodden handkerchief as she reviewed the events of the previous night and talked of her three years on the force as a policewoman.

Always Helped Girls

"I was a policewoman here for three years," she said, "and I loved the work. Many's the time I have worked on this ward for twenty four hours on a stretch with poor kids who had gotten into trouble of one kind or another. I always felt so sorry for them and tried to help them as much as I could.

My special job was rounding up delinquent girls, and I have brought hundreds of them through the doors of the station.

But I never thought that I would be in a prison cell except to help some other poor girl," and she began to sob again. "That's the most pitiful part of all!"

Windsor Evans, of the Atlanta police force, was shot and killed Tuesday night, and his wife asserts that the killing occurred accidentally when she attempted to wrest from his hand the gun with which he was threatening to "end it all."

Thinks Only Of Husband

Despite the fact that she is held on serious charges pending an investigation by the police, Mrs. Evans says she can think of nothing but her husband and wishes that one of the bullets could have been for her.

"Windsor was like a daddy and husband to me," she sobbed. "He was lots older than me and I married him when I was fifteen. I never had any other sweethearts but him, I was so young.

"But he got funny spells.

"Lots of times he threatened to 'end it all,' but I never believed that he'd try to do it. Once he threatened to shoot me, but I ran from him. Twice he took Martha and Marion away and kept them four days till I was distracted, but in between times he was good to me. When I'd ask him why he did so mean, he'd say, 'Oh, I don't know.'

"And then last night he had been drinking. He sat in the dining room and drank nearly a whole quart, except the little bit that's left in the bottle. The detective department has it now. I tried to make him stop and come to bed, but he wouldn't. He kept insisting that he was going back to town and get some more when he finished that bottle.

Begged Him to Stop

"When I kept begging him to stop drinking and come to

bed, he got nasty and said: 'Well, I guess I'm going to end it all now.'

"He reached down and on his left side, and I thought his coat was caught under the cushion. I was sitting on the arm of his chair, and when his hand came up with the gun in it, I threw myself across his arms and grabbed his hands.

"We struggled just a minute and then the gun went off. My hands were over his but I know he pulled the trigger. I know it. Why couldn't one of the bullets have been for me?"

—*August 30, 1923*

Two New York Girls Out-Walk Death

Doctors Told Martha Bozeman and Betty Sweitzer That They Had the White Plague. Both Donned Knickers and Set Out to Walk Back to Health. Now, After Hiking From New York to Galveston, They Are Returning, Completely Cured.

Timid girls who are afraid to be out alone after dark without a big strong man to protect them—take note, please!

Delicate damsels who can't even run for a street car—attention!

Betty Sweitzer and Martha Bozeman, both of New York City, hiked from their home city to Galveston and are now on their way back north.

A desire to see the world, to make money enough selling magazine subscriptions to pay their tuition at Columbia University, and to fight off the grip of tuberculosis sent these two plucky girls on their hiking tour a year ago.

Both are young and pretty, bobbed haired and bright-eyed, tanned by sun and exposure to all weathers; and the health that glows in their cheeks is sufficient evidence that the game fight they have put up against the White Plague has been successful.

Attired for the road in trim knicker suits and boys caps, with eight-pound packs strapped on their backs, the two intrepid wayfarers arrived in Atlanta on their long hike back to New York City where they both expect to enter the Columbia School of Journalism in the spring. Whatever Betty wants to do, so also does Martha and vice versa, for the vicissitudes of the road have bred a deep affection and congeniality between the girls that is evident in every glance they give each other and in the care with which each looks after her comrade's health.

The long trail from New York to Galveston and thence south to Texas has not been without its adventures, its fun, and its tragedy. In their experiences they number long hours spent in country jails when they were "taken in" as runaways; the sorrow at the death of Helen, the third member of their trio; meetings with tramps, wild bulls, and a wilder Indian oil millionaire.

Offered $500 to Make Trip

Betty, who has long silky lashes that sweep over her tanned cheeks, explained how they started on their lonely hike.

"I was working in a magazine house when Martha and I decided to take to the road to save our lives," she said. "Martha was a certified trained nurse and had served overseas in the Salvation Army but developed T.B. on her return, so that she couldn't nurse anymore. I had had several tubercular glands removed from my neck," and she turned back her shirt collar to reveal several tiny criss-cross scars. "So I wasn't good for much either.

"One day, I heard of a man who took a long hike on a thousand dollar bet and I sighed and said that I'd hike to Borneo for that!"

"And the boss of the syndicate Betty worked for heard her

and gave us the chance," interrupted Martha in the characteristic way girls have of taking the words out of each others' mouths. "He said he'd give us five hundred dollars if we'd hike across country selling subscriptions to magazines and, as we wanted money to study journalism at Columbia University, we jumped at the chance."

"Of course we couldn't do very much at first," admitted Betty. "Just a few miles a day and lots of rests between, but soon we became stronger. We slept in barns and haystacks and farmhouses when we were in the country and sometimes outdoors under the open sky. We make our expenses selling subscriptions and we don't accept any donations or even rides in automobiles unless it is storming so hard that we really need shelter."

Betty's Tears; Martha's Wallop

"We started from New York in September and spent New Year's Day in Chicago. Up till that time, we had very little trouble either in making expenses or in handling police or tramps we met on the road. But when we left Chicago and went South, trouble began.

"The houses were far apart and no one seemed to want magazines or else they had all that they could read. We met many tramps but found out that no matter how tough a man is, if you appeal to his better nature, he isn't going to hurt you."

"And Betty can cry so easily," sighed Martha, enviously. "Whenever any tough would start to bother us, Betty would look up appealingly at him and break into heart-rending sobs that always made men let us alone!"

"It wasn't my tears half as much as your 'wallop,'" insisted Betty. "Why, you know you knocked a deputy sheriff down!"

"That was when we were arrested in a Missouri town," explained Martha, whose sweet face belies the 'wallop' with which her friend credits her. "We were taken up by the sheriff because we answered the descriptions of two runaway girls he was hunting for. He took us to jail and despite all of the police credentials we showed him, he insisted on locking us up.

"And his cute little deputy made a fresh remark when the sheriff's back was turned and Martha lost her temper and knocked him flat," said Betty. "Then we were scared to death because the sheriff said that we had struck an officer in the pursuit of his duty and we would be sentenced to jail for years and years! Of course, he was joking, but we didn't know it and when he put us in a big cell with girls who were dope fiends, pickpockets, and vagrants, we felt pretty blue.

"Perfect Ladies'" Certificate

"But we cheered up when we thought about what a fine experience this was and how we could use this adventure in a story when we became full-fledged writers. So we talked 'hard' as if we were in the habit of spending most of our time in jails and the girls opened up and were perfectly natural. We learned more about human nature and the seamy side of life in the six hours we spent in that jail than during the whole of our previous life."

"We also lost money by our sojourn in jail," added Martha. "The prisoners put us through 'Kangaroo Court' and fined us three dollars apiece. 'Kangaroo Court' is the self-appointed court made up among prisoners in a main cell. They try all of the newcomers before a mock court and fine them money to buy cigarettes and candy for the gang. Our stay in jail cost us exactly six dollars."

"Which was all we had!" declared Betty, with a grin. "When the sheriff finally did let us out with profuse apologies for his mistake in detaining us, we were nearly broke! The sheriff gave us a note to the rest of the sheriffs we might meet certifying that we were 'perfect ladies' and packed a wicked wallop and to keep all deputies away from us!" Betty dug into her crowded pocket and produced the odd recommendation of the sheriff who had a sense of humor.

"We landed in Kansas City without a cent," continued Betty. "No money, no friends, no place to stay and an awful appetite with us. I thought we'd have to get arrested to find a place to sleep, but instead we went to the biggest hotel in town and talked the management into letting us check in for the night! I don't know how we did it; it was because we were desperate that we put it over, I suppose.

"And the next morning we each took a big drink of ice water for breakfast and went out to work the town. And would you believe it? We made more in Kansas City than we had ever made before! The orders simply rolled in as fast as we could write them down. We felt enormously rich and ordered a steak four inches thick.

Helen With the Dimples

"It was in Kansas City that we met Helen Patterson, our other buddy. She was selling magazines when we met her and as she was interested, we took her with us. She was so pretty— wasn't she, Martha?"

Martha gouged into her pocket and brought out a snap of a slender girl with dimples in both cheeks. "That's Helen," she said, shortly. "She died in San Antonio, of typhoid."

"Texas was a bitter disappointment to us two New Yorkers, brought up in the wild and woolly idea of the West. We didn't see a single cowboy the whole time we were there. We thought we saw one once but he turned out to be a farmhand.

"A wild bull had chased us across a meadow and we had hastily climbed a tree. Every time the bull would saunter off, we could climb down. As soon as we got to the ground, back he would charge and take up his stand under the tree, shaking his head and bellowing—looking up at us with his red eyes till we were lots scareder than when the sheriff had us.

"Then this noble youth whom we took to be a cowboy rode up and drove the bull away and helped us down. It broke our hearts when he turned out to be the 'hired man' on a near-by farm instead of a cowboy!"

"If we didn't have any luck with cowboys, we certainly got our share of Indians," declared Martha. "An Indian oil millionaire fell in love with Betty and wanted to marry her. He was worth about a thousand dollars a day or something fabulous and he was a Cornell graduate and terribly nice. We nearly got into serious trouble about him for he insisted on following us from town to town—"

"Martha, you know it wasn't that bad!" objected Betty, blushing under her tan. "Things didn't get bad till his former sweetheart turned up."

Kisses Instead of Bullets

"It did look serious for a while," said Martha reminiscently. "We were at a hotel in Tulsa when this pretty little Indian girl came to our room and announced that she was going to shoot Betty!"

"I was so petrified that I didn't know what to do," admitted Betty. "But I asked her what she was going to shoot me for and she told me that he'd have married her if I had not come along. I told her that she could marry him. Then she broke down and cried on our necks till we were terribly embarrassed.

"We decided to inveigle him into marrying her so that he'd stop following us around. So one night when he turned up at the hotel drunk, we married him off to his Indian fiancée and left town hastily."

At the present, the two knickered travelers are somewhere on the road between Atlanta and Chattanooga, swinging down the highway, packs on backs, and the carefree spirit of youth in their hearts.

September 16, 1923

Novelist Loved Atlanta Girl's Picture

F. Scott Fitzgerald, who originated the flapper, once fell in love with the picture of an Atlanta girl.

Fitzgerald, author of *This Side of Paradise* and *The Beautiful and the Damned,* never saw the original of the photograph, but he became so enamored of the picture that he wrote verses to the girl whom he never met.

Martin Amorous, who has returned to Atlanta from New York to open a studio in the Connally Building, was a roommate of Fitzgerald's at the time at the Newman School in Hackensack, N.J., and he tells here about the novelist and the photograph— the original of whom was "Anne." Can you guess the rest of the name?

Martin Amorous spent several years in New York designing costumes for plays and revues, and in addition to reminiscences of his famous schoolmate, he has brought back to Atlanta original ideas as to how the Atlanta girl should dress.

"When Scott and I were roommates at Newman," said Mr. Amorous, "I had the picture of a very lovely Atlanta girl on the mantle piece in our room. Her name was Anne and though she is married now, she was one of the belles of Atlanta then and a very prominent worker in the Junior League.

"Scott was much impressed with her beauty and wanted to meet her. He used to look at her picture and talk to me as if he knew her. Finally, he began writing poems 'To Anne.' I have one of them in my scrap book."

He opened a book lying on the table of the studio and turned to a page where a poem, scribbled in blurring pencil was pasted.

To Anne

1
Like the mellow wisp of an ancient moon,
On a night of long ago,
Like the fragrant breeze of a by-gone June,
When the wee winds whisper low,
Or wild in a night of pleasure gay
Or sweet in the calm of an April day—
Dear Anne!

2
Girl of my dreams, 'neath the midnight gleams.
A whisper echoes "Anne," an answer echoes "Anne."
Enveloped by all romance, fair in my fancies flight,
Star shot by legend and slowed by tale,
Queen of some fair tonight, dear Anne!
Queen of some fair tonight!

3
Some time when the stars kiss the roses,
We'll meet in the never land,
When the violet night discloses
I'll take you by the hand.
Dear Anne! Some day and some day!

Fitzgerald Always Argued

"Scott and I were very good friends," continued Martin Amorous, "but like most roommates, we never could agree on any subject and consequently led a cat-and-dog life. He was always arguing. He would argue with anyone who would listen to him, and the disconcerting part about his arguments was that he never stayed on the same side of a subject more than five minutes.

"At first this confused and annoyed me 'till I discovered that he switched from side to side in arguments, not for the love of the fight, but to get other people's viewpoints. I think it was in this way that he obtained much of the material he used in his stories.

"Scott was good-looking, attractive, and quite egotistic. He had the most impenetrable egotism I've ever seen, but we made companionable roommates because neither of us could ever say anything that could get under the skin of the other.

"I have a few verses that Scott wrote to some Hackensack girls, who for various reasons were not on speaking terms with him—a fact that worried him not at all! He went down the list of girls who had snubbed him and detailed all of their shortcomings—and ended the verses in this way—

'For the lands of the village triumph,
Honest, not brilliant like me,
So I turn again to St. Paul
For my old popularity.

For handsome is as handsome does,
And the hands of time won't turn back.
Girls, be they friend, crush or sister,
Don't love me, in Hackensack!'

"My most vivid memory of Scott is meeting him in New York before *This Side of Paradise* was published. He was tired and discouraged, had been writing good stories and couldn't sell a one. He had been from publisher to publisher and had a stack of rejection slips that he swore was a foot high.

"He told me that he was going to quit the advertising concern for which he was working and go back home to Minnesota. Nothing was going right and he was tired.

"The next thing I knew, *This Side of Paradise* met with a success that was phenomenal—and Scott was made. Then he sold all of his rejected stories to the very editors who had turned them down."

Personality and Dress

After his experience as a New York designer, Mr. Amorous has returned to Atlanta to preach a doctrine of individuality in dress.

"It is very trite to say that women should dress to suit their personalities, but that still is and always will be the secret of the well-dressed woman's charm," he began. "Women never seem to realize that, however. Chubby little girls always want to wear low-cut gowns with hoop skirts, just because such costumes look well on tall, willowy friends. And tall, skinny girls are always after cute clothes. Women must be educated to the right kind of clothes, or else they will sink their personalities in garments worn simply because Irene Castle or some other actress looks well in them.

"Northern women discovered this some years ago, hence the number of dress designers in New York. Southern girls are naturally prettier than Northern girls, and it doesn't take so much trouble for them to make a good appearance. But the New York woman always shows up for her pains by looking well-groomed in a way that few Southerners ever attain.

"A well-dressed New York woman would as soon think of wearing an organdie dress in mid-winter as a costume that is contradictory to her personality. Just think of the sheer waste when a girl, whose charm lies in her simplicity or her boyishness, tricks herself out in ruffles, or the mistake when the exotic type selects simple, tailored lines!

"Since returning to Atlanta, I have designed dresses for Atlanta women, and some of them have been a struggle because the girls wanted me to sketch dresses for them just like so-and-so's. I wouldn't, and that sometime made them angry.

"A designer has to study each woman, her temperament, and her personality, as well as consider whether she is tall or small. Women who are accustomed to grabbing dresses off a hook in a department store usually snatch the dress that they think will look best on them and wear it. It never occurs to them that if they look well in long dresses, that they should wear long dresses whether it is the style or not—or short dresses if short dresses are becoming."

Concerning his work in New York, Mr. Amorous told of costumes designed for Hazel Dawn's production of *The Winged God*, for flower choruses at cabarets, and displayed his sketches for *The Bird Wedding*—a revue where the bride, groom, and wedding party were birds of various species, in gorgeous colored costumes, with the wedding taking place in a glorified canary cage.

He gave an account of a talk with Paul Poiret, on the latter's last visit to New York, and described the King of Styles as a very "Frenchy" Frenchman, who wore clothes as exotic as those he designed for Parisians.

—September 30, 1923

Martin Amorous was the subject of an earlier Sunday Magazine *profile entitled "The Only Atlanta Man Designer of Women's Clothes." Fitzgerald's* This Side of Paradise *and* The Beautiful and the Damned *appeared in 1920 and 1922 respectively. Fitzgerald attended the Newman School from 1911 to 1913.*

Fulton County's First Woman Treasurer

"**A** telephone call for the county treasurer!"

A motherly woman, clad in mourning, smiled in quiet triumph as she knocked on her young daughter's door at nine o'clock in the morning after the recent state and county election.

This was the first intimation Miss Margaret Culberson had of her success in the campaign for the office occupied by her late father, H. L. Culberson. While many other candidates sat up all night, alternately soaring and dropping in spirits as the returns came in, she went to bed at 9:30 and slept until her mother wakened her in the morning to answer the congratulatory phone calls that came pouring in.

"Don't think I went to bed peacefully because I was so sure that I would win," explained the new county official, "I simply realized that by 9:30 all the balloting was finished and that my fate was decided. Either I was elected or I wasn't and it would do no good for me to sit up all night worrying. So I went to bed."

Politicians, take note! Candidates, please copy! It is hard to believe, but it is true. The fact that Margaret Culberson went to bed early, on the eve of her election, proves the coolness and balance of the new county treasurer.

Will Handle $2,500,000

She is tall and slim and her whole bearing is one of pleasant dignity. Her face is small, the features delicately cut, the profile with its thin, high-bred nose, in particular, possessing a cameo clearness of outline. Her eyes are serenely gray-green, level in their gaze, the eyes of a woman whose poise is founded on a quiet self-confidence, born of experience. One feels instinctively that hysteria and indecision in the face of emergencies are strangers to her. There is firmness of character in every line of her face and sweetness of disposition in each glance she bestows upon her mother, to whom she displays a rare devotion.

It is upon the slim shoulders of this girl that the duties of county treasurer devolve. Through her hands must pass approximately $2,500,000 with which the county pays its innumerable bills. She must be accountable for every cent of the sum, be able to produce signed vouchers, balanced accounts, receipts, etc., at the end of the year—a responsible job that few women would care to undertake. But Margaret Culberson is modestly confident of her ability to handle the position.

Miss Culberson has lived in Atlanta all her life, as have her parents before her. After graduating from Girls' High School with one of the best records ever achieved there, she attended Smith College at Northampton, Massachusetts, where she was awarded Phi Beta Kappa and highest academic honors. Having received a scholarship from the French government, Miss Culberson studied abroad at St. Germain for a year and then returned to the United States to teach at Agnes Scott. After two years as an instructor, she went to Columbia University in New York for further post-graduate work.

Called Home to Attend Mother

While studying at Columbia she was called home by a serious accident to her mother. Scarcely was her mother nursed back to health before her father, then county treasurer, fell ill. During the five months of sickness prior to his death, Miss Culberson acquainted herself with her father's work and became thoroughly familiar with the routine of duties at his office.

After the death of Mr. Culberson, scores of friends came to the bereaved family and urged his daughter to enter the race for treasurer, pledging their aid.

"At first I could only look at them, speechless," said the

young official with tears in her eyes at the memory. "It was so dear of them and it made Mother and me so happy to know that Father was so loved and well thought of. They urged me, and so I consented."

Miss Culberson presents the paradoxical situation of a woman who went into politics because she felt that her "place was in the home."

"If I had not been elected, in all probability I would have been obliged to go back up North to work, as I had given up my position in Atlanta to nurse my father. That would have meant leaving Mother practically alone and she has been very ill.

"I could not leave Mother, so when Father's friends came to me, after his death, and suggested that I run for the office, I saw the solution to my problem. I could carry on my father's work and stay at home with Mother, too."

On the matter of political careers for women, the new treasurer was noncommittal. She is neither a radical, modern woman nor a retiring Victorian in her views on women in public life.

"It's more a matter of individual circumstance," she said. "Some women belong to the home. They would be lost in a legislative body or an office. Other women make mistakes in trying to domesticate themselves if their bent lies in another direction.

"As for me, the force of circumstance threw me into politics, and I have no desire for a further political career. I simply want to run my father's job to the best of my ability. I am not a politician."

When it was pointed out that she was a very successful politician when she carried the wards of both her opponents, Miss Culberson disclaimed any credit with a characteristic modesty that is one of her greatest charms.

"That wasn't due to any of my campaigning, but to the dear friends of Mother and Father! You see, I did not start an active campaign until two weeks before the election. The summer was hot and so many people were away from town and I felt that if I started off with a whoop-la several months before the elections were called—and then trailed off weakly, it would jeopardize my cause. So I waited until two weeks beforehand and then campaigned."

Will Buy New Clothes

The mother of the county treasurer beamed.

"Margaret," she said, "made speeches both in and out of town and she was as cool and unself-conscious as if she had been stumping all her life."

"But Mother," protested the winning candidate, "of course I wasn't self-conscious! After a few years' experience in teaching, one naturally becomes accustomed to speaking before crowds. I'm not much of a hurrah orator," she explained. "I just had one thing to say—and that was that I knew the job and believed that I could handle it satisfactorily. After I'd said that, I stopped talking."

"That's probably the reason you were elected," observed Mrs. Culberson, briskly, "and now the first thing I am going to do is take the county treasurer downtown and buy her some new clothes. Between nursing us and campaigning, she hasn't had any new clothes for a year. Yes, buying clothes will be her first official act."

"Yes, Mother," said the treasurer, demurely, but with a twinkle in her eye.

—June 21, 1924

Grandma Veal Speaks Her Mind on Her 102nd Birthday

Grandma Virginia Elizabeth Veal, of Braselton, Georgia, celebrated her 102nd birthday on September 27, by speaking her mind on bobbed hair, short skirts, fast cars, trousers for women, and similar "abominations."

Grandma Veal's birthday party, given at the home of her "baby girl," Mrs. T. T. Cooper, age fifty-nine years, of Braselton, was very different from a similar celebration held by Mrs. Myra Able, ninety-nine-year-old flapper, of Ashtabula, Ohio, who observed the day by bobbing her hair.

Five generations of descendants gathered at the family reunion, listened to Grandma Veal's opinions on votes, trousers, and short hair for women.

Mrs. Veal, who has reached the age of 102 years with all the faculties unimpaired save for a slight deafness, presents a remarkable picture of a strong mind dominating a worn-out, century-old body. Her memory for exact dates would shame a history professor; her strength of will and clearness of mind, despite her 102 years, are those of a middle-aged woman.

Lots of Pep

Grandma Veal is a slight, tiny figure, yet erect of carriage. Her small face is wrinkled and faintly yellow, but marked with strength and determination. Her nose is curved, strong and clear cut, the nose of a pioneer woman who feared no hardships and did her full share of the work in days before modern conveniences were dreamed of. Her eyes, undimmed by age, gleam vivaciously over her spectacles and her small hands are constantly in motion as she talks. Grandma Veal, to quote a modern phrase that she scorns, has "lots of pep."

The mother of fourteen children, of whom five are now living, Mrs. Veal has sixty-two grandchildren, 179 great-grand-children, and eighty-seven great-great-grandchildren, that she knows of.

"Of course there may be a lot more that I don't know about," she admitted, her eyes sparkling youthfully as she looked around the crowded little house at the relatives who had gathered to celebrate her birthday. "Every time I hear of a new one I put it down and I try to keep track of the families. But there are so many of them."

When told of the ninety-nine-year-old flapper of Ohio who celebrated her birthday by bobbing her hair, Grandma was scandalized. No woman ought to bob her hair, whether she was nineteen or a hundred and nineteen, she stated in uncompro-mising accents.

Bobbed Hair, Derby Hats, and Votes

"If I bobbed my hair," said Grandma Veal, vigorously comb-ing up her back locks with a tortoiseshell comb, "I'd expect my folks to get me a derby hat and a pair of pants and make me vote! Vote—just that! The women who bob their hair VOTE!"

There was utter scorn in her tone as she retied her soft black silk kerchief about her white hair. The bobbed-haired grand-children and great-grandchildren ranged about the walls, ducked their shingled heads guiltily and grinned at grandma as her piercing old eyes sought them out. The matronly daughters and granddaughters who had obviously exercised their preroga-tive of suffrage, smiled and clucked reprovingly at Grandma.

"I didn't want to see suffrage come, Mamma," mildly said Mrs. J. D. Deanton, one of Mrs. Veal's daughters, now living at Flowery Branch, "but now it's here, I think we women ought to vote for the right things."

"Woman's place is in the home," stated Grandma with final-ity, waving back the suffrage members of her family. "It's her place to stay there and make a home and raise the children and let the man do the bossing and voting. No good can come of women aping men, running around the country, riding in fast cars, cutting their hair, voting, and wearing pants. PANTS!" Her tone breathed the anathema at *pants* as it had done at *vote*.

"Now, Grandma, knickers aren't pants!"

"Knickers are pants and pants on women are a scandal and a disgrace," said Grandma with such decision that one felt that the Supreme Court of the United States had made a ruling, "and it's against the Good Book," she finished, triumphantly. That settled the question and the young and irreverent generation was quelled.

As the old lady talked, the automobiles and wagons filled with cousins, in-laws, grandchildren, and great-grandchildren continued to arrive, for despite the driving rain and the knee-deep mud, the entire family wanted to make Grandma's birthday party a success. Soon the small house was filled to overflowing, the men, crowded out, ranged themselves on benches on the porch where the rain dripped from the eaves; little boys, some barefoot and in overalls, some uncomfortable in imprisoning stiff collars, overran the wet yard despite the rain, and prowled into the barn; the women crowded the small rooms, grouped about Grandma, who presided in the semi-circle of smiling relatives like a queen on a throne; small girls, red-haired, black-haired, curly, and bobbed, ringed around the old lady, with fingers in mouths and curious eyes wide as she talked on about old times and old customs, pausing every now and then to stroke with a thin, yellowed hand the soft hair of some great-grandchild.

Old Paths are Lost

"The old paths are all lost," said she, her voice rising shrill above the patter of the rain on the roof. "No one follows the old paths now, no one loves the old meetings. I've been going to meetings all my life and they aren't like they used to be.

"Now, Mamma, there's lots of good meetings now!"

The old lady paused, in fairness, "Yes, I guess there are good meetings, now days, but the old days and old paths seem best. They always do—to old folks. But it does seem to me that there's more wickedness these days than there used to be," she reflected, "but that's because there's more folks to be wicked now than when I was young."

"When I was young there were mighty few folks living around here. Of course there weren't any railroad trains through here. My goodness, no! I remember when the first railroad came up through this part of the country and how everybody came for miles around to see it. I remember one old lady shouted out loud when she saw the engine coming, '"My land, the poor thing must be tired! Just listen to how it's a-panting!'"

Grandma Veal clapped her hands and laughed gleefully, her eyes sparkling as she looked at the five generations, listening with breathless interest. "Wasn't that silly of her? But, you see, she hadn't ever seen a train before. We used to do all our traveling by mule wagon or ox cart."

Mrs. Veal's father owned a store near what is now Braselton and when he went to trade in Augusta, the nearest large town, he took his whole family and most of his household goods with him, for the journey required some weeks. In those days the roads were uncertain and sometimes there were no roads at all. The Indians had been removed but there were still a few left on reservations and at times they were dangerous. There were also bridgeless rivers and trackless forests, and so traveling when Grandma Veal was a child was a dangerous undertaking.

"Cherokees used to come over the mountains to trade at Pappa's store," continued Grandma Veal. "They traded moccasins and skins for food and clothes and hung around the place, in silence, watching the white folks and grunting every now and then. The Indians around the store are about the first thing I remember—except I do remember something when I was two years old!"

"Why, Grandma," gasped a great-great-grandchild at her knee, "can you remember a hundred years ago?"

"Of course. No trouble at all," replied the old lady briskly. "I remember when I was two years old that Mamma was milking the cow and I was on the other side of the fence from her. There was a crack in the fence and I kept slipping my little tin cup through into the bucket and drinking the milk as fast as she milked it.

When the Stars Fell

"I remember when the stars fell, too, for I was older then.

"Oh, Grandma, did any stars fall smack into the front yard?" eagerly questioned the six-year-old, at her knee, pressing closer for information.

"Oh, no, they didn't fall to the ground. They just fell though the elements like the shooting stars you see. It was before day that it happened. Mamma was up stirring around early like folks did then, to get things ready for the day, and her moving around woke me up. I saw funny lights outside, and peeped through a crack in the wall and saw the sky full of falling stars. They dropped into the elements like comets. No, I wasn't scared. It takes a lot to scare me. I watched them till the sun came up and faded them out."

Grandma Veal married when she was sixteen, which was not considered too young at that time. She made her own wedding dress, a gown of double-woven imported Irish linen, fashioned after the quaint style of 1838, with a basque waist unbelievably small in these days of unrestrained figures, wide hoop skirts, short puffed sleeves, and a neckline off the shoulders—a graceful garment that even after eighty-six years breathes the atmosphere of an older, quieter day and the charm of the spirited sixteen-year-old who wore it.

In the years following her marriage, Virginia Elizabeth Veal saw, step by step, the complete industrial revolution of the world. The sewing machine, the cotton gin, and the railroad impressed her as being the most remarkable inventions of all.

Seed Picked From Cotton by Hand

"The idea of being able to separate the seeds from cotton by machinery was hard to believe, at first," said she.

"We were so accustomed to doing it by hand. We used to give cotton parties where everybody had refreshments first and spent the evening picking the seeds out of the cotton. I have some quilts now that are made of hand-picked cotton. My mother made them, a hundred years ago.

"Of course, the railroad and the gin were about the most re-markable things that I've seen since I was a child, but because I'm born and bred a farmer, I'll say that plenty of good bread and meat and good farms now in this state are the things that have impressed me more than any of the inventions of recent years."

After Grandma Veal had talked at length on old days and old customs and had spoken her mind with some freedom and pungency on the modern days and ways, "Uncle Taylor" Cooper, twice her son-in-law, with whom she now makes her home, pushed his way through the crowd of fourth-degree cousins who were making Grandma Veal's acquaintance for the first time, and shouted above the hubbub that the dinner was ready.

The Birthday Dinner

The old lady, scorning any more assistance than her hand on

her son-in-law's arm, walked into the kitchen and seated herself at the head of the long table. On account of the rain, the annual out-of-door barbecue that is usually the main feature of her birthday parties had to be foregone and an indoor feast was spread. The table ran the full length of the long kitchen and was crowded to the edges with examples of the "Southern cooking" that has made Georgia cooks famous the nation over.

Each family had brought its own lunch and each vied jealously with the others in having the most tasty basket to spread before Grandma. Fried chicken predominated at the repast, with roast fresh pork and roast hen running it a close second. Pies of every description crowded the table, from succulent grape pie to lemon pie with fluffy meringue billowing up lightly like tan clouds. Grandma's own personal birthday cake, iced to snowy whiteness and studded with candles, occupied one end of the table and marshaled beside it were cakes of every color and flavor. Pickles rubbed elbows with jars of brandied peaches, sandwiches were flanked by glasses of homemade jam, and stuffed eggs spread their golden filling wherever they could find room amid the cakes.

An opening prayer was made by W. H. Mahafney, thanking the Lord that He had permitted the beloved old lady to see another birthday with her five generations of relatives around her. Then Grandma Veal rose and asked grace, briefly and in a strong voice that carried all over the little house and did not falter as she prayed that she might be permitted to ask grace at her 103nd birthday party.

Children First

Then the numerous little great-grandchildren who had been holding themselves politely but impatiently in restraint reached the table first and began the assault, unchecked by smiling parents. Castor oil could come thereafter, but Grandma's birthday happened but once a year and parents could afford to be indulgent.

When the children had retired to the wet porches, hands full of cake and pickles, mouths blissfully greased with fried chicken, the grown-ups gathered about the table, eating and getting acquainted. Some relatives had come from afar to this reunion. Miss Corine Roberts had traveled all the way from St. Louis, Mrs. W. C. Pirkle, from Hedrick, Oklahoma, and the Hugdins family, from Abbeysville, Alabama.

Seven Southern states were represented at Grandma Veal's party and five generations of direct descendants attended, so naturally there were many questions of, "Are you Cousin Will's son, or are you one of the other Coopers?" "Are you one of the Winder family, or are you all from Flowery Branch?" And many were the little children hauled from quiet corners where they were devouring chicken to be presented to strange cousins with question, "Do you think he favors me, or his father?"

"I've got the best-looking kinfolks in the world," boasted Grandma Veal, with pardonable pride, as she looked around the room at the smiling faces. "And I guess I've got the most kinfolks of anybody around here, because if the rain hadn't come there'd have been a thousand here. Well, better luck next year," she finished philosophically.

—*October 12, 1924*

647-Pound Girl Deplores Short Skirts

I t is axiomatic that the world pities, hates, or fears people who are different from the general run of mankind.

In the case of the sideshow freaks who come to Atlanta every year with the Southeastern Fair Midways, the crowds who stare at them usually feel a sort of superiority.

But the sentiment is wasted, for the freaks don't feel freakish themselves. When the bearded lady or the midgets do their stuff, or the snake charmer caresses the scaly throat of a six-foot pet, or the Senegalese fire-eater puts a red-hot poker in his mouth, most of the audience cluck commiseratingly and murmur, "Wouldn't it be awful to be like that?"

That's just the egotism of the world. Freaks, under their grotesque bodies, and for all their amazing capabilities, are not different from the average Main Streeter. They have their families and their homes, and their social life, their likes and dislikes and interests just like normal individuals have. The fact that JoJo, the Dog-faced Boy, has a face that will give a child fits, and Baby Alice, the 647-pound fat lady, has eighteen dimples and three chins, does not keep the one from being interested in the World's Series and the other from getting excited over the return of high waistlines and short skirts.

As Professional as Undertakers

Baby Alice, who was in Atlanta at the Southeastern Fair, said that being a sideshow freak was as much a profession as being a minister or an undertaker. Nature predisposes some people for the freak profession, added Baby Alice, with the gurgling laugh that has won her the title of the "World's Fattest and Jolliest Girl."

"But Nature doesn't change our hearts one bit," she continued. "I am just as crazy about housekeeping and cooking and sewing as any one-hundred-pound girl would be—and just as crazy about my husband," she added, dimpling. (It's very easy for Baby Alice to dimple. It is the easiest thing she does.)

"I don't usually admit that I'm married," she went on. "The boys who come in here don't like me so well if they know that. They like to think that I'm still single and looking for a sweetheart," the Fat Lady grinned expansively, and lifting up the canvas flap of the sideshow tent she showed a smaller tent pitched directly in the rear.

"That's my home," said she. "At least while on the road. I have my own chairs and trunks and bits of furniture that I always travel with there. I'm home-loving, I am. If I couldn't have the things I love around me, I wouldn't like my life in the sideshow.

Outshouting the Igorot Tom-Toms

"As it is, I like work in a show. The only thing that bothers me is my voice. I have to talk as loud as I can to be heard above the tom-toms in the Igorot tent next door, and almost scream to be heard when the bally-hooers are shouting. It wears my voice out," she finished plaintively. "But its's a good life and I like it. I've been in sideshows for ten years, and I guess I ought to know.

"I haven't had a chance to get into Atlanta while I've been here, and I do need clothes so badly. I've been so busy I haven't bought any fall clothes. I hate that skirts are getting shorter and waistlines higher. I hate that. I never did look well in high-waisted dresses," and the Fat Lady sighed with all the mental attitude of a hundred-pounder.

The Fat Lady's next door neighbors, a midget troupe composed mostly of Germans and Belgians, were lively and talkative, and as mischievous as monkeys, joking and pushing each other about like care-free children. None of the six midgets was over three feet tall, but all were well proportioned and intelligent of face. Of the three men, two were droll and solemn of manner, and one, a boy of sixteen or seventeen, was a "monkey-shiner," to quote the disapproving words of Albertini, the tiny, fifty-six-year-old midget, who seemed to be the official chaperone of the group.

Lucille and the Monkey-Shiner

The dwarfs spoke only a few words of English, but their

conversation was translated by the German woman who looked after them, cooked and sewed and comforted them. "On the lot," the midget troupe dressed and ate in a large circus wagon, and slept at hotels at night. In the wagon was a stove with pots and pans simmering and the comfortable woman who managed the troupe moved about stirring the dinner.

When the little group broke into chatterings and the pretty Lucille pouted and climbed down the wagon steps, her infinitesimal nose in the air, the German woman spoke reprovingly to the "monkey-shiner," but smiled as she explained.

"Always they are teasing little Lucille, who is pretty and knows it. This time the monkey-shiner was asking her if she did not want to get married, and telling her that he knew someone who would make a good husband.

"Little Lucille thought he was talking about himself and was much set up until he told her that it was the Igorot Head Hunter in the next tent. Now they don't speak to each other all day."

"Lucille and Igorot," squeaked the little man after her, and the three-foot debutante turned and put out her tongue at him, in unmistakable disdain.

Midget Babies

"They quarrel and make up and love and get married just like big folks," said the midgets' manager. "Their marriages are real social affairs, too, and every one on the lot is invited, from the bearded lady to the snake-charmer. The midgets are solemn and cunning in dress suits and wedding veils, for, though they are small, they feel just as intensely as if they were normal sized.

"And their little babies!" She threw up her hands and smiled. "They are so tiny you can hardly see them—wee, precious little things. See now," she broke off, "there goes the monkey-shiner to make his peace with Lucille." The little fellow had slid out of the wagon and was trotting across the dusty grass after the petulant small beauty. "He is like big people. He likes Lucille more than anyone in the world, but he teases her and makes her mad, so he can make up."

What could be more normal and unfreaky than the "kiss and make up" instinct?

It is difficult to imagine that a man who makes his living by bathing himself in flames, putting hot irons in his mouth, and walking over hot bricks, can be a normal individual. But the "Senegalese Fire-Eater," soft of speech, swarthy of face, and silky of hair, graduated from the University of Chicago, likes to read poetry and can't smoke cigarettes. That is his only abnormality, he says.

Fire Has Never Burned Him

Brought to this country from Ceylon with his parents and five brothers in the Buffalo Bill Wild West Show in 1908, the Fire-Eater was left without a family when his parents and brothers died in an epidemic. He is not only a graduate of an American college, but he has taken out his citizenship papers and is changing his name from an unpronounceable Oriental one to the less romantic but more practical George Williams.

As to his strange immunity from burns, he cannot explain it—or will not—but merely shakes his head and smiles blandly as is the way of the Orient.

"How can I tell?" he asks, spreading out his hands. "In my country some people think that fire is a god, for it gives light and heat and all things that are desirable and beautiful, as well as all things devastating and terrible. Perhaps fire does not harm those who do not fear it." He smiled, but there was an un-Oriental twinkle in his eye.

"See, it does not hurt me," and picking up a bit of red-hot iron with tongs from a brasier glowing near by, he passed it over his arms and bare legs. "It never hurts me. Even when I was small fire never hurt me. When I was a little boy, I used to dance on red hot stones. In my country people do not think it is strange. In this country people say *freak*. To me it is nothing freakish. It is natural. I have never known anything else."

Girl Who Reads Minds

Of similar opinion was Eva Crewse, a shy girl of seventeen, who performed a remarkable mind-reading act. It embarrassed her to be questioned on how it felt to be able to read other people's minds.

"But I really can't tell what people are thinking about, except at the very time they are thinking it," she protested. "That is just mental telepathy. I always have been able to tell what people were thinking about at the instant the idea flashed into their heads. I never thought anything of it till it began to be noised about that I was telepathic. Then it began to dawn on me that perhaps I was a little different from other girls along that line, but not along any other.

"Yes, it is embarrassing sometimes to know what is going on in people's heads."

The "snake lady" was perhaps the most normal-looking of the midway artists. Usually snake-charmers are of soubrette appearance, blondined and bobbed, Oriental of figure and costume, blasè of appearance. Mrs. Rutherford, wife of the "Cigarette Fiend," luridly depicted on the canvas front of the tent across from the snake pit, was more than middle-aged and growing old gracefully and without a struggle. She stood in a pit, with a thirty-pound python sleeping near her foot and a writhing heap of hissing rattlers in one corner, their rattles buzzing like dried peas in a pod.

She was quietly dressed in a navy blue twill, her thick, gray hair bobbed but unshingled, her nose glasses sliding perilously near the end of her long nose—for all the world a school teacher explaining a difficult problem to a class. In this case, the "class" was the crowd who hung over the pit and fell back with screams of alarmed joy every time a rattler coiled and struck upward in an attempt to reach some of them.

But Mrs. Rutherford picked up the enraged snakes with careful fingers, clamping their jaws from behind their heads, and stroked their throats until they subsided with mollified hisses. She has been a "snake worker" all her life, and has given study and thought to the habits and peculiarities of the different breeds. Fear has never entered her mind. To all appearances she seems to be a motherly woman who would doubtless be interested in federated club work and bridge, but never snakes. As a matter of fact, Mrs. Rutherford IS interested in club work and bridge, but snakes are her pets.

—*October 19, 1924*

Harry Thaw Sees Atlanta's Battlefields

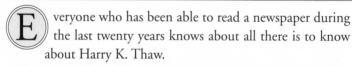 veryone who has been able to read a newspaper during the last twenty years knows about all there is to know about Harry K. Thaw.

But when Harry Thaw and three companions motored to Atlanta recently and spent two days at the Biltmore Hotel, a new sidelight on his character was revealed which heretofore had escaped print.

Everyone who can read knows of Thaw's eccentricities and irresponsibilities, his money, his wife, Evelyn Nesbit Thaw, his shooting of Stanford White, his trial and incarceration in an insane asylum, his escapes, his final successful fight to be adjudged sane, and to gain his freedom.

But no one credits him with being a deep student of American history, particularly Civil War history, and that he has given years of his life to the study of obscure details of dim and almost forgotten battles—particularly, no one who knew him in his wild, younger days.

He is certainly not the slim young man who went to Matteawan asylum nineteen years ago for the killing of Stanford White, New York's most famous architect, nor is he the carefree young millionaire whose exploits rocked the White Way in the early 1900's. The Harry Thaw who motored into Atlanta to spend a few days looking over Civil War battlefields and memorials bears no resemblance to the man who won front page notoriety by his legal fights to escape the gallows and, later, the insane asylum. The Pittsburgh millionaire of 1906 would never have had a thought of dates and battles, statistics and personalities of the Lost Cause, nor would he have retraced with such absorbing interest Sherman's march through Georgia and the campaigns in the valley of Virginia.

Thaw at 50

Harry Thaw, at fifty, is tall and fleshy, though not fat, brown-faced and unlined of cheeks. His eyes, the most arresting feature of his face, are large and hazel-brown, wide of pupil, and twinkling in stare. They are set remarkably far apart, as is generally the case in those gifted with such unusual memories as his.

His hair, still a thick shock which he brushes straight back in a long pompadour, is neither white, salt-and-pepper, nor iron gray, but an odd slate color, the even gray of a Maltese cat. His quick, noiseless movements are cat-like, too, as if the years of confinement had bred in him a nervousness, an abruptness, bordering almost on suspicion, although his manners are courteous and his smile most pleasant when once assured of the friendliness of his surroundings.

The voice is so rapid and eager, the words coming so close together, that there is an inclination toward stuttering when excited. His questions—and there were many—come as suddenly and explosively as machine gun reports and just as close clipped. He asked questions but mostly to justify his own information, as his knowledge of Civil War incidents is most exhaustive and accurate. There is probably not one man in a hundred in Atlanta who knows at exactly what spot General McPherson was killed in the Battle of Atlanta, what mount of food stuffs was in the Confederate commissary before Atlanta fell, what was the religion of General Lee and "Jeb" Stuart, how early in the war Ashby, "that cavalier of the cavalry," was killed, what railroad Sherman cut at Jonesboro, Georgia, eventually causing the loss of Atlanta to the South, and a thousand other historical items large and small—few Atlantans would know them all, but Harry Thaw knows them.

Learned in Asylums

"No, I didn't learn them in school. No one ever learns anything in school when they are young," he said shortly. His years at Matteawan and other asylums where he spent his time reading every American history he could lay hands on and studying minute details of Civil War campaigns account for his remarkable knowledge. The years behind walls reading, studying, and thinking bred in him a desire to visit the places made familiar through 10,000 pages, should he ever gain his freedom.

Dressed in a dusty and inconspicuous suit and wearing a gray felt hat, shapeless and ripply of brim, stained about the band with sweat and exposure to all weathers, there was nothing about him, or any of his party, to suggest a million. That is, nothing except his car.

It was battleship gray, large and underslung, equipped with enormous tires and enough accessories to set up a "parts and accessories" shop, upholstered in a warm gray and filled with a number of wooly lap robes and blankets of paisley design. In this powerful car, with the top down, Thaw, his secretary, and two companions have motored southward from Virginia, stopping at every town of historical interest that lay in their path, to visit graveyards, read carvings on memorials, examine historical tablets, and consult with the "oldest inhabitants" who "fit with Lee and Johnson."

His desire after arriving in Atlanta was to view the Stone Mountain Memorial and to travel the road on which so much bloody fighting took place in 1864, when Sherman's armies attempted to enter Atlanta from the northeast.

Once at Stone Mountain, he was not content to view the unfinished memorial from the easy cushions of his car, but climbed a hundred yards through straggling blackberry bushes to an elevation directly in front of Lee's head. Upon the rise of ground was an old tally-ho, weatherbeaten and rusty of wheels, which some thoughtful person had dragged thither so that spectators could obtain a better view. Thaw climbed up into the driver's seat and viewed the mountainside with Lee's head standing out clearly, with a blurred, indistinct mass of cuts and lines about it, in absolute silence for five minutes.

How Head Looked to Thaw

"It looks," he said abruptly, "like the Prince of Wales."

"Who?"

"Albert Edward, of course! Doesn't anyone remember the Prince of Wales? I forgot, he died before all you were born. At any rate, his head is on tobacco cans, you see," and then broke off into a rapid string of questions. How high was the monument? How high was the mountain? What were the dimensions of General Lee's nose? Who were the generals who were to be carved on the mountain, and in exactly what order did they come?

There is something about his intense stare and his rapid-fire questions that elicits an equally rapid response, but also causes a sinky feeling akin to that of a schoolgirl who has turned up for a history final without "cracking a book or cramming a line." If the answer is incorrect, Thaw says with decisiveness, "No, that's all wrong. Johnson should have never been deposed. Johnson could have saved the Confederacy," or "You made an error there, General Jeb Stuart was killed at Yellow Tavern the year following the date you said."

Then a deep and gloomy realization of ignorance spreads over his audience. The only person who escaped this inferiority complex about Confederate history was the white-bearded veteran, the custodian and lecturer at the Cyclorama at Grant Park, who "marched along with Jackson and climbed the heights with Lee."

Of course, after seeing Stone Mountain from every angel, Harry Thaw had wanted to spend several hours at the Cyclorama, that being one of the main reasons for his visit. The "vet" who took him and his party through, explaining every detail of the magnificent picture, had no intimation of the international notoriety of the tall visitor with the odd gray hair, but gathered from his accent that he was a "Yankee." Probably he had never before had so interested a listener to his lecture, for Harry Thaw, noiseless of footsteps and shining of eyes, was at his shoulder every moment.

Thaw's Questions

"But I don't understand" said he suddenly, pointing to one part of the canvas whereon was depicted the closest hand-to-hand fighting of the whole picture—the incident in the fight around the unfinished brick house, on which a shell-torn Red Cross flag waved, and about which rifle pits and cotton bales made barricades.

The remnants of a shattered battery were there, caisson wagons splintered and wheelless, horses and men piled in heaps, cannon pointing in all directions over the breast works, smoke rising above the fighting men.

"But I don't understand. Why are those earthworks thrown up on the northeast, and why do the cannon face both north and south? The Federals held that earthwork first and dug those pits."

"The Confed-rits retook the battery," kindly explained the "vet," passing on to the next incident.

"But why are the guns thrown out all in all directions? Are some of them from the Confederate battery?"

"No," said the veteran, accommodatingly. "And now on the summit of the hill, we can see the reinforcements of..." But the listener with the New York accent still leaned on the rail, at the same place, his eyes riveted on the puzzling battery, with the life-like smoke curling from the muzzles. It was near the closing hour, the lecture was to be finished, the other members of the audience were restless for the lecturer to go on.

"Come on," invited the veteran to Harry Thaw, who seemed not to hear but was checking up in his mind whether or not his historian had been at fault, or an error had been made by the painters of the picture in having two cannon pointing toward Stone Mountain instead of toward Atlanta.

Finally, the veteran gently poked him in the ribs with his cane and remarked, "Young fellow, if you want to learn anything about this war, you'd better follow me and pay attention to what I am going to tell you."

Aroused, Thaw turned and looked at him steadily for a moment and then laughed aloud suddenly, and followed the white-bearded lecturer.

When the "spiel" was over and the onlookers were leaving, the veteran plucked at the sleeve of Thaw's secretary, who was the last man to go down the steps.

"Who was he...the big man who laughed?"

"Him? The one you poked in the ribs? Oh, that was Harry K. Thaw. He's spent fifteen years studying Civil War history."

—*May 17, 1925*

Atlanta Doctor at O. Henry's Deathbed

Sydney Porter, newspaper man, author, convict, now immortalized under the name of "O. Henry" as the world's greatest short story writer whose royalties since his death have run into the hundreds of thousands, died in a New York hospital with only twenty-three cents in his pockets.

This information comes from Dr. Charles Hancock, who was the physician in attendance on O. Henry at the time of his death. Dr. Hancock, who with his brother, Dr. T. H. Hancock, is joint owner of the Atlanta Hospital, at 20 Crew Street, was formerly instructor in surgery at the post-graduate school of the New York Polyclinic Hospital, and it was in his capacity as surgeon that he took O. Henry's case, although he found the writer too far gone for surgery to save.

"It was through a patient of mine, Miss Anne Partlan, a newspaper woman, that I was called in on O. Henry's case," said Dr. Hancock. "I had been her family physician for some years and knew her well. Miss Partlan was a very attractive young woman, and a clever writer. I learned afterward that many of his clever ideas were originally suggested by her. She was certainly a true-blue woman and a loyal friend to O. Henry in his last illness, when he refused to let anyone else know how serious was his condition.

A Dying Man

"It was after midnight some seventeen years ago, I think, that Miss Partlan called me on the phone, and begged me to come and take the case of a friend of hers, Sidney Porter. He was very ill, she said, and she had decided that he was not receiving the proper medical attention. I must admit that I had never heard of him, and, in fact, had never read any of his stories, so the name, 'Sidney Porter,' meant nothing to me. Perhaps, if she had said 'O. Henry,' it might have sounded a familiar note. However, I dressed and went hastily to the street number she had given me.

"The sick man was in a room at the Calidonia Hotel, and as I entered I couldn't help noticing that it wasn't an especially good room or well suited for a sick room. However, not knowing who the man was, I thought at first that it was some poor devil of a newspaper friend of Miss Partlan, sick and broke and down on his luck. But as soon as I spoke to the man and saw his face, I realized two things. First, that I was in the presence of a great and powerful personality—and next, that here was a dying man.

"There was something sparkling about him. His face was expressive and humorous despite the fact that he was dreadfully ill, and his mind was keen as a sword where any other man, suffering from the same complication of diseases, would have been in a state of coma. He joked with me and with Miss Partlan as if we had met at a tea.

Not Afraid of Death

"I examined him and asked a few questions and was almost stunned to find that this alert, scintillating fellow had sclerosis of the liver in an advanced stage, nephritis, and diabetes. After his death, I discovered that another load he labored under was the most dilated heart I have seen in all my practice. As a general thing, any one of these diseases, in the last stage, will cause coma or at least stupidity and torpidness. But in O. Henry's case, there was no indication of slackening powers. Of course, it was nothing except his will and his powerful brain that was keeping him going.

"When I saw his condition, I knew it was only a matter of days, and I started to tell him as gently as I could that his death was near. But before I could say anything, he waved his arm at me and grinned.

"'Never mind that, doctor. I know all about it. I'm going to die very soon and I'm not especially bothered.' He paused a moment and added, 'And not afraid, either. I guess when I die, I'll go where all the other "good fellows" go.'

"Wishing to make his last days as easy as possible, I told him that I would take him to the hospital. But did he go in an ambulance? Oh, no. He called a taxi, walked out into the hall, went down the elevator, and climbed into the car. The three of us rode to the old Polyclinic Hospital, then at 218 East Thirteenth Street, Anne Partlan steadying him on one side and me on the other, while he talked casually about the things we were passing—things he knew he was seeing for the last time.

Joked with His Nurses

We arrived at the hospital, and he walked into the desk where the registrar asked his name.

"'William Sidney Porter!' said O. Henry. 'But tomorrow it will be 'Dennis!' Then he felt in his pocket and pulled out twenty-three cents and held them out, laughing, to Miss Partlan.

"'I've heard of people being worth thirty cents and here I am going to die, and only worth twenty-three!'

"I got a good room for him and two nurses and put him to bed. During the next three days, I gave up my other patients and worked with him day and night in an effort to make his passing easier.

"Still, I didn't know who he was. I only knew he was the most remarkable patient I had ever had. He kept the nurses in gales of laughter all the time. Some of the jokes he cracked would have made a dog laugh. If I had only known who he was, I'd have jotted down some of his witty remarks, for they were worthy of saving, but I was so busy trying to help him that I only had time for admiration for his nerve. He joked about everything, life and death, and his humor was at times biting and keen.

"It seems strange to think that while the man who was afterwards hailed as America's greatest short story writer lay dying, no one knew of it except Miss Partlan. I discovered afterward that he didn't want anyone to know. He was so popular with the newspaper people and the literary set that they would have camped all over the hospital, anxious to do something and getting terribly in the way. He seemed very happy as he lay there at the Polyclinic, and to my knowledge did not ask for anyone or send any messages, although his wife and daughter were somewhere in the South, unaware of his condition. He made no disposal of property of any type or of trinkets. He had no property, or keepsakes or anything, he told me.

"I've often thought it odd that he should die penniless when his royalties should have been large.

"Afraid to Go Home in the Dark"

"I kept waiting for the collapse that should have taken place days before, and expected every moment that he would slide into an unconscious state from which he would never awaken, but he remained keen up until the very end.

"The end came about in this way. There were two lights in the room, one a bright one and the other low and green-shaded. The five of us were in his room, the two nurses, Miss Partlan, O. Henry, and myself, talking and, I must confess, laughing at his jokes, when one nurse rose and turned off the bright light.

"'It's so bright it might hurt your eyes.' she said.

"'Turn it back on,' he ordered, and smiling, added a quotation from a song then current, 'I'm afraid to go home in the dark!'

"His heart stopped then, and his brain and body died at one and the same time.

"Some hours afterward, when I was trying to catch up on the sleep I had lost during those three days, the phone rang. Reporters, of course, wanting to know about Mr. Porter. I told them briefly what I knew. More called and more and more phone calls poured in. Finally I located Miss Partlan.

"'Who was Mr. Porter?' I asked her.

"'He was the world's greatest short story writer,' she told me, and that left me flat. I don't suppose that if the President of the United States had been my patient there would have been any more people seeking information about him. Reporters, magazine writers, friends who were heart-broken that they had not been notified, kept me so busy morning, noon, and night that it was a week before I could get time enough to look up his books and begin to read them.

"Afterward, I talked to Miss Partlan about O. Henry. She had worked on the same paper with him fairly well. From her I learned much about his life, his writing, his prison experiences.

"Since talking to her, I have never believed that he was guilty of the forgery for which he did time. In his Texas days, O. Henry drank more than was good for him, and I believe that it was while on a 'bender' that his troubles began. He had a very good friend, of whom he thought the world, and I believe he sheltered that friend. He always claimed he was innocent of the crime for which he was punished, but he never gave the name of the guilty man.

"I have read all his stories over and over since then and never tire of them. I think, perhaps, I can appreciate them better than most people, having seen the gay way in which their author met death."

—January 2, 1926

5

Flappers & Sheiks

This photo of A. S. Weil and Mitchell illustrated a 1923 *Journal Magazine* article,
"From Toddle to Tango."

Laundry List Sung by Atlanta Sub-Deb

—◈—

The Rat Court, the Three-Legged Race, and the Football Game Played With an Old Galosh, Are Some of the Other Funny Things Described by Atlanta College Girls While Here for the Holidays.

—◈—

"Galli Curci has nothing on me," declared Ruth Ridley, during the holidays spent with her parents, Mr. and Mrs. R. H. Ridley. "She may be able to take 'high C' in grand opera, but I'll wager she couldn't hold a candle to me when it comes to singing a laundry list to the tune of the Marseilles before an audience of strange girls when I was being hazed at Linmoore Hall this fall!"

"But I think of being the middle girl in a three-legged race, as I was at Goucher." This from Constance Cone, daughter of Mr. and Mrs. E. H. Cone.

The girls' finishing school of the conventional type where correct young lades were taught how to enter rooms and ascend staircases with no end of grace, where they acquired stilted mannerisms and a "Don'tchaknow" attitude toward life seems to have passed totally out of existence, if we are to believe that the experiences of some of Atlanta's sub-deb school girls are typical. Holidays are really a most commendable institution, if for no other reason than that they bring these young girls back to brighten the town for a week or ten days.

Sophomore Hazing

"It seems from what they say that girls' schools nowadays are places where all manner of important things are learned by our sub-debs, things that will fit them for something more valuable to the world than merely adorning a ballroom or scintillating at bridge. And when they play, they play hard, and college spirit is as big a thing to them as it is to their brothers at Tech and Georgia. They do have fun, part of the time at least, and many a frolic is mixed in with their study and work.

"There never was a girl yet," said Constance Cone, "who went off to college and didn't believe in her heart of hearts that she was going to be president of the freshman class, captain of the basketball team, and head of student council—all in the first week of college! But when you do get there, there are so many girls and they all are just as sure that they are going to be class presidents, etc., and so many other things to do that you finally realize that you haven't a chance. Then you settle down to enjoying college life.

"The first thing that takes the high falutin' idea out of a freshie at Goucher is the annual sophomore hazing. Of course the sophs never do anything really mean or that would hurt you—it's all in fun—but it does make you feel a little less important! They have almost stopped hazing at Goucher, and have narrowed it down to one day—but that day is a gala occasion. By sophomore edict, all freshies turn out with their hair skinned back in two pigtails, their middies on backwards, and their faces painted white. You can't imagine the effect when so many girls look so terribly!

Ordered to "Scramble Like an Egg"

"The sophs line up in two long lines facing each other and make their victims 'run the gauntlet.' Every soph yells a different order—and the freshmen have to obey them. When I started down the line, first, someone yelled, 'Why don't you smile?' and when I grinned, half a dozen cried indignantly, 'Wipe that smile off your face!' Then it was 'Stand on your head!' 'Dance a jib!' 'Hop like a frog!' and a dozen other silly orders, coming so fast that I hardly knew what to do next. Really, it was lots of fun, but some of the timid little girls were so confused at the excitement and crazy orders that they broke down and cried out loud.

"All the rebels who refused to obey were reserved for 'Rat Court' that afternoon. That was really the best fun of all. The sophs held court and solemnly passed judgment on the disobedient freshmen. Some of the most defiant had to stick their heads in a bucket of water, others had to 'get down on the floor and scramble like an egg' or 'develop like a film.' I think that I drew the worst. I was in a three-legged race! I was the middle one and as the other two girls with me were excited, I couldn't manage them at all.

"'Start off on your left feet!' I'd hiss at them and they would start off on their right and as a result, poor little me had to keep both legs moving at once—in fact, I just leaped like a frog, and, of course, all of us pitched over on the ground, to the intense glee of the assembled multitude.

"But when 'Rat Court' was over, the sophs gave us a party, and at that party we had the ceremony of burying the hatchet. After that they were lovely to us. That is why Goucher has so much college spirit, because everybody helps everybody else."

They Ended in the Infirmary

Frances Traylor, daughter of Mr. and Mrs. George M. Traylor, who is a student at Mary Baldwin at Staunton, Virginia, talked with characteristic school-girl hyperbole of the beauties of her school and its mountain scenery.

"It's just perfect," she said, "except for one thing," and she smiled. "That is that you have to enjoy the scenery from a respectful distance! They are very strict about letting the girls go away from school, even into town, except on weekends. That strictness brought us to a bad pass one day.

"It was a Sunday afternoon and all of us wanted some candy. We didn't have any or anything to make candy out of or even any way to get the 'makings.' I did have a little sugar and my roommate had some 'Sterno.' We scraped around and found another girl and her roommate who had a bag of pear chips. We decided to mix these all together and cook them. But we didn't have anything to cook them in. Then my roommate proved her ingenuity by producing a tin candy box with Rudolph Valentino's picture on it. Wasn't she self-sacrificing?

"We mixed up the sugar and pear chips and some water in the box and watched it cook, thinking all the time of all the millions of boxes of candy in the world and how horrible it was that we couldn't get any.

"Finally we couldn't wait any longer, and taking the mess off, we sampled it. It really tasted worse than anything I've ever eaten, but none of us would admit it. It tasted like tin, and paint and 'Sterno' and syrup, and was quite sickening. But we ate it.

"Then we all went to the infirmary."

Singing the Laundry List

"Freshman song try-out at Linmoore Hall is the occasion when strong freshmen turn pale and weep," said Ruth Ridley. "Song try-outs are traditional at Linmoore, and to be chosen song leader of the freshman class is one of the biggest honors in school. Then, too, it is an honor to the house you live in; so the sophs at my house gathered all the freshmen together, the day of their arrival, and began to teach us college songs. None of us looked forward with any joy to the occasion, for the idea of getting up and leading two hundred strange girls in songs didn't appeal to any of us.

"When the big night finally came, we were all frantic with fright and declared that we simply wouldn't go. The sophs said the honor of the house was at stake, so eventually, by arguing and cajoling, they rounded us up and escorted us to the chapel.

Overwhelmed with Fright

"The whole school had turned out to see the fun. Even the faculty was there, occupying the front seats. We freshmen were lined up in alphabetical order and waited, milling around like uneasy cattle. When everything was settled, the four judges mounted the platform and called up the first candidate.

"She was so overwhelmed with stage fright that her knees were shaking, but she was 'game.'

"'Sing *Jingle Bells,*' commanded the judges.

"The poor kid faced the audience and after waving her hands back and forth, in the approved song leader style, began to sing in an unnaturally high pitch.

"'Jingle bells, jingle bells on the icy air!'

"When she took the high notes, her voice broke and without waiting for the audience to join in the second line, as was the rule, she turned and fled ignominiously. The audience cheered loudly.

"At this, I broke into a gentle perspiration from sheer fright. I can't even carry a tune!

"The fun grew furious as the poor freshies were butchered to make a Linmoore holiday. Some girls did very creditably, pitched their voices in the correct key and led the crowd in a way that brought forth real applause. Most of us failed miserably. Some sang a line, burst into tears and ran. When my time came, I decided to pitch my voice very low, so that it would not break ridiculously.

"'Do you know the *Marseillaise?* asked the judge.

"Yes," I admitted, quailing.

"'Then sing this to the tune of the *Marseillaise*, and she handed me a piece of paper.

"I glanced at it. It was as laundry list!

"'Go on,' urged the judges, and I plunged into it.

"'Six nightgowns, ten pairs stockings,' sang I, and the hall broke into roars. Even Mrs. Timmer, the principal, had tears of laughter in her eyes. I was shaking with fright, but my courage was up and I caroled on.

"'Four shirtwaists, two middies,' on to the very end, then I rushed off the platform, in the midst of howls of laughter. All the rest of the freshies had to sing the list, too. But can't you imagine how I felt, when I found out the next day that I had been chosen as one of the assistant song leaders!"

Where the Galosh Landed

"I went to Randolph-Macon for two years," said Caroline Beckham, daughter of Mr. and Mrs. W. E. Beckham, "and I loved it, but I decided that if I went there four years, all I'd have when I got through would be a diploma. Of course, it's wonderful to have an A.B. degree, but I wanted to do something practical, so now I am going to school at Beechwood, near Philadelphia. It's a vocational school, and there you learn how to do everything imaginable.

"They have secretarial courses and home economics, dress designing, and hat trimming," she patted a pretty toque she wore. "In fact, they teach everything practical there is to be taught."

Ann Harriet Shewmake, daughter of Mr. and Mrs. Claude Shewmake, one of the throng of Atlanta sub-debs who was home from school during the holidays, told this story. It seems the girls of her floor at Mary Baldwin Seminary decided on football as a good reducing exercise, and after a fashion they played football with an indeterminate number of the girls on each side, with the corridor as their gridiron, and the time of play from "lights out" in the evening, until the matron arrived to stop the game. "Tech" and "Auburn" were the names adopted by the rival teams, and the games were quite as interesting as the one we saw out on Grant field on Thanksgiving—and the best sort of reducing exercise.

The nightly game was the popular school sport until Ann Harriet made a forward pass with the galosh, which was serving as the football that evening, at exactly the right moment to hit the matron in the face as she opened the door. After that there were no more Tech-Auburn games at Mary Baldwin.

—*January 14, 1923*

Atlanta Sub-Debs Pass Up Tutankhamen

I t's all a matter of viewpoint.

While the whole world has been watching from day to day the progress of the excavations that are to bring to light the mummified remains of Tutankhamen, King of the Egyptians, a party of Georgia girls just back from a tour that included the Land of the Pyramids had to arrive in Atlanta before they realized that the event was creating such a stir.

"Oh, no, we couldn't be bothered with watching them dig up dead people. Too many live things were happening," remarked Margaret Elder, one of the girls.

Which isn't so very surprising when these Georgia peaches in the short five months of their tour had tea at Oxford with a pair of Russian ex-dukes of the pre-Bolshevistic nobility, saw the King and Queen open Parliament, sailed the Mediterranean with Elsie Janis, attended the opera in Naples as the guests of an Italian count, and rode camel-back into the desert with an honest-to-goodness, sure-enough Sheik, all of which is of far greater importance to the All-American girl than the privilege of standing around while prying scientists dig into the grave of an ancient monarch.

And with a Sheik for a guide! A dead King couldn't be expected to be nearly so interesting as a live Sheik, could he?

"He wasn't exactly what we expected," Margaret Elder said. "He was very dark, and his robes weren't so very clean, but then he was a Sheik and he had that—you know, 'Sheikish' look in his eyes. We went by the place where they were digging the King up and we saw the crowds there, but we didn't go over."

Sheiks, Counts, and Dukes

The girls in the Georgia party were Miss Elder, daughter of Mr. and Mrs. Sterling Elder; Miss Telside Pratt, daughter of George L. Pratt; Miss Winnie Belle Davis, daughter of Mr. and Mrs. Wade H. Davis; Miss Margaret Colbert, daughter of Mr. and Mrs. Roy Simms, all of Atlanta, and Miss Mary Mack, daughter of Mr. and Mrs. E. E. Mack, of Thomasville. Mrs. John T. North chaperoned the party.

The Sheik and the Count and the Duke and the King weren't all the interesting things that happened to them. There was an audience in Rome with the Pope, and the funny little Italian guide who let Telside Pratt's horse get away from him and nearly carried her into the crater of Vesuvius; the Herr Conductor who became excited and polysyllabic because they weren't able to get enough sleeping-car reservations on the way from Berlin to Frankfort so that four of them had to sleep in a space none too large for two, to say nothing at all of Montmartre and the Follies Bergere in Paris, those wonderfully blue moonlight nights on the Mediterranean, and the rugged green beauty of the Isle of Wight as they first sighted land and sailed into Southampton after a stormy trip across.

"Things started happening as soon as we sailed," said Margaret Colbert. "It was just a few days out when we, or rather the captain of our ship, got an SOS that an Italian ship was sinking somewhere.

What Happened in Brussels

"Our boat rushed to the rescue. It was more exciting than any race I had ever seen because we knew if we didn't get there, many lives might be lost. But we reached the sinking vessel in time and we got everybody off before the boat went down, all except a Collie dog. Such a pretty one too!"

England didn't make a very favorable impression on the All-American girls. "The women dress so awkwardly," as "Peggy" Davis expressed it, so they gave Southampton a hasty once-over, shopped a bit in London's Regent Street, tea-ed at the Trocadero, dined at the Savoy, and were off to the Continent, after finding out that "Oxford isn't a bit like Tech or Georgia, and the students are lots different from our college boys."

"The funniest thing that happened was in Brussels," said Telside Pratt. "The morning after we got there from Paris it was raining, and as we didn't have any heavy shoes, we all wore our galoshes and went flapping down the street with the straps unbuckled.

"You wouldn't think that people who wear wooden shoes would see anything odd in galoshes, but they did. We noticed passers-by on the street looking at us and laughing, but we couldn't figure out what it was all about. Pretty soon there was a regular crowd following, and we dodged into a shop to get away from them.

"When we came out, the crowd was still there waiting to see the strange American girls with their stranger shoes. Then we realized what it was all about, because we noticed them pointing at our feet. We were attracting more attention than we ever could by wearing the most fashionable gown on the Peachtree promenade. After that we wore our galoshes with the straps buckled."

Why Italians Don't Get Drunk

In Italy, the Atlanta girls found out why there was so little drunkenness, in public at least.

"The Italians think the American prohibition law is ridiculous," said Margaret Elder, "but they have a way of stopping people from getting drunk even though the cafes sell everything alcoholic. When the Fascisti police find a man drunk on the street, they stop him and give him a chaser of castor oil they carry. Imagine such a thing at one of the Atlanta dances!

"Since the Fascisti took charge in Italy everyone wears black shirts, even to fashionable affairs. It looks odd, but the people seem pretty well satisfied with the way they are running things."

"I didn't much care for the Fascisti guide who let go of my horse's tail while we were climbing up the side of Mount Vesuvius!" declared Telside Pratt. "The ascent is very steep, and these little guides always go up the mountains hanging on to the tail of the horse they are guiding. I don't see how the horses stand it for the guides pull out great handfuls of hair and keep yelling, 'Onh! Onh!' to make the horses go faster.

"While we were clattering up the side in a bedlam of *Onh, ohn*s! my horse bolted, with the bit in his teeth, leaving the guide sitting in the middle of the path, looking silly. Vesuvius is in semi-eruption now, and the crater is a vast, seething cauldron of molten lava with vapor and smoke swirling 'round. The silly horse kept tearing on up with me sticking on somehow, till we passed some Italian soldiers. Of course, I thought they'd see how scared I was, even though I was too scared to yell. But instead of stopping the horse, they all yelled 'Onh!' and the horse

*Onh*ed right on up till just as I had lost hope, some guides lined up across the path and yelled 'Ump!' (At least, that was what it sounded like!) and the horse stopped so suddenly that he stood straight up. If I had only known enough Italian to say 'ump' in the first place!"

"But camel-riding on the Sahara was much more exciting," said Margaret Elder. "There is something fascinating about the desert, just as it is in books. Then, too, we had a Sheik as a guide, which made it much more exciting. His name was Harsernanikh-atab, and though he was a little too dark to be romantic, he had wonderful manners and was splendidly educated. We rode on camels out to the pyramids and the Sphinx with Elsie Janis in our party. She is so adorable! No, we didn't waste any time on Tutankhamen. We couldn't be bothered."

Breaking Jerusalem's Speed Laws

"I had the thrill that comes once in a lifetime when I drove a Buick at top speed through the streets of Jerusalem with my hat off and my red hair flying!" said "Peggy" Davis. "The Eastern women are so subservient, they are always veiled and silent and afraid to call their souls their own. We could see them peeking out at us in horrified awe as we tore around in the car, without hats or veils, honking the horn, and being generally noisy. They came to the windows and stared and whispered till I felt sorry for them.

"The natives aren't used to autos, and the camels are such dumb brutes that they can't ever learn anything. A camel will get in the middle of a narrow street and stand across it, gazing absently into space, chewing his cud, and no power on earth can convince him that it's against traffic regulations to block the streets. When we drove from Jerusalem to Bethlehem, we could see the caravans of camels ahead of us being driven off the road into the fields. The drivers screamed excitedly and beat the camels, who rushed off in all directions, their enormous loads bobbing up and down as they fled in terror at the horn. We certainly had the right of way in the Holy Land!"

Is it any wonder that these All-American girls, who breezed through Europe with typical American insouciance, laughing at inconveniences and dangers, having tea with nobility, shocking the veiled women of the East, should have more interesting things to do than watch Tutankhamen dug up?

—*March 11, 1923*

Interest in British Egyptologist Howard Carter's November 26, 1922 discovery of the tomb of Tutankhamen (c. 1370–1353) in the Valley of the Kings was still at fever pitch in 1923. Mitchell wrote several articles about prominent Atlantans who visited Egypt during the period, and about the local craze for clothes and beauty products influenced by the Art Deco version of Egyptian taste.

Tech Boys Tell Why Girls Are Rushed

One girl gets a rush. Another, just as pretty, doesn't. Why?

The mystery isn't solved when you ask Tech boys. They only know that the popular girl gets the rush, and that fact, in itself, increases her popularity. Why should they trouble with trying to find out what makes them like her?

However, when urged, some members of the Tech student body "spoke their minds" on what they like in a girl, and what is their "ideal."

Asking serious questions upon such a weighty subject and getting serious answers are two entirely different matters when dealing with college students.

On the porch of Kappa Sigma fraternity house on North

Avenue lounged a dozen or more of the celebrities of Atlanta's younger set, the Tech boys—bare-headed and careless, pipes in hands, feet on banisters, hands clasped behind heads. The warm spring weather was not conducive to effort of any kind.

The occasion was graced by the presence of "Sugarfoot" Raiford Gaffney, he of the famous black mustache; Charlie Lyons, who captivated young Atlanta in the Follies; John Staton, whose name strikes terror to the hearts of all enemy football players; the famous Moore brothers, Mac and Larry—and many others too numerous to mention.

The Sheik Speaks

"Here is 'Sheik' Saunders!" cried "Sugarfoot" Gaffney, as an immaculately-groomed young man sauntered up the Kappa Sig walk. "He's the original man who understood women. Let him tell what he likes best about girls."

"Gentlemen, I thank you," said the Sheik with becoming modesty. "Frankly, I like sweet girls with big, trusting eyes. I like girls that I can write letters to—for it's much more satisfactory to write to them than to see them."

"No letters for me," remarked Larry Moore in positive accents. "I'm a firm believer in 'Do right—and fear no man. Don't write, and fear no woman!' "

"You just don't understand women," explained the Sheik. "Now, the kind of girl I really like best is the girl who isn't eternally expecting you to make love to her. It's awful to feel like women are always wanting you to make love to them—and I don't want to be making love all the time. I—I just want to be—you know—friendly with girls."

"I never saw a woman yet who wanted to be friendly," said Fred Moore, gloomily. "However, girls are all right if they aren't athletic. My ideal is a very feminine, unathletic girl who has got some sense, but who isn't convinced that she can take care of herself and is always going around telling everybody at the top of her voice that she can."

Loud cheers greeted this statement. Sol Davis was very definite in his view on the One Woman.

"I like 'em modern to their finger tips, bobbed-haired blondes are my specialty. I like a girl who has lots of pep and loves to dance, but who gets a little tired after the first two or three dances and enjoys sitting out looking at the moonlight."

"I like girls who appreciate a little air during dances, too," cried Mac Moore, and a unanimous murmur of approbation went up.

Tall Girls

"I like modern girls, too," declared "Sugarfoot" Gaffney, stroking the black mustache that is the pride of North Avenue. "That is, if they are sincere about their modernism.

"But I don't like girls who do things just as a pose. It's my belief that most modern girls who smoke wouldn't do so if they were alone. Of course," he admitted seriously, "I have never been with a girl when she was alone with herself, and so I can't speak with absolute authority on the subject."

By this time the Tech boys on the neighboring frat house porches had hastened over to join in the discussion, and those passing down the street had wandered in to swell the throng and air their views (and those of their neighbors!).

"John Staton likes them tall," volunteered Larry Moore.

"I'm not so tongue-tied that I can't tell what kind of a girl I like, myself, without any help from you," declared John Staton, giving Larry Moore a poisonous look. "I do like tall girls and detest these little 'cute' ones. But I don't like them skinny. I like them to have just enough weight to be—err—"

"Yes, yes! Go on! You interest us strangely!" chorused the crowd.

"I like them to have just enough weight to be substantial," finished John Staton, with dignity. "But the thing I like best about a girl is pretty teeth. I like a girl who has shiny, glistening teeth."

"Hurrah for beautiful dumbbells!" cried Squire Allen. "They are so much less trouble and infinitely more appreciative than sensible girls."

"Save us from dumbbells," prayed John Staton fervently. "There is nothing more terrible than a dumb girl—even a dumb man can't compare with one. I like for a girl to have something to say when she opens her mouth."

"Oh, yes, I like for a girl to know how to talk," admitted Larry Moore, "but I don't like a highbrow or an intellectual—they are terrors. There really is nothing sweeter, though, than a pretty girl who can talk sensibly. I think every man likes that kind of girl."

A Blighted Life

"I love them trusting," mused Charlie Lyons. "One thing I always fall for is that sweet trusting look in their eyes. Sweet eyes and trim red shoes, now, that's the kind of girl I like."

Ed Merritt snorted in disgust, "Trusting! Who wants a trusting girl? Give me a Tech girl, one who runs with the college set and likes—"

"And likes college boys—particularly Ed Merritt," interrupted the obliging Mr. Gaffney. "I suppose one may gather that Merritt likes the ladies."

"Of course you don't like them," pointed out Fred Saunders, who was so friendly disposed towards the feminine sex.

"I have a blighted life," said "Sugarfoot" with dignity. "I have no definite statement to make concerning my particular likes and dislikes where women are concerned. However," he brightened, "I can give you her address."

"I want a girl who hasn't already been trained up in the way in which she should go," declared "Joe" Hill. "It would be a calamity to get a girl and then find out that somebody else had 'brang her up' differently from what you want. The girl I'M going to have isn't going to let anybody bring her up but me!"

"Your faith is simple and beautiful," jeered Ed Merritt.

"What's all the racket about?" yelled a 180-pound blond on the porch next door.

"Come and tell the lady about your ideal woman," commanded Gaffney.

"Not me," said the blond, calmly.

"He's married," explained Gaffney in a loud stage whisper that reached to the next porch. "Very much married and has four children. So you see, he feels that he hasn't the right to make a statement on women."

"Hey, I'll talk! I'm not married!" cried the blond, hastily vaulting over the banisters and joining the crowd to the edification of Mr. Gaffney. "I like modern women—terribly modern women. My name is J. E. Jackson."

At the mention of the name, there was an indignant gurgle from the porch of the frat house, a scuffle, and four boys hastily escorted a small freshman into the house.

"Is that really your name?" questioned the interviewer, dubiously.

"Oh, yes," vouched the crowd.

"Well, don't any of you want a girl of sweet old-fashioned type who meets you at the front door when you come home at night and asks 'is my darlin' tired?'" queried the interviewer.

There was a moment's silence, and then as if by tacit consent, Raiford Gaffney became spokesman.

"Why, that is exactly the kind of girl we have all been talking about for the last half an hour," he said, in pained accents.

—*June 3, 1923*

Road Show Girls Record Dressers

S eeing a play "back stage," from the wings, robs it of some of the glamor of unreality that the stage always has, even for the most sophisticated. But unlike most things seen from a different angle, the new viewpoint is worth the loss of a few illusions.

However, unless one is a member of the cast, a stage hand, or a reporter, it is next to impossible to see a play from the wings. There are three guardians to be passed before obtaining a coveted position back stage, from whence the action of the play can be viewed close-up. First, there is the Argus-eyed "door keep," who guards the entrance to the stage door and subjects all strangers to a third-degree which makes the methods of police force pale to insignificance. Second, there is "props," the property man, a kind-hearted, hard-boiled individual who presides over all the "properties" to be used in the play. Third, there is the stage director, who has no love for strangers who "clutter up the wings."

A "road show" is different back stage from a stock company and vastly different from vaudeville. There is the element of hurry, as if haste of the "quick jumps" from town to town had communicated itself to stage hands and chorus alike. Before the curtain rises, the stage hands move swiftly about erecting scenery, placing furniture, laying down rugs. The members of the cast who are in costume roam about the stage talking, trying out their voices, humming over their songs. From men's dressing rooms comes a startling outburst of sound as the baritone and the tenor try to out-sing each other while making up.

Dim, Unreal World

"Back stage" seems a dim, unreal world, the ceilingless heights of which are filled with hanging back drops and suspended scenery, a world peopled with shadowy figures of chorus girls who flit up and down the narrow concrete steps and stage hands carrying "props" to be used in the next scene.

Then the "call boy" makes his rounds, five minutes before the curtain, yelling names at the door of each dressing room at the top of his voice, so that the cast may assemble.

The chorus takes its place. The overture ceases and the curtain goes up.

From "out front" comes the sound of the unseen orchestra and the chorus breaking into the opening number, something about spring and robins nesting again and love, as opening numbers always are.

Then, the shuffle and patter of feet. The first dance has begun. From the wings, only the backs of the dancers can be seen as they dance close to the footlights, coquetting with the lukewarm front row. As they dance back—skirts snapping out as they whirl, ballet slippers scuffing the floor—the spotlight in the wings throws them into vivid relief. The side view from the wings above shows up the red dots in the corners of eyes, and the heavy beading on lashes and the abrupt line at the neck and ears where the heavy rouge stops, none of which is visible across the footlights. The "spot" and footlights which give garish effects are kind when viewed from "out front."

Then the sound of applause drifts back to the wings, the scanty applause of an opening number, faint as the patter of rain on dry leaves, the discouraging greeting from an audience that is still whispering to its neighbors and opening candy boxes. The chorus rushes off breathless as the tenor male lead addresses the leading lady, "Where are you going, my pretty maid?"

Once in the wings, the bright smiles fade, rouged lips droop, and sibilant whispers begin.

"Dead house." "That didn't get over at all." "It never does get over." "Wonder why they don't take that number off?" "Oh, they'll warm up."

Nose Powdered Instantly

"Hurry up, you girls!" whispers the voice of authority from back stage. There is the smell of heavy theatrical powder as they crowd by and a whiff of mingled perfumes as they hurry up the narrow steps. The dressing rooms of the chorus are on the third floor, necessitating speed in climbing the three flights, speed in changing the fluffy costumes (which mercifully are equipped with few hooks and are donned in a thrice), and speed in descending the steps and dancing on again.

When the play calls for three and sometimes four changes of costumes in an act, the trips to the dressing room degenerate into a series of mad dashes up and down the cement stairway. The dressing rooms are flooded with a glaring white light that is reflected back from the mirrors above the narrow shelves. On the shelves are boxes of powder and rouge of all shades, varying from faint green to delicate lavender, powder puffs smeared with rainbow tints, grease rags covered with remains of a dozen make-ups, cold cream in cans, lipsticks and blue "eye pencils" rolling together in disarray, hairpins scattered among a varied assortment of combs and brushes, bright costumes hanging one on top of another, ready to be snapped on at a moment's notice.

While the audience out front applauds the clever quips of the comedian or breathlessly listens to the melodious tenor as he breaks into "the big song" of the first act (there always is a "big song" in the first act), they never think of the fact that three stories above, fifteen girls are jumping into costumes, with a speed that belies the axiom that it takes a woman an hour to powder her nose. What would seem confusion to an outsider is really chorus efficiency.

"Get that hook between my shoulders, won't you, Ruth? Why weren't my arms longer? Never can reach it."

"Dumbbell, you've torn my hair net, and Heaven only knows there's no time to change!"

"Lend me your puff—somebody's dropped mine!"

"Time! Hustle along, girls."

"Smile and Fake It"

As the girls descend the stairs, patting their hair into place, "props" hands each a basket of flowers with a ribbon handle that they are to use in the next number, and then he retires gloomily to his bench. The electrician floods the stage with a blue "moonlight" light, the orchestra bursts into a catchy dance which sounds strangely soft in the wings. The chorus simultaneously assumes baskets and dazzling smiles and trips out to be greeted with an enthusiastic applause.

"They are warming up," whispers the soprano lead in relief to the tenor as they stand listening in the wings.

He clutches at his neck, clears his throat, runs up the scale of notes softly, and groans.

"Listen to that voice! It's getting worse, I tell you. If this cold doesn't get better, I'll never sing tomorrow!"

"Fake it out somehow," advises the soprano sympathetically as the chorus dances off amid vociferous applause.

"Take this encore!" orders the stage director, and obediently the girls dance out again, singing "For we are the girls of—" (they always are "the girls of something-or-another" in encores.)

"I don't think that was applause enough to warrant an encore," declares the soprano venomously.

"Shush!" hisses the director. "Hire a hall."

Mournfully, the tenor warbles a tentative scale, with head cocked to one side, listening for hoarseness—and finding it, to his dismay. However, as the time for his entrance comes, his "won't-come-off" smile appears and he strides onto the stage, "faking it" as best he can.

The Real Chorus Girl

There is much gameness, like this "smile and fake it" of the tenor who could have relinquished his role to an understudy and rested his aching throat. One "poney," hardly five feet tall, has a bad "cold in her chest," as she laughingly explains it. But "props," who, despite his gloom, is kind-hearted, takes off his coat and puts it around her, lest she take more cold in the drafts back stage.

As her turn to go on arrives and she relinquishes the coat with a grateful smile, "props" remarks, "Some folks always talking about wild chorus girls. Take that little girl now—sick and won't quit because she's sending money home to put her sister through school. Don't eat enough to keep a fly alive. Road show girls don't ever get time to be wild, I guess."

Having delivered himself, "props" slouches off as if regretting his outburst, but leaving his coat where the "poney" can get it when she comes off.

When the play is over and the curtain rung down on the last encore, the scene shifters make quick work of dismantling the scenery that looked so substantial from the audience. Back and forth run the stage hands, under the bellowing directions of the chief shifter, carrying furniture, laying sections of scenery against walls, pulling up backdrops, rolling up rugs.

Amid the confusion stands the company, talking and joking like a large family, leisurely moving toward the dressing rooms to which they rushed so frantically during the acts. The tenor is applying an atomizer to his throat, the "poney" with the cold has "props's" coat wrapped around her, the soprano lead is talking about friends in Birmingham and New Orleans and giving thanks that they are playing there, soon.

Up the stairs they go, cheerfully, to pack their make-up boxes and suitcases and go back to their hotels. The next day will mean a train and a long, tiresome trip to another town where there will

be another "three-night stand" before moving on again.
That's life in a "road show."

—November 11, 1923

Only One Atlanta Girl Likes Whiskers

W hiskers are stylish again—England has decreed it, and America is on the trembling edge of taking them up!

No longer will flapper granddaughters stealthily unhang enlarged chromos of Grampa, brave in the whiskers and checked pants of the nineties and hide them in the attic when company is expected. No longer will Grandma be viewed with pitying smiles by the younger generations when she reminisces of how her heart fluttered like the wash on the line when General E. B. Stuart, of the Confederate cavalry, dashed by her house in 1862 with long red curling whiskers blowing back over his shoulders like the original Seidlitz Powder ad—"The perfect cavalier, the most beautiful whiskers in the Confederacy—so long that he could tuck them in his sash!"

For whiskers have come into their own again after years of humiliation and contumely with no less famous personage as their sponsor than Lord Arthur Ponsby of England. After Lord Ponsby's declaration that the reason the modern woman dominated the man of today was that he was too effeminate to command her respect and that only a return to whiskers could save civilization, many young Britishers have gone in seriously for whisker-raising. Neat and refined whiskers will be the keynote for the coming season; untrellised and flamboyant beards of the Bolsheviki variety will be stricly banned.

As all English fads spread swiftly to America, the whisker epidemic seems at present to be on the verge of an American debut, to the great indignation of the various barbers' associations, razor manufacturers, and, most of all, the ladies.

"The Ladies" Condemn Beards

The ladies of Atlanta, at least, seem to have nothing in common with their grandmothers who buried their heads coyly in bushy whiskers on their husbands' chests. They condemn beards from every angle—aesthetic, hygenic, utilitarian, and comfort. Whiskers will meet with a cold reception in Atlanta, even if so dear an institution as Georgia Tech should sponsor them.

In all Atlanta there is only one girl original enough, or bold enough, or Victorian enough, not only to like whiskers, but to come out publicly in favor of them. She is one of this season's prettiest and most talented debutantes, Eugenia Buchanan, 1211 Peachtree Road, who has combined a popular social season with her vocal studies. Her sub-deb sister, Corine Buchanan, attributes Eugenia's predilection of hirsute masculine adornments to the fact that Eugenia has been too much influenced by the grand opera roles she has studied—each of which is usually the foil of some bewhiskered tenor.

"I think whiskers are perfectly darling," declared Eugenia Buchanan, "and it isn't because Lohengrin or Rhadames wore them. I always did like whiskers on middle-aged and elderly men, because they lent so much dignity and made them look so impressive, and though I've never seen any young man with a full beard (except boys who'd been on camping trips and been too lazy to shave), I don't see why they shouldn't look stunning on young men. I don't mean wild and untamable whiskers, but nice, sleek whiskers, whacked off squarely at the bottom. They are so masculine looking."

"They Tickle"

But the sub-deb sister who declared that the very thought of whiskers made her flesh crawl, summed up her objections to them in two terse words:

"They tickle," she said.

Of like opinion was Anne Couper, daughter of Mr. and Mrs. John Couper, 194 Juniper Street, who, fresh from a round of college dances and house parties, calmly greeted the news of the whisker epidemic with an ultimatum.

No hairy-faced he-men need ring her Juniper Street doorbell and expect to find her at home. Genuine Arabian sheiks might be able to get away with murder, despite their bristling beards, but she doubted that the Sheik Americanus could do the same and still retain his charms.

"Why, I never even had any romantic yearnings to be cast away on a desert isle with a dearly beloved, no matter how dashing he might be, because I know three days away from a razor would take the dash out of any beloved, no matter how dear!" she explained. "And after the conventional twelve or fifteen years that always elapse between the time you're cast away and the time the ship comes into view to rescue you—just think what he'd look like! A tropical underbrush would have nothing on his face.

"No, this whisker craze is simply banana oil."

"I couldn't ever love a man with whiskers," sighed Louise Bradbury, daughter of Mr. and Mrs. O. H. Bradbury, 1291 Peachtree Road, "no matter whether they were parted in the middle or cut on the bias, they'd be a handicap to any boy. I don't see how a man with streamers on his face could be any more attractive than one with a harelip!"

Might Be Grown Gradually

"I think it would be an awful struggle to decide if you could still love your husband if he grew nasty whiskers," said Virginia Stone Williams, daughter of Mrs. Lucille White, 54 Juniper Street, who has such large, appealing, dark eyes that no husband, no matter how brutal, could think of turning his face into a perambulating doormat without her consent. "Of course, if you loved him a lot maybe you could put up with them if he grew them gradually and didn't spring them on you all at once. A little moustache first and then a Van Dyke (they do look aristocratic on SOME boys), and then his sideburns a little longer, and then let the sideburns grow to meet the moustache. Maybe you could get used to it that way, but I doubt it."

"It may be the English fad to sprout whiskers, but don't let's ape the English," said Isabelle Howard, daughter of Mr. and Mrs. C. B. Howard, 725 Piedmont Avenue, alarmed at the news of the coming whisker crop. "Just think how dreadful it would be if Tech heard about it and took to it as they did to yellow slickers and corduroy pants! Imagine going to a dance and having all the boys breeze in with long, waving whiskers. Bobbed-haired girls and bewhiskered boys! No, let's hope it doesn't become a fad in Atlanta. I think," she finished cryptically, "that no girl over sweet sixteen could ever be thrilled by whiskers."

Caroline Howard, her sister, agreed with her that there could be no thrill in a dance where one looked up into the eyes of one's partner and saw only flaunting whiskers, jerking at every move of the dance.

"I'm 'fraid of men with whiskers—even moustaches, "confessed Ethel Palmer, daughter of William Palmer, Vedado Way, "because when I was a little girl, my old mammy used to rock me to sleep and sing me an endless song. I never stayed awake long enough to hear it all, but the last words of every verse were something like this:

Now all you young gals, take my advice—
Don't never trust a man with a black moustache.

"There must be something in this psychological stuff about early impressions, because all my life I've had a sort of fascinated horror of men with black moustaches. They look so wicked, you know, and untrustworty."

"No, I'm not in favor of whiskers for men any more than long hair for women. It's too much trouble," said Anne Armstrong, 248 East Fifth Street. "Men take long enough time to get to dates now, what with slicking down their hair and talcuming their faces. Just suppose they had a couple of yards of hair on their chin to tend too! Why, they'd never get to dates at all—and think of how husbands would be taking money that wives could use so well in beauty parlors to get permanent waves in their whiskers! You know how vain men are! Women can't hold a candle to them. I somehow can't see myself hustling through my dressing and going to parties looking like a fright because I had to take three hours curling my husband's whiskers over my finger with a brush!

"Not me!"

—March 8, 1925

What It Costs to Rush a Girl

nyone old enough to remember will recall that poignant ragtime lament from some musical show of the 1914–15 era—

The high cost of living is only a joke
The high cost of loving, it's keeping me broke.

Recently, the same plaint has been raised among the young men of Atlanta, on the "high cost of rushing." Modern girls, according to Atlanta boys, are no longer satisfied with a pound of candy, an occasional movie, and much small talk about a little cottage for two.

They insist on "going to places and doing things," and these places and things consist of eating, dancing, eating some more, going to theaters, riding in taxis, wearing flowers, and acquiring extensive collections of jeweled fraternity pins. The boys declare that they are not stingy, but the pace is too much for young-sters. It has been rumored that a union has been started among the boys to limit expenses to five dollars per date instead of twenty-five!

Several young Atlanta boys, all intelligent and popular, are outspoken on the subject of the "rush price." According to them, the day when the woman paid and paid is a thing of the past.

"Where Do We Go?"

"I only know one place in town where I can go on a date and not find the girl waiting in the front hall, with her hat on her head and 'Well, where are we going?' on her lips," declared Donald Keller.

"The high cost of rushing is due to the fact that girls don't want to stay at home for dates. The day of calling on a girl, bringing her a box of candy, and spending a nice evening by the fire has passed. Why, girls are insulted if you bring them candy.

"I know of only one family where the girls will stay at home on dates and not insist on being tead, danced, theatered, and fed in rapid succession. But these girls are so popular a boy has to date them up way ahead. Believe me, boys appreciate that sort of girl!

"I've noticed in the last year or two the growing reluctance of boys to take girls to dances and the delight with which stags accept their stagdom. The reason is this: a boy is told to take a girl to a dance. First, that means flowers, and flowers pretty enough to compare favorably with those of other girls. Then a taxi, if you don't happen to own a car. Then the dance. And after the dance, there is food. Always, there is food. And I do not refer to a lettuce leaf and a sandwich. I speak of a dozen raw, a planked steak, and a pound or so of French fries."

"Her" Increasing Appetite

Garland Walraven says that the cost of courting and rushing is now almost prohibitive. "The main reason for this," he declared, "is that girls WILL eat. I've often wondered if most girls eat enough at home. Take them to a movie and they MUST have a meal afterward. Gone are the days when simple ice cream satisfied! Take them to a dance and send them flowers with your last cent—and afterward, they faint from hunger unless you pass around the food. I don't see how the modern girl retains her modern figure and eats the way she does!

"I have heard of old-fashioned girls who would not accept any gift from a man except candy and flowers," said Sherwood Higgs. "But I've never met one—and I've never met anyone who has met one! I've hear'n tell of girls who said, 'Oh, let's don't go out tonight! We've been out so much.' But I think they stopped making them, because I've never met one of them, either. And I've never met a girl who wasn't always hungry and who didn't want to go to the most expensive dances and theaters.

"The cost of taking a girl around these days is more than most young men can stand. Modern life has speeded up so much and people are all hunting excitement, so girls want speed and excitement too. And those are two very high-priced commodities.

"I don't suppose girls today think of what would happen if they married a boy and tried to live on the same amount of money they so blithely use for rushing about!"

"Girls Expect Too Much"

Ted Atkinson had evidently given the idea deep thought,

because he had gone into the economic side of the rapidly-climbing cost of entertaining girlfriends and into the far-reaching social consequences.

"The girls are the ones who are raising the standards of entertainment. Formerly, when social life was not so complicated, a movie or a play, an occasional dance, and the usual candy and flowers made a girl feel that she had a real Romeo after her. But they want more now.

"They don't take into consideration the fact that most of the boys and young men with whom they play are just out of school and are spending their entire salaries on entertainment. They don't take into consideration that they have raised economic standards so high that most young men can no longer rush girls around or marry them. Girls expect too much.

"So, most nice young men who would like to marry young and marry nice girls and start out on a modest salary, like Dad and Mother did, are confronted with the fact that they can't give their girl a two-and-a-half carat diamond, a gold mesh bag, a summer ermine coat, and a closed car. So they don't marry. That forces girls to marry the older men, who have made money and are established and can give them what they want. And the higher the girls raise the standards of entertainment, the older the 'husband age' will become."

—January 10, 1926

6

About Atlanta & Georgia

—⁓—

Mitchell sometimes posed with the subjects of her magazine stories. Here she stands beside Rebecca Latimer Fulton, a Georgian and the first female U.S. senator, for a photo illustrating their 1924 interview.

Spring

In the spring a young man's fancy
(So the story goes)
Lightly turns to thoughts of love,
And a woman's thoughts to clothes.

S pring has a way of slipping up behind you and slapping you for a row of castles in Spain. And you feel *tra-la* and you want to write spring stories, the sort that just won't spring when the weather stays cold and the man who sells daffodils on the street corner has the collar of his overcoat turned up around his ears.

Here's how it happens. You've just about decided that there isn't going to be any spring. And people are going to keep on having "spring codes," and coughing and sneezing at the theater at the psychological moment to interrupt the most dramatic scene in the play, and the coal supply in the cellar day by day is getting thinner and thinner, but if the furnace isn't kept all steamed up you nearly freeze, and you really do freeze when you go out for what you hoped would be a nice warm ride in the nice warm weather. And when that sort of thing happens for weeks and weeks after the scheduled date for the arrival of the season of poetry and *tra-la*s, then you give up hope.

But one morning the sun is shining brightly when you wake and you notice something different in the air even when you are hurrying to get dressed and down to work on time. And you rush into the office and slam your hat and coat on the nail and try to go to work.

Spring and Cinders Enter

But you want to do everything else but work, and while you're wondering what's the trouble you realize that spring is knocking at the window.

Up goes the window. Out goes the dead air that's been accumulating all winter. In comes spring in a show of cinders. Only you don't mind the cinders that blow in because of the breeze they blow in on. And then maybe the cinders won't always blow in because they're going to build a plaza (name of Bleckley) just outside your window some day, maybe.

And it's spring!

So you tuck a photographer under your arm and wander up and down the streets of Atlanta, joyfully sighting evidences of spring that you have yearned for during the muddy months of winter.

Just a few blocks away a bunch of kids are playing the first game of marbles—

And around the corner is the man with his basketful of gay yellow daffodils (and no overcoat at all)—

And down on Decatur Street is Mehitabel herself, the alley cat, carrying one of the spring crop of kittens to its new home under the Courtland Street viaduct—

And up the street is a crowd of small boys and full-grown men with their noses respectively pressed against the window of a shop where there is displayed no end of fishing tackle—

And walking along the street, arm-in-arm, are couples; from all indications the young men's fancy isn't at all disapproved of as it lightly turns to thoughts of love—

And the traffic cop has a flower in his buttonhole—

And out in the parks the grass is green and the flowers are

blossoming and in Druid Hill the dogwood trees are beginning to bloom—

And there's a soft warmness like velvet in the air that rubs itself against your cheek and makes your soul sit up and purr.

Park Benches Are in Demand

Out Peachtree Road, the Sunday band of picnicking flivvers proves that spring is not only for the Young Man and his Fancy. Father sits at the wheel, somewhat perspiry, with Mother close beside him, holding the lunch basket on her lap, while the back of the flivver overflows with squirming children.

And a flop-eared hound, the family pride, hangs a grinning head over the side of the car.

The benches in the park are in great demand, particularly the secluded ones, while the perennially popular swings, screened by shrubbery, are occupied from twelve to twelve.

Small boys haunt the sides of the vacant swimming pools, eagerly comparing notes on the date of the prospective opening of the "ole hole."

And little girls wander off into the long park grass and ruin perfectly good handmade dresses with grass stains, while their colored nurses exchange persiflage with chauffeurs.

And it's spring!

Tra-la!

Spring, of course, is a state of mind. The young man's fancy can, and frequently does, turn to thoughts of love during three other seasons of the year. There are flowers that blossom in the winter time and in the lush warmth of the mid-summer that are more beautiful than the hyacinths, buttercups, and daffodils of spring. There are months when life is permitted to make far more rapid progress toward the serious things of existence than during the season when distracting, balmy temperamental, enticing spring holds sway. But no other season can make us feel *tra-la!* That's the special prerogative of spring and the sort of thing that one waits a year for and is out of sorts and peevish if it fails to arrive on time.

Peevish we were when the opening bars of this selection were being played on a chattering typewriter to the accompaniment of chattering teeth. But since that all too unpleasant event, spring has come! Glorious, gay, exhilarant spring!

—April 14, 1923

Hanging Over Atlanta in Borglum's Swing

"Oh, Mr. Gallagher!
Oh, Mr. Gallagher!
Did you see the human fly a-climbing high?
Oh! He took an awful chance
When he hung there by his pants.
Feats of daring, Mr. Gallagher!"
"Plain d—n foolishness, Mr. Shean!"

No, Sir or Madam!
In the immortal words of Bert Williams, "Somebody else, not me," is going to have to do all that carving on the side of Stone Mountain that is expected to bring into existence the world's most magnificent monument to the Southern Confederacy. As long as the trip down the side of the mountain has to be made in a diminutive swing about as large as the palm of your hand, one candidate for fame and glory has been thoroughly and completely eliminated.

A highly laudable ambition to convey to readers some idea of the perils and hazards in the ways of completing the Stone

Mountain memorial suggested the idea of taking a trip over the side of the mountain in the swing that has been constructed for the workers to sit in as they carve the figures of the Confederate leaders out of the face of the living rock.

Whereupon, on a bright, sunshiny morning, when life seemed most attractive, and not the sort of thing one·might wish to lose, one found oneself being strapped in the swing and shoved out a window on the very top floor of a very high building which had been selected as an imitation Stone Mountain.

Bump!

The swing was designed by Captain J. G. Tucker, who is Gutzon Borglum's first assistant in the work, and was constructed by M. G. Caldwell, of the Crumley-Sharp Hardware Company. Aside from the fact that it has a leather strap that fastens under one's arms, it is just like an ordinary swing, with a narrow piece of board to sit on and leather straps instead of ropes which join above one's head in a steel ring, in which slides the cable that lowers the swing over the side of the mountain.

Captain Tucker presided at the ceremonies. "Where is that cable?" called he, with a show of irritation.

"It doesn't seem to be here," said Willis Timmons, who was present to see that the swing didn't receive any damage. "Guess we'll have to use a piece of rope. This quarter-inch manila ought to be strong enough."

"Wel-l-l, maybe," Captain Tucker said with an alarming show of doubt. "I suppose it will have to do."

Even with assurance of this sort that there was absolutely no danger at all—oh, no!—one doesn't feel so very good when one is shoved out of the window of a skyscraper, especially when one has never been shoved out of any sort of a window before.

In an enormous pair of size-forty overalls, kindly lent by Mr.

Timmons (which gave the effect of a deep sea diver's costume) and with a hammer and chisel to complete the workmanlike rig, I was strapped in and swung far out of the window.

A dizzy whirl—building, windows, a glimpse of the sky, anxious faces at the windows, all jumbled up for an instant of eternity, a feeling of nauseau, then BUMP! completed the first swing in the air and came up against the side of the building with an awful wallop.

The wall felt good. It was rough and it had hit me a jolt, but it was solid and secure. Before I could catch hold of it, however, Newton's third law of motion asserted itself—for every action there is an equal and opposite reaction—and, pendulum-like, we started to swing out over the great wide world again.

Smile!

"Hey!" shouted a distant voice. "Look down this way and smile!"

Smile! Ha! Smile! Imagine that at a time like this! Except that both hands were so busy holding on to the leather straps I would have laughed in my sleeve at him. I glanced down to give him the most cutting, scornful look in repertoire, and— What a sensation!

The realization of how high above the world I was hit me with a jolt. There was a sickening sensation in the pit of the stomach. I jumped. The seat of the swing slipped from under me, and for a terrible instant I hung there, spinning, with only the strap under my arms between me and the hard, hard street two hundred feet below.

Fortunately, Mr. Timmons had fastened me in so tight I could hardly breathe and the strap held.

They lowered me down the side of the building and swung me around some more, and after a while they decided that the cause of journalism had been sufficiently served and they consented to pull me back up to the window, and the thing was over. Trembling, I'll admit. But the feel of a solid floor beneath my feet brought back the jolly old bluff and I managed to pull a weak sort of smile and announce—

"Oh, it wasn't so bad!"

But about that time the photographer arrived.

"Say, you'll have to do it all over again; the slide in my camera got jammed and I don't think I got any good pictures!"

I turned and faced him.

"If the fate of the whole Confederacy rested on my being hung six stories from the ground again," I declared firmly, "Sherman would have to make another march to the sea!"

Painting the Mountain

Captain Tucker, who has been working for several nights, "painting" the mountainside, used the same type of swing in which I had been swung above the town.

"It is tedious work," admitted Captain Tucker, "for where I was working last the mountain wall is absolutely perpendicular, and so that prevents me from bracing myself against the rock by stretching out my foot. I have to use my knees as a brace while I 'paint.'

"An ordinary steeplejack uses just a swinglike contrivance for his work, but we have more to contend with on Stone Mountain than steeplejacks ever encounter. We have to think about the wind on the mountain as well as the fact that we have to work there so long, and a swing would not serve our purpose.

"A broad strap, like that used in an aeroplane, seemed the most feasible solution, so Mr. Caldwell made the whole contrivance out of heavy harness leather. This belt gives the worker something to lean back on as well as a place to stick his flashlight and tools and hang his paint.

"We are having several of these made up now and will have to have about a dozen before we finish," continued Captain Tucker. "In two weeks, we expect to have the steam drills busy on Stone Mountain, cutting out the rough blocks for the chiselers to work on. When they have finished laying out the figures in large detail, then Mr. Borglum will do the artistic work of the finishing touches.

"Now, this swing does look risky, I'll admit," laughed Captain Tucker, "but it is really the only thing that we can use. There will be a steel cable running through this ring at the top and it will be attached to the steam engine on the top of the mountain. The engine will raise or lower the workman in the swing as high as he desires.

"I don't see why you think that the swing doesn't feel safe," finished Captain Tucker. "It doesn't worry me at all!"

Yes, but probably he was heavy enough to hold down the contraption and keep it from sliding treacherously from under him!

—May 5, 1923

The Stone Mountain Memorial Carving, depicting the profiles of three Confederate generals, was carved into a massive granite outcropping outside of Atlanta beginning in 1923 and is the largest relief sculpture in the world. Its sculptor, Gutzon Borglum (1867 - 1941), is best known for his work on the Mount Rushmore National Memorial.

Georgia's Empress and Women Soldiers

When Mrs. W. H. Felton took her place in the United States Senate as the first woman in the nation to receive this distinction, she was carrying on the tradition of Georgia's noble womanhood.

From the early pioneer days until the present, Georgia women have made the tradition a glorious reality. Born and bred in a

Southern civilization where womanhood is exalted and knightly regard for the protection of women is the first mark of a gentleman, Georgia women have not been merely beautiful chatelaines, but have been gifted with brilliant ability and a capacity for assuming difficult responsibilities when the need arose.

Among the pioneers, they fought side by side with their men against the hardships of that day; in the two wars which swept over the state they did their part nobly; in the fields of art and literature Georgia has produced notable women; and in this present day they have also attained eminence in public affairs. A few of Georgia's notable women and some of their achievements are told of here. A discussion of the state's women writers has been reserved for a later article in this series.

Mrs. Felton's Career

Ex-Senator Felton, whose name is known round the world as the first woman Senator in the history of the United States, was a "new woman" long before the "new woman" arrived.

Reared and educated in the country, Rebecca Latimer Felton married at the early age of eighteen, and for the next eight or ten years she was so absorbed in her children that she hardly ever ventured outside her own gate. But during those years she read omnivorously of medicine, politics, history, and fiction, laying the foundation for the public life that was to be hers in the later years.

After the Civil War, in the "starvation times" that marked the Reconstruction period, she taught school, studied, reared her own children, and in general kept up with the times, until Dr. Felton's name was mentioned for Congress. With her husband's career began her own career, and there has been no more interesting figure in Georgia politics for thirty years than she.

In the hot campaign that elected him to Congress, Dr. Felton took the stump to speak and Mrs. Felton took up her pen. Night and day, the indefatigable wife wrote letters to four-teen counties, and toward the end of the campaign she kept a man on horseback at the door to catch every mail train. She made appointments for speeches, answered vitriolic newspaper attacks, and kept a brave face to friend and foe.

But the election of her husband did not end her career in pol-itics. When he attacked the convict lease system or fought for reformatories for children and separate prisons for women, Mrs. Felton was behind him, writing and speaking until she began to be felt as a definite force in Georgia politics and reforms.

When the late Senator Watson died in 1922, Governor Hardwick appointed Mrs. Felton to serve out the unexpired term, and she went to Washington as the first woman Senator of the United States.

Cross-Eyed Nancy Hart

Very different from Georgia's woman senator was Nancy Hart, one of the famous characters from the state's early history. Nancy Hart stood six feet tall, was broad and muscular in pro-portion, red-haired, and cross-eyed. Her neighbors were often given to saying that her disposition was cross-gained, too, and though she was the best mother and the best cook in the neigh-borhood, her personality left much to be desired where sweet-ness was concerned.

Through the distressing times into which Georgia fell during the Revolutionary War, there was no need for sweet dispositions and a great need for more fearless souls like Nancy. Georgia was overrun with marauding bands of Whigs and Tories. The Tories burned and killed, regardless of age and sex, but when everyone else trembled at the very name of Tory, Nancy only vociferously voiced her hatred.

Among the many stories of this remarkable woman, who feared neither Tories nor devils, the most famous is that of her single-handed capture of six Tories who had tried to eat her pumpkin pie.

Nancy was a famous cook and "could do more with a pumpkin than any woman in Georgia." One day when in the midst of preparations for a large meal of pumpkin pie and turkey, news came that pillaging Tories were in the neighborhood. Nancy's unheroic husband and the neighbors fled to the swamps.

"Oh, drat the Tories," said Nancy. "I won't leave my pumpkin pie to them," and she kept on with her cooking. When the Tories arrived, they were in high good humor at the feast they saw in preparation, and, stacking their rifles, they ordered Nancy to continue with her work.

She pretended to obey them, grunting and grumbling the while, as she worked around to where the rifles were stacked. When seeming to reach for a pot, she grabbed one of the rifles and instantly covered the startled raiders. One of them, not knowing Nancy's reputation for sharpshooting, tried to rush her, but she coolly shot him down.

Whether the others were unnerved by her suddenness or by the certainty of death at the hands of the Whigs, or the incongruity of her cross-eyes that seemed to make each one the object of her ferocious gaze, suffice to say that they made no further resistance.

Sending her little girl after the neighbors in the swamp, she guarded the soldiers until help arrived.

"I wasn't goin' to have any Tories eatin' my pun'kin pie," she remarked when the excitement was over.

Private Bill, Soldierette

She was known as Private Bill Thompson and not until her "buddy" was killed at the second battle of Bull Run was she revealed as a woman—and her "buddy's" wife, at that.

Mrs. Lucy Mathilda Kenny, of Savannah, Georgia, enlisted with her young husband in the first volunteers that went off to the Civil War from Georgia. She was large, masculine in appearance, a fine rifle shot, and absolutely fearless. It was only necessary for her to cut off her hair and put on a suit of her husband's clothes to complete her transformation from a very proper wife to a very good soldier of the Confederacy.

As Private Bill Thompson, she fought by her husband's side through battle after battle, thereby proving that the Russian Women's Battalion of Death in the recent war [World War I], did not include the first women soldiers.

Not only did this woman soldier face the dangers of battle, but she was constantly confronted with long, forced marches, little or no food, and exposure to wind and rain, sometimes with no overcoat and a thin uniform. Yet she passed through hardships that would have unnerved and killed most women and never whimpered. It was her cheery laugh and gay jokes that kept up the morale of the men when hope was low. No one ever knew that she was a woman—or if they did, they never told the officers. Every rifle was needed and she was a good shot.

She was seriously wounded by bursting shells at Sharpsburg, and lay in a hospital for months, but on recovering she slipped away from the authorities who would have sent her home, and rejoined her company.

At the second battle of Manassas her husband was killed. Only then did she reveal the fact that she was a woman, so she could take his body home. The company with whom she had fought bade a sorrowful farewell to the brave "soldierette" who had gallantly fought shoulder to shoulder with them, and she set out on her sorrowful journey to North Carolina to bury her husband at his old home as she had promised.

This "daughter of the Confederacy" was animated by no less brave spirit than the maid of Orleans herself, yet strangely enough very little is known of her.

Mary Musgrove, Empress

Other states have had governors, mayors, and even presidents, but Georgia is probably the only state that has had emperors.

In the early days of the young colony, when Oglethorpe was attempting to cement the uncertain friendship of the Creek Indians and the colonists, he discovered at Yamacraw a young Indian woman named Mary who could speak both Creek and English. On discovering that she had great influence among the Indians, Oglethorpe spared no pains in winning her good will with gifts and flattery.

Mary was a woman of great personal magnetism and the idol of the Creek nation, but despite her years of life among the civilizing influences of the colony and her three successive white husbands, she remained an untamed savage until she died.

Mary Musgrove, as she is usually known, married the Reverend Thomas Bosomworth, a clergyman of the Church of England, who was her third husband, and from the day of their marriage, they kept the Georgia colony in a constant state of commotion. Prior to this marriage, she had been content to give her services wholeheartedly to Oglethorpe, and had kept the relationship between the Creeks and the whites both pleasurable and friendly.

But Bosomworth, having fallen into debt and seeing no chance of extricating himself, encouraged Mary to declare herself the Empress of the Creek Nation, and demand from the white people all the lands that the Indians had formerly held.

Naturally, the idea appealed to the untamed soul of Mary, for by direct line she was descended from an old Creek emperor, and, summoning all the Creek chieftains, she made them an impassioned address. She set forth the injustice of the colonists' treatment of the Indians, and, firebrand that she was, so inflamed the warriors that they pledged themselves to stand by her to the last drop of their blood.

So Mrs. Bosomworth was crowned in great state as empress of the Creek Nation.

Borne up on a surge of power, Mary sent an insolent messenger to Oglethorpe, announcing that unless he yielded all the lands that she demanded, she, the Empress of the Creek Nation, would summon her hosts of warriors and destroy the little colony with "torch and tomahawk."

This ultimatum threw the little band of colonists into wildest confusion and fright, for, cut off as they were from help by England and the other colonies, such warfare would mean the complete extermination of the town. Indians on the warpath meant night attacks, ambuscades, scalpings, burnings at the stake, and other unpleasantnesses that the president of the colony was anxious to avoid.

The garrison of the fort numbered only 120 men, but they put the town in the strongest possible condition and then sent a messenger to Mary, requesting that she come and bring her warriors to a conference.

Mary arrived at the head of her braves. The townspeople had drawn themselves up in as formidable array as possible, but they dwindled to insignificance before the long lines of brightly painted Indians. Mary swaggered into the town, resplendent in barbaric finery followed by the Reverend Bosomworth. By Oglethorpe's orders, Bosomworth was entrapped, unknown to Mary, and put in confinement, lest he stir up more trouble.

Before the council, Mary was anything but reassuring. She announced that, despite her former friendship, she had not the slightest scruples about torturing and scalping the townsmen unless they acceded to her demands. Unfortunately for the white people, she knew how easily her warriors could be bribed, so she kept them under her eyes every moment.

As all men were on guard, the women and children cowered in fear in the houses. The rumor arose that the president of the colony had been beheaded with a tomahawk, and this disquieting news was intensified by the fact that the excited warriors of Empress Mary began to race up and down the streets, making the air hideous with their yells and whoops.

Fearing for their families' safety, the colonists could scarcely be restrained from firing on the savages, but realizing that this would probably mean a massacre, Oglethorpe decided to win the fight by strategy.

He announced that a huge feast was being prepared for all the "visitors," but Mary, deeply suspicious, refused his invitation. Mary, drunk with power, delighted herself by reviling Oglethorpe, King George, and the whole colony, stamping her foot on the ground and shouting that every foot of earth she trod on was her property.

It was a ticklish moment, with the fate of Georgia hanging on the whim of a drunken savage, but Oglethorpe carried the situation off by inveigling the braves, hungry after the long conference, to come to the feast. While they enjoyed themselves, gorging on food, Mary was captured quietly and sent to join her husband in jail.

During the progress of the feast the president of the colony addressed the savages and in a long harangue convinced them that their beloved empress was the victim of her husband's self-seeking schemes.

More kindly disposed toward the colony after such a bountiful feast, the fickle savages were roused to ire against Bosomworth and were disposed to scalp him instead of the colonists. By promises, presents, and flatteries, their departure was accomplished. A much chastened empress was released, too, and to reconcile her again to the young colony, the island of St. Catherine was given to her.

Here she spent the remainder of her life in distinctly unregal circumstances, and the little colony that she threatened with annihilation grew into a great state.

—May 20, 1923

Camp Meeting at Mount Gilead

A mong the quaint old Southern institutions that have survived from the early days of Georgia history down to the present time is the custom of the annual "camp meetin'." When the Creeks and Cherokees were still viewing with amazement the preaching and hymn-singing of their white neighbors, the camp meetings were an established custom and they have changed very little from 1824 to 1924.

Outwardly, the Georgia camp meetings have changed in that the visitors no longer arrive in ox carts, nor are the evening services lighted by tallow candles and pine torches. Basically, they have not changed at all. The soul of religion, the reverence, the spirits of friendliness and of open-handed hospitality that characterized the meetings in the old days, is the same.

The most famous and the oldest camp meeting ground in Georgia is that at Mount Gilead, two miles from Ben Hill. It was established ninety years ago when Mr. John M. Smith, one of the pioneers of what was then Fayette County, now Fulton, donated a tract of land, amounting to 202 acres, to the Mount Gilead Methodist Church to be used for camp meeting purposes.

The annual camp meeting at Mount Gilead is held always on the third Sunday in August and the Monday following and attended largely by Methodists from all over the state. Automobiles by the hundreds pack the woods near the camp ground, and the red dust under foot rises in faint clouds as the crowds carrying lunch hampers make their way leisurely toward the center of the ground where the sermons are preached in the "arbor."

No Shouting Now

The "arbor," as the long open shed is called under which the meetings are held, stands in the center of a circle of "tents." The "tents" are wooden shacks, unpainted and weather-beaten, with shingles curling from age and plank walls gray and splintery from the rains of many years. These shacks have sheltered the visitors to camp meetings for two generations and are filled to overflowing every year. When there is no room under the "arbor" for those who wish to listen to the sermons, they sit on the porches of the "tents" and listen as the words of the preachers ring out across the intervening space.

The "arbor" itself is long and cool, and beneath the rows of benches, sawdust and hay straw muffle the sound of many feet. On the raised platform is the minister's table bearing the Bible and hymnals. The choir is grouped behind the platform near the small organ and the sweet sound of old hymns floats across the cleared spaces of the meeting ground and is taken up by those seated on the porches of the encircling "tents." When the hymns are ended and the preacher takes the platform for the first sermon of the day, the entire congregation leans forward expectantly for the first words.

The congregation gathered at the Mount Gilead camp meeting represents the pick of a prosperous community. Here are found well-to-do farmers and their families, small-town merchants with their comfortable-appearing wives, bobbed-haired flappers from Atlanta, and even people from as far away as Macon and Augusta. They sit in the cool of the arbor, little children wriggling uneasily beside their parents, white-haired, white-whiskered men from the country with brown, gnarled hands cupped over their ears. Prim country wives, hatless and with hair drawn on top of their heads in severe knots, little girls in white organdie and blue satin sashes, small boys in stiff Buster Brown collars, sleek businessmen, young men and women whose straying fingers touch slightly and then withdraw. . . .

Palm-leaf fans and folded newspapers wave slowly back and forth, a baby cries fretfully somewhere in the congregation and is hushed softly by its mother as the voice of the minister goes on, ringing and clear, preaching a gospel of honor and truth, of simple living and fear of God. There is a complete absence of the "shouting" that characterized the camp meeting of a generation ago. At particularly stirring points of the sermon, masculine voices rumble "Amen!" and are echoed by feminine "amens" from far corners of the "arbor." The present generation seems to take its religion as seriously as did its predecessors, but more quietly.

"Dinner"

When the first sermon of the morning, beginning at eleven, is finished, dinner is served in the open on long barbecue tables, and "no one shall go away hungry" is the motto of the camp ground. Fried chickens by the dozen grace the tables, barbecued hog and roast beef, pies fluffy with meringue, and cakes studded with nuts or frosted high with icing range side by side with platoons of sandwiches and stuffed eggs—all of which makes the visitor realize that Georgia has the best cooks in the world.

Uncle Andy Lee, a grizzled old Negro who has attended to the cooking of camp meeting food for many years, stated emphatically that nowhere else was such cooking to be found, or such religion. Uncle Andy should know, for "I bin a-comin' here with the Peacock family for nigh onto seventy-five years. For the last fifty years I bin fixing and frying chickens for the Peacock family. I spec I'll still be a-fryin' chickens when Mount Gilead ain't no more."

After the midday meal, and the midday siesta, comes the second sermon of the day, at 2:30. There is a third sermon at four, then a supper rivalling, if possible, the dinner, and at eight o'clock the last sermon of the day. Ministers from all over the state are invited to attend the camp meeting to preach and many stirring sermons are delivered beneath the old "arbor" that has heard sermons for the last fifty years.

Today, many good Methodists attend the Mount Gilead camp meetings in automobiles and seldom stay in the weather-beaten "tents" encircling the "arbor," because by the speedy transportation of their cars, it is easier to go home overnight than to remain on the grounds.

But when Mount Gilead camp meetings were first established, people came by the scores and stayed the whole length of the meeting, sometimes five days. Families came in slow-moving oxcarts or in mule-drawn wagons. The young "blades" arrived on horseback and the less fortunate walked weary miles to the "meetin'." But one and all, the Methodists gathered from the entire state for the yearly meeting.

In the days when transportation was slow and people seldom saw anyone but their immediate neighbors, camp meetings were a social as well as a religious gathering. It was the one season of the year when the Georgia farmers took a vacation. The crops needed very little attention during the middle of August and the cotton was not ready for picking. Camp meeting time was also "get together" time.

Families came from all over the state, bringing their servants and even their dogs. At one time there were forty "tents" and all were filled to overflowing. It was the season when housewives, freed from household duties, gathered to gossip and exchange recipes between sermons, or to create envy by the cakes and pies they baked on the open stoves in front of the "tents." It was the time, too, when the young people became acquainted and did their courting and marrying, when the men did their "politicking" and when everyone "got religion."

Old Time Religion

"When people 'got religion' back in those days, they really got it," said Mr. J. L. Peacock, who has been attending meetings for sixty years. "The ministers didn't mind preaching scorching hellfire and damnation sermons and sometimes they fairly blistered the sinners. Those were the shouting days. You could hear a camp meeting a half-mile away by the shouting and singing. Nobody except a few old-timers shout now, but back in the old days, folks didn't mind shouting right out in meeting when they got religion and coming down the aisle to the pulpit to profess their faith.

"I recall one time in particular," continued Mr. Peacock, "when five or six people got religion at one of the night services. They knelt at the altar nearly all night, in the light of the flaming pine knots and bonfires while the preacher prayed over them and the fires had burned to ashes when the meeting at last broke up."

"The night meetings were usually lighted by bonfires and tallow candles and some of us were always rising to relight them or to throw more wood on the fires surrounding the arbor. But that never disturbed the preachers. Nothing much bothered them once they started. I remember one time a black snake, as long as my arm, swung down from one of the cross beams by his tail and Brother Robbins snatched him down and, running outside, popped the snake's head off—and never disturbed the meeting at all.

"And food!" Mr. Peacock sighed in memory. "This section of the country always did have the best cooks in Georgia, and in those days when every family killed a hog and lots of chickens and the women vied with each other in making cakes and pies, well, camp meetings were worth attending!"

Another interesting fact beside the recent camp meeting is the centennial celebration to take place August 31 and September 1 at Mount Gilead Church, two miles from the camp grounds. Founded in 1824, shortly after the Indian removal, Mount Gilead Church is celebrating its birthday of a century by a Home Coming Day for all the old members of the congregation and for all the ministers who have ever held the pastorate of the church.

The program will last two days, and one of Mount Gilead's oldest members, Mr. John M. Baker, will feature the history of the church. Sermons will be preached by Bishop Warren A. Candler, by the Reverend Frederick Sparks, present pastor, and by various visiting ministers, while the old members will get together for a general exchange of reminiscences of the days when people "didn't mind shouting right out in meeting."

—August 24, 1924

Crooks, Debs, and Financiers Seek to Read Future

"If I could read the future!" There is probably not a person in the world who has not thought that at one time or another. And because of that yearning in the hearts of all ages and classes to lift the grey veil that is Tomorrow and read the future clearly, all the world, at some time, has set in a palmist's seat, listening eagerly or grinning cynically as the seeress poured over the lines of the hand or gazed into a bottomless crystal.

One may believe or not believe that some people have gifts that permit them to "look through strange windows" into the future and see things that are hidden from the eyes of ordinary mortals. But believers or skeptics, the fortune-tellers of Atlanta always have more business than they can attend to.

"Is my wife (or husband) true to me?" is the question most frequently asked them.

After that, inquiries concern love affairs; next, business; third, sickness; and, fourth, questions of the afterlife, and of lost articles.

Dr. Himibia, the Hindu clairvoyant, living at 331 Lakewood Avenue, uses a 600-year-old crystal to read the future for those who come seeking to know their fates. He has prophesied the

Harding election, the famous Hall-Mills murder that puzzled New Jersey officials last year, and deaths of many prominent persons.

Letters From Mrs. Mills

"The Hall-Mills case was one of the most interesting I ever handled," he said. "I was in communication with Mrs. Hall before the murder, for distance is no obstacle to me in reading people's futures in my crystal. She wrote me from New Jersey of her love affair with Dr. Mills, saying that she was worried because love letters which they had kept in a secret box in the pulpit had been stolen. She wanted me to tell her whether Dr. Mills' wife had discovered them and was preparing to make them known.

"I wrote her that I saw nothing of the wife in my crystal, but that a dark, foreign-looking man had found them. She wrote back in great distress that she had once known such a man, that he loved her and that she feared for her life if he had come into possession of the lost correspondence.

"When she wrote me again, it was to ask if Dr. Hall would keep all his promises to her. She said they had planned to run away to the Orient and that he had planned to send for her little girl, Charlotte, after they had reached the East. I wrote her that I saw only her death in my crystal, and the death of her lover at the hands of the foreigner and great shame for all concerned. The next week came the news of the double murder. . . . I have the letters from her to prove my predictions.

"While in Marion, Ohio, a few years ago, before the Harding-Cox campaign, a young woman came to me and asked me to predict the next president, and furthermore asked whether Marion would ever send a president to the White House? I told her that a Marion man named Warren Harding would be the next president. She laughed and I found out later that she was Mrs. Harding's daughter."

A crystal-gazer, according to Dr. Himibia, is as great a repository for secrets as a doctor or a priest, particularly for criminals.

Whisperings of Murderers

"Criminals lead a devilish life," he said. "Always in fear of getting caught, generally ridden by an inner conscience that is more terrible than any fear of the police. They feel an urge to talk to someone—to tell their stories to one they can trust. They are anxious to know whether the police are on their trail, if they will ever be caught, and if so, how long their prison terms will be.

"Murderers lead lives that no one would envy. They come here and whisper that they not only fear jail and hanging, but they fear that if they die, they will encounter on the other side of the grave the spirits of those they murdered. Most murderers want to be assured that there is no afterlife—that this life is all, for they cannot face those they have wronged. And when they are told that there is another world after this, they become frantic at the thought of Eternity spent with their victims.

"I was called to a prison, not long ago, at the request of two condemned men who had refused either to listen or to talk to ministers of any faith. They had committed terrible crimes and were unrepentant. Their only regret was that they had been caught. They were about to die without belief in a hereafter, God or anything. But they sent for me and my crystal, and what do you suppose they wanted to know?

"Both murderers asked if their dead mothers know anything of their crimes! I told them that of course their mothers knew—that mothers always knew what happened to their boys. At that they broke down and cried, called for the ministers they had laughed at, and be [   ] as they dream them, or the opposite."

Madame Foneda, who tells fortunes in her striped tent at Buckhead, near Pace's Ferry Road, is Irish by birth. She asserts that gypsies and East Indians are not the only races who have the key to the future in their grasp. A nation that boasts of banshees and leprechauns cannot help but be "fey," says Madame Foneda, smiling out of her keen blue eyes.

Sick people and people who have lost articles of value are Madame Foneda's specialty, although unhappy lovers and sad people seeking communication from those who have "crossed the border" are very numerous. Among other odd customers she receives are frantic parents who want to know where their lost children have gone, wives who sob out that their husbands didn't come home to supper and want to know whether they are out with blond women, adventurous boys seeking buried treasure who demand Madame Foneda's opinion on the exact location, blasé-looking flappers who nevertheless want to know whether their "knight will ever come riding"—and Madame Foneda adds with a genuine Irish smile—"and whether or not he'll come riding in a Packard or a Ford!"

"The question that every lover and every married man or woman wants to know is 'Is my loved one true to me?' That question is as inevitable as the sunrise and the sunset.

"Love and death occupy most people's minds—the desire for love and, in some cases, the desire for death. All ages and classes want love, real love, and seek after it, consciously or unconsciously, all their days. They peer ahead into the future, wondering if love will ever come to them and in what shape. Then they come to me, and I read their eyes and palms and tell them what I see. Sometimes it is very hard to tell them the truth— that love will never come to them, or that it will bring them unhappiness, or shame, or death. But I must tell them what I see in their hands.

"About death, people are divided. When I say, 'I see death—' they cry hastily, 'Oh, Madame! Don't tell me when I am going to die. I don't want to know!' Others consult me for the sole reason of finding out how or when they are going to die. They want to know all the details and even what happens after death, but that I cannot tell them.

"Sometimes I see danger, violence, or even suicide in a palm, and tell the owner, 'If you do thus and so, it will drive you to suicide, so take care and avoid this and that condition.' Usually they look up startled and whisper, 'How did you know I was going to kill myself?'

"And the desire to know about the hereafter! It seems to be deep in every heart, a bewildered wondering if those who they loved and are now dead still know and love them, and if they will ever see them again. But no one can read the future beyond the grave."

—January 4, 1925

Atlanta's Favorite Limericks

W hat's your favorite limerick? Is it about the "young lady from Siam," or the skinny young maid from Lynn, or the irrepressible flapper from Birmingham?

Interest in limericks has been revived by the publication of a volume, *The Complete Limerick Book,* by Langford Reed (Putnam), which is a compilation of the limericks of all nations and periods. It is surprising to find that the author includes every class of men, no matter how austere or respected their calling—from Dean Inge, George Bernard Shaw, and Robert Louis Stevenson, to nameless and numbered prisoners in penitentiaries.

No one seems to be exempt either from the lure of manufacturing limericks or from committing them to memory, for there is a greater satisfaction in the crisp, terse line of the Nigerian tragedy of the young lady who rode on the tiger than can be found in all the tragic cantos of Dante.* Atlanta people seem to think so, for every one has some favorite limerick, from poets and painters to doctors and sub-debs.

Miss Mary Brent Whiteside, one of the South's best known poets who is at present working on a series of "Palestine Sonnets" (the local color of which she gathered on her recent trip to the East), is not above the frivolity of a limerick, even if her bent is toward more classic forms of verse. Her favorite is about the much rhymed young lady from Lynn, who seems to appear in limericks more than is proper and lady-like.

"There was a young lady from Lynn
Whose form was so terribly thin
    That when she assayed
    To drink lemonade
She slipped through the straw and fell in."

Miss Carolyn Coles, pretty daughter of Mr. and Mrs. Russel Coles, 604 North Jackson Street, favors a limerick concerning an unfortunate Savannah girl (perhaps "Hard Hearted Hannah" herself, getting her just deserts).

"There was a girl from Savannah
Who slipped and fell on a banana.
    She fell upside down
    And lit on her crown
And saw more stars than the 'Star-Spangled Banner.'"

Dr. Sydney Jacobs, manager of the Whitehall-Mitchell branch of Jacobs' Pharmacy, was inclined toward the limerick about the city-bred young man.

"There was a young man from the city
Who found what he thought was a kitty
    He gave it a pat

And said, 'Nice little cat.'
And they buried his clothes out of pity."

"Mine's about a young lady very much like myself," said Miss Yolande Gwin, daughter of Mr. and Mrs. James L. Gwin, 1035 Peachtree Road. It goes:

"There was a young lady named Gwyn
How she loved to dance was a sin
    From dusk until dawn
    Without ever a yawn
She danced till the stars went in."

"I like the one about the lady who had a rough sweetheart named Priam," said Adalia Witham, daughter of Mrs. Dean Witham. "Mother says it's a most inelegent ditty to quote, much less to print":

"There was a young girl from Siam
Who had a rough lover named Priam
    'I don't want to be kissed,
    But if you insist
God knows, you are stronger than I am.'"

Tom Connally gave as his favorite the verse concerning the two irreverent Birmingham girls.

"There were two ladies of Birmingham
I know a sad story concerning 'em.
    They stuck needles and pins
    Into the right reverend shins
Of the bishop engaged in confirming 'em."

"I have a limerick about myself," said Ruth Miller, daughter of Mr. and Mrs. E. H. Miller, 46 Lombardy Way, "that I have to admit is original":

"There was a young lady named Ruth
Who always told the truth
　　When asked for her age
　　This wise little sage
Said, 'Add a year to my first baby tooth.'"

[The article goes on to quote eight limericks from Reed's book.]

—April 5, 1925

A caption for a drawing illustrating the article contains this limerick:
"There was young lady from Niger, who smiled as she rode on a tiger.
They came back from the ride with lady inside, and a smile on the face of the tiger."

Georgia Generals for Stone Mountain Memorial

Georgia has chosen her five Confederate generals to represent the state in the immortal granite of the Stone Mountain Memorial. The choice has been wise, and these five men—Generals John Brown Gordon, Ambrose Ransom Wright, Pierce M. Butler Young, Thomas R. R. Cobb, and Henry Lewis Benning—all gallant soldiers, selfless statesmen, and courteous gentlemen, deserve fully this honor of honors which grateful Georgia bestows upon them.

Following is a sketch of the lives of General John B. Gordon and Pierce M. Butler Young. Next Sunday, the *Journal's* magazine section will tell the story of the lives and achievements, both in war and in peace, of General Thomas R. R. Cobb, General Henry Benning, and General Ambrose Ransom Wright.

General John Brown Gordon

General John Brown Gordon, the "Bayard of the Confederacy," whose equestrian statue now guards the entrance to the state capitol, and after whom Gordon Street, in Atlanta, was named, was a handsome man, pleasant of smile and possessed of great dignity of bearing. He was magnetic, drawing all hearts and eyes to him, and when he spoke, all others were silent to listen. A stranger coming into his presence could not but realize that he stood before a great man.

But the best summary of the hero is this—
"His men loved him—and so they followed him."

He was born in Upson County, July 6, 1832, the son of the Rev. and Mrs. Zacharia Gordon.

He entered the University of Georgia and graduated in the class of 1852. He read law and was admitted to the bar a few months later, and between the years of his graduation and the outbreak of the War Between the States, he practiced law, quietly but with success, after the manner of many young Georgians who were fated in after years to carve glorious names for themselves—and for the Confederacy.

When war broke out and regiments, companies, and "legions" were being organized on all sides, the young lawyer entered the "Raccoon Roughs" as a private, but was speedily elected captain. In fact, within a year of his enlistment with the "Raccoon Roughs," he was a full-fledged colonel. In December 1861, he marched away with his men as lieutenant colonel of the Sixth Alabama regiment of the Rhodes brigade of General D. H. Hill's division.

The young soldier distinguished himself from his first rush with the enemy, but his spurs were won at the Battle of Seven Pines. General Rhodes, who was fiercely pressing the enemy, was seriously wounded at the crucial moment of battle, when victory and defeat hung in the balance.

General Rhodes was carried to the rear, and the command devolving on the senior colonel, young Gordon stepped into the command with coolness and thorough competency, and led the brigade with the brilliancy and dash which characterized his whole career. He was only thirty years old at this time, and the whole Confederacy rang with applause and pride at the exploits of the daring young Georgian.

He commanded the brigade at Malvern Hill and, later, led it in the great charge of Hill's division against the Federal positions at Sharpsburg where the most desperate and bitter fighting of the whole war took place. The Confederate troops numbered approximately 60,000 and those under McClelland were nearly 105,000. It was in this "great drawn battle of the War" that the courage and endurance of the leader was displayed as never before.

No man who could still keep his saddle must leave the field, were the words of Gordon, spoken in the thick of the fighting, when with smoke swirling about his horse and blood streaming from two wounds, he refused to go to the rear. Urging his men on, a bullet pierced the top of his cap and then he was wounded again. Still he remained in the saddle, giving orders to couriers who dashed up through the smoke, as cooly as if he were in his own law office. But when the fifth wound came, he fell unconscious.

In recognition of his rare generalship and his matchless courage in remaining with his men, though bleeding from five wounds, he was promoted to the rank of brigadier general of the Georgia brigade which was composed of the thirteenth, fourteenth, thirty-first, thirty-eighth, sixtieth, and sixty-first Georgia regiments. In this gallant brigade was the flower of Georgia, for here men of wealth and position fought as privates in the ranks, proud to wear fading grey and butternut uniforms—and to call Gordon their leader. Their worth was proved in the Battle of the Wilderness, when Ewell's corps struck Grant's lines. The Confederate tide swept up but swayed back, as the troops of General Jones faltered under the Federal punishment. The Confederate lines were broken, and for the moment defeat, like a dark cloud, hung ready to break over the Confederate army.

But Gordon's brigade, thrown into the front by the falling back of Jones' men, stood firmly and refused to give an inch. The Federals were repulsed and the Confederate lines reestablished. This was not the last evidence of Gordon's dashing leadership in this battle. For on the following day, with two brigades, he made a sudden attack on Sedgwick's position and drove the enemy from the works. In this sally he captured six hundred prisoners, among whom were General Seymour and General Shaler. For this exploit he won the praise and commendation of Lee himself.

But despite the brilliancy of this victory, the achievement for which the South loves Gordon the most is the incident at Spottsylvania Court House. Gordon was leading Early's divisions into the fight which, at the onset, seemed fated to be a Confederate defeat. General Lee rode quietly to the front and announced his intention of entering the battle at the head of his troops.

In all the history of the War was there ever another cry so fraught with courage and with love of a leader as that which went up from a thousand throats—

"Lee to the rear!"

And Gordon, catching at his general's bridle added his voice to that of the men—

"Lee to the rear!"

Then, swept to heights by the courage of Lee, he turned to his men, crying, "Follow me!" and led the charge with such a fury that the Federal troops were driven back from the base of "The Bloody Angle." For this charge he was promoted, a week later, to the rank of major general.

As a major general, he fought through the Battle of Cold Harbor and then followed General Early in the brief campaign in Maryland. With Early he fought through the Shenandoah campaign and especially distinguished himself in a victorious engagement with Sheridan at Cedar Creek. Returning to the lines before Petersburg, he was assigned to the command of the Second Army Corps of the Army of Northern Virginia. Shortly after this he became a lieutenant general.

And then the sad days fell. In March 1865, with half of Lee's skeleton army under his command, ill fed, badly equipped, he led a desperate sally and captured Fort Stedman, in front of Petersburg, and lines to the left and right of it. With reinforcements he could have held the position, but there were no reinforcements, and, lacking strength, he was forced to fall back.

What had happened in his command was happening all over the Confederacy—the spirit was valiant, but the flesh was weary and hungry and the gaps in the ranks could no longer be closed up. Gordon held the last lines at Petersburg and maintained his position with the stubborn fierceness of a bulldog, over every inch of ground. He seemed never to sleep or to eat, for he was everywhere at all times.

In the fated retreat from Petersburg, he again seemed omnipresent on the fighting line, a smile for the footsore soldiers, a handclasp, and a word of cheer for the wounded and the weary.

It was Gordon who led the last charge of Lee's army at Appomattox.

His days as a soldier and a general passed, Gordon's usefulness did not end nor his wisdom falter. The surrender no sooner over, he marshaled his men and gave them advice, as a father might speak to many sons who were to fare forth into the world, far from his sight. They had fought well, he told them, defeat carried no stigma of shame with it. But the war was over and now they should go home in peace, obey the laws of the conqueror, rebuild the country, and work for the future.

No other words could so well express the conduct of General Gordon in the bitter days that followed the surrender. He went home and worked for the good of his state and his people. In 1866 he represented Georgia in what was known as the "National Union convention" in a futile effort to better conditions in the state. In 1868 he was Democratic candidate for governor against Bullock and was, in all probability, elected but counted out.

It was 1873 before Georgia came into its own, out of the wreck of Reconstruction. Gordon was one of the candidates for Senate, with Alexander Stephens, Benjamin Hill, A. T. Akerman, and Herbert Fielder. Gordon was elected, and the recent soldier's career in the Senate was notable, especially for his efforts to promote better feeling between the two sections of the country.

He was reelected to the Senate in 1879, but resigned after a year of service in order to rebuild his fortune, for during his unselfish and untiring work for the state, his private affairs had fallen in a bad way. The president of the L&N railroad offered him the position of general counsel, which he accepted, and for the next few years he distinguished himself as a railroad builder in connection with the Georgia Pacific railway.

But in 1866 he was again called from private life to serve Georgia, this time as governor. He took his seat as governor with an inaugural address that won praise from all over the union. The *New York Sun* remarked in an editorial that it was "worthy of Thomas Jefferson."

He was reelected governor in 1888, and in 1890 was again sent to Senate. The United Confederate Veterans were organized during that year, and by unanimous vote, the commandership was given to Gordon. He held this post until his death, although he frequently protested that he had held it long enough and that some other man should have the honor.

His last term in the Senate completed in 1896, General Gordon spent the remainder of his life in traveling and delivering his now famous lecture, "The Last Days of the Confederacy."

His death came in 1904 in Florida, where he had gone for his health, and his passing cast a pall over the whole nation, who now united to mourn and praise the "Bayard of the Confederacy"—a gallant gentleman and a perfect soldier, who added to his four years on the battlefield thirty years of selfless service in civil life for the good of his state.

Pierce Butler Young—"Beau Sabreur"

General Pierce Butler Young was the only one of the five generals selected by Georgia to be immortalized on Stone Mountain who was a soldier by profession.

Born at Spartanburg, S.C., Nov. 15, 1839, he attended school first at the old Georgia Military Academy, at Marietta, Ga., and then entered West Point. A few months before his graduation he resigned to join the army of the Confederacy.

He was a handsome man, of courtly manners and magnetic personality. Men followed him eagerly and without question, for in him the traits of a shrewd strategist and leader were mingled with the dashing temperament of a cavalryman. He was indeed the ideal cavalry leader, the "Beau Sabreur" of the Confederacy, and ranks with Stuart, Forrest, Hampton, and Wheeler as one of the great cavalry leaders of the Southern forces.

After resigning his West Point commission, Governor Brown offered him a first lieutenancy in the First Georgia infantry, which he refused, as he wished to take a second lieutenancy in the artillery. After his entry in the Confederate army, he served, in rapid succession, as engineer on the staff of General Bragg, at Pensacola, aide on the staff of General W. H. T. Walker, adjutant of Cobb's legion, lieutenant colonel of the Seventeenth Georgia infantry, colonel of Hampton's brigade of Stuart's cavalry, and brigadier general of Hampton's old brigade. By the time he had reached his twenty-fifth year, he was a major general—the youngest man in the Confederacy to hold this honor.

His promotions came as a direct result of gallantry in action under the eyes of Stuart, who will live long in history as a smiling cavalier and a matchless cavalryman. At the battle of South Mountain, General Young led a desperate charge on the enemy and carried his men through their lines. He was wounded at the moment of victory and carried to the rear, but not before General Stuart had given him the highest praise and personal compliments. Before he had recovered from this wound, his promotion to the rank of colonel arrived, and after the Battle of Fleet Wood (or Brandy Station, as it is sometimes called), he was made a brigadier. His new command was composed of Hampton's old brigade, in which were the First and Second South Carolina regiments; the Cobb legion, the Jeff Davis legion, and the Phillips legion.

Upon the death of General Stuart, when General Hampton succeeded to the command of the cavalry, Pierce Young temporarily succeeded to Hampton's command. However, in 1864, when Sherman was menacing Georgia, General Young was sent to Augusta to gather reinforcements to aid in the city's defense. He was promoted to major general before the defense of Savannah, and, in the closing campaigns of the war in the Carolinas, he again saw action under his old leader, General Hampton.

With the surrender of Lee, the spirits of the young general were not crushed. He came home to a state torn by Reconstruction, and with the same dash and humor and bravery that had endeared him to his cavalrymen, he applied himself to bringing order out of the chaos in Georgia.

In 1868 he was elected to federal congress from the Seventh Georgia district, being the first representative admitted after the war from that district. He was reelected in 1870, 1876, and 1880. In 1878 he was commissioner to the Paris exposition, and in 1885 President Cleveland appointed him United States consul general to Russia. Ill health caused his return to America, and on his recovery, in 1893, President Cleveland gave him another foreign appointment, this time as minister to Honduras and Guatemala. But in Central America his health failed him, and he made a speedy return to the United States, anxious to return to his Georgia home before the end. But he died in New York City in 1896.

—November 29, 1925

In 1925, it had been announced that each Southern state would be represented by five of its generals in the Confederate Memorial being carved on Stone Mountain by Gutzon Borglum. The articles on the lives of the generals selected to represent Georgia garnered favorable comment when they appeared in 1925. The introductory paragraphs of the first article above stated that the Journal *originally planned to publish only two articles. But the series ended up running in four installments and more space was given the later articles than the first. Mitchell's first article had made the* Journal's *editors and readers eager for more.*

When General Cobb Wrote the Georgia Code

In the lives of most great men there is only one great achievement, one great moment. But in the life of General Thomas R. R. Cobb there are many great moments and three great achievements, all of which will live in history.

He codified the laws of Georgia.

He swept the state out of the Union and into the Confederacy by his eloquence.

He died in the Sunken Road at Fredericksburg after repulsing six attacks of Federal troops.

Thomas R. R. Cobb, son of John Addison Cobb and Sarah Robinson Cobb, was born in Jefferson County, April 10, 1823. When still a child, his parents moved to Athens, Georgia, where they owned a large estate. The Cobbs were one of the wealthiest families in Georgia, owned wide acres of cotton, dozens of slaves, and were noted throughout the state for their culture and for their hospitality.

Thomas Cobb attended the University of Georgia and graduated with first honor in the class of 1841. He was brilliant in his studies and exemplary in conduct, for in his four years at the University he did not receive a single demerit or reprimand from his instructors.

Soon after his graduation, a financial depression swept Georgia, crashing many old fortunes, and the Cobb estate was one of the first struck. During this panic, cotton fell to three cents a pound, slaves to one-fourth of their value, and even fertile land could find no buyer. The proud Cobb estate went under the hammer of the auctioneer and young Tom Cobb went into the office of William L. Mitchell to study law. He was both quick and profound, and in 1842, when not twenty years old, he was admitted to the Georgia bar. After this, he formed a quasi-partnership with his brother, Howell Cobb, but this was soon ended, for Howell Cobb went to Congress.

Married Marion Lumpkin

In January, 1844, Tom Cobb married Marion Lumpkin, daughter of Chief Justice Lumpkin, of Lexington, a girl not only beautiful of face and of personality, but of a Christian character that had a marked effect on the life of the future general. It was through Marion Lumpkin Cobb that he became interested in the work of the Presbyterian Church and Sunday School and in the Georgia Temperance Society.

He was elected vice president of the Temperance Society, was made assistant secretary of the Senate, and was offered an appointment on the staff of General Taylor. This last he refused, saying that he had no desire for any fame save in his own profession.

As the years went on, Tom Cobb advanced in his profession by leaps and bounds, until he became the most brilliant legal light in Georgia. He studied the genius of the law and was never a case lawyer; he sought to know what was right and then found a law for it. A wide reader, he soon became cognizant with all the old statutes that had been handed down in Georgia since Colonial days. He was made reporter of the Supreme Court, in 1849, and it was while holding this office that he was appointed by the General Assembly of Georgia, with two other men, to codify the state laws. To Cobb's lot fell the civil and criminal laws.

His work, slightly revised and amended, still remains the Georgia Code and is one of the most remarkable pieces of legal work ever executed, for Cobb did for the laws of Georgia what Justinian did for the laws of Rome. Up until this time, the laws of Georgia had been in a somewhat disorganized state, consisting, as they did, of all the old Common Law, the statutes passed by the Legislature since Georgia began, and the decisions of the Supreme Court. In order to find anything, lawyers were forced to wade through all of these hundreds of records and old papers.

Code Unanimously Adopted

Cobb brought order out of this chaos. His knowledge of the Roman Law, of the Code Napoleon, his wide studies of our own statutes, familiarity with Supreme Court decisions, supplemented by a judicial conscience, enabled him to do in a year what no other man could have done in ten. He condensed, changed the verbiage, simplified the expressions, and constructed definitions.

So overjoyed and amazed was the assembly at such erudition and at the enormous amount of ground covered in so short a time that they unanimously adopted Cobb's code and made it the Code of Georgia. This state was the first to have a Code and is still one of the few in the union enjoying so compact and lucid an exposition of its laws.

Being a prolific writer, Tom Cobb produced many other literary works of religious, political, and legal character. His *Cobb's New Digest of the Laws of Georgia,* published in 1851, is still one of the most valuable law books of the state. His *Cobb on Slavery* is the only book extant which gives a complete comprehensive and accurate view of slavery both from the historical and legal aspects. *Letters of an Honest Slave Holder to an Honest Abolitionist,* was copied all over the world, even in the *Bombay* (India) *Courier. Religious Papers* were a true reflection of the Christian character of the man.

Cobb founded Lucy Cobb Institute for Girls, at Athens, Georgia, and was its mainstay in its early days. He was a trustee of the University of Georgia for many years and, while occupying this position, urged state-wide free education for grammar schools, secondary schools, and colleges. In the lines of law, education, literature, and religion, this remarkable man had already made, before 1860, a name that would have lived in history, even had he died before the War Between the States broke out.

Secession Convention

On January 16, 1861, the Georgia Secession Convention met to decide the fate of the State. Here, according to those who were privileged to see this fateful convention, occurred a "battle of the giants" when those favoring the secession movement spoke against those who desired to settle amicably the differences between the North and South without severing the Union.

Alexander Stephens, Johnson, Means, and Hill spoke with fervor, advocating some manner of compromise for both sections. Cobb, Nisbet, Toombs, Reese, and Bartow rose, with fiery eloquence, and harangued the convention for states' rights. Although all the speeches made rang with sincerity and with conviction, none swept the delegates as did that of Cobb. It was Cobb's impassioned oration that carried Georgia out of the Union for the keynote of it all was this:

"We can make better terms out of the Union than in it!"

"And this one sentence," said Alex Stephens, after the convention was over, "did more toward taking Georgia out of the Union than all the wordy speeches that went before!"

Cobb's enthusiastic eloquence, like Patrick Henry's, "Give me liberty or give me death!" changed the fate of a state and Georgia voted for secession. After the convention, Cobb returned to Athens and organized Cobb's Legion, a body comprising three branches—cavalry, artillery, and infantry.

Thomas Cobb had had no previous military experience. He was not of a war-like nature, for all his instincts were those of kindliness and dignity. But he studied the manuals of his three branches of the service as thoroughly as ever he did his law books, and so competent did he become that General McGruder gave him high praise.

Made Brigadier General

In 1862 Colonel Cobb was promoted to brigadier general, for his handling of men in action surpassed even his handling of cases in court. He was a stern disciplinarian, yet a just officer.

His soldiers knew that the general would take care of them—knew, too, that General Cobb would never order them into any dangerous place unless he was at their head—nor would he enjoy comforts and privileges that his men could not share.

The brilliant career of this Georgian came to a close on the fatal day in December, 1863, at Fredericksburg, on the old Sunken Road where thousands of others lost their lives. His brigade was stationed behind a stone wall in the old road, the target of six consecutive attacks by Federal troops. Far away across the battlefield stood "Old Federal Hill," the girlhood home of General Cobb's mother. It was from this old house that she had married and it was in the yard of the estate that the Federal batteries were planted—the batteries that were raining on Sarah Robinson Cobb's son.

General Cobb had dismounted from his horse, in one of the intervals of fighting, and was walking down the road behind the wall, encouraging the men, giving orders for the removal of the wounded, checking up, with saddened heart, the number of dead in the Sunken Road, when a bullet struck him. It severed a femoral artery and the general lived only a little while, dying on the battlefield with the roar of the guns in his ears.

Perhaps General Robert E. Lee summed up the Georgia hero better than anyone else—

"Of his merits, his lofty intellect, his accomplishments, his professional fame, and above all his Christian character, I would not speak to you who knew him so well. But as a patriot and a soldier, his death has left a gap in the army which his military aptitude and skill render it hard to fill."

—December 6, 1925

General Wright:
Georgia's Hero at Gettysburg

mbrose Ransom Wright, soldier, orator, statesman, lawyer, and editor, died at the comparatively youthful age of forty-six years, having accomplished more in the service of his state, both in civil and military life, than most men could in a century.

Born at Louisville, Jefferson County, Georgia, April 26, 1826, the first son of Ambrose and Sarah Hammond Wright, he displayed from earliest youth great mental precocity. At the age of fourteen, he read law under Hershel V. Johnson (later governor), and showed a marked aptitude for legal things. When seventeen years old, he married Mary H. Savage, daughter of Dr. William Savage, of Augusta, Georgia, and half-sister of Annie Polk, Johnson's wife.

Because of the extreme youth of the couple, both families objected strenuously to the wedding, but the young groom, in no way disheartened by parental disapproval, bought a small trace of land on which stood a cabin and here brought his young bride. He continued his legal studies and read law by the light of flaring pine knots until he had learned enough to be admitted to the bar.

He practiced both in Dooly and Jefferson counties with more success than is usually attained by young lawyers, and was well on the way to legal prominence when the death of his father, in 1850, brought him a large share of the Wright estate. After ten years of married life, the young wife of Ambrose Ransom Wright died, and in 1857 he married a second time, Carrie Hazlehurst, daughter of Robert Hazlehurst, of Brunswick. During the years between 1854 and 1860, he distinguished himself notably in his profession and became especially famed for the brilliance of his oratory, both in law courts and in the political world.

Commissioner to Maryland

When the first small clouds of the coming war rolled upon the horizon, Ambrose Ransom Wright came out in favor of secession. Lincoln's election having precipitated the South into turmoil, Wright was sent as commissioner to the Maryland legislature, then in session in an effort to bring that state into the Confederacy. The people of Maryland were, for the most part, sympathetic to the cause of the South, but their chief executive, Governor Hicks, shrewdly maneuvered matters until Federal troops had overrun the state and there was no chance for the fiery eloquence of Wright to take effect.

The Georgian returned home and enlisted as a private in the Confederate Light Guards, of Augusta, which was one of the companies of the Third Georgia Regiment. Almost immediately they were ordered to Portsmouth, Virginia, and there, in April, 1861, Ambrose Ransom Wright was elected colonel of the Third Georgia Regiment and joined the brigade of General Albert C. Blanchard.

The gallant record of the Third Georgia Regiment is well known, but perhaps the best recommendation it ever received was that of the Confederate Congress, in a joint resolution bestowed in 1864.

Resolved by the Congress of the Confederate States of America, that the thanks of Congress are due and are hereby tendered to the officers and men of the Third Georgia Regiment, through its representatives in Congress, who were the first to leave their state to battle on the soil of Virginia, whose gallant dead have been left on many of her historic battlefields, which entire regiment, to a man, has cheerfully and unanimously reenlisted for the war, resolving as they were the first to take up arms in the cause of Liberty and

Independence, they will be the last to lay them down.

Approved, February 15, 1864

Attack on Island

Ambrose Ransom Wright, like General Cobb and General Benning, his brothers in arms who will be carved on Stone Mountain, had no previous military experience when he enlisted, but, like Cobb and Benning, he quickly applied himself to the study of the military manuals and soon perfected himself. He looked every inch a soldier, for he was of impressive and commanding mien. A stern disciplinarian, he nevertheless was absolutely just in his judgments and his men respected him, knowing that they would one and all receive impartial treatment from him.

His first active service came in the fall of 1861, when he carried off brilliantly the raid on Chicamicomica Island. This island, off the North Carolina coast, was held by the Federals, and here they had gathered a large supply of army stores. Colonel Wright, with two companies of Confederates, secured a small Confederate steamer and attacked the island.

The federal steamer *Fanny,* loaded with munitions and supplies, was captured just before the party landed, and this whetted the appetites of the attackers. The federal troops made a stand when the attack opened, but soon fell back into the marshes, losing a number of men and several hundred stacks of arms. It was in this encounter that the personal bravery as well as the leadership of Wright was apparent, for while the federal rout was in progress he spurred his horse after four of them and demanded their surrender. They replied with pistol shots, killing his horse, but undismayed, he sprang from the ground, and seizing one of the Federals drew him against his breast, and using him as a living shield, brought about the surrender of the other three. His gallantry on this occasion won the complete confidence of both officers and men and the highest praise from General Blanchard.

One of the best examples of the cool nerve of Ambrose Ransom Wright was his exploit at Elizabeth City, then occupied by federal troops. The exact strength and intentions of the enemy were unknown, and it was imperative that they be discovered immediately. Colonel Wright and Major Lee, of the Third Georgia, volunteered to perform this dangerous duty, and, changing their uniforms to civilian clothes, they entered the city. For some hours they remained there, talking freely with citizens and soldiers and then, eluding the pickets, made their way out of the federal lines, where capture would have meant the most ignominious type of death.

Promoted to Brigadier General

Shortly after this he returned to Virginia and was in the retreat from the Peninsula before the army of McClelland. After this, he engaged in the Seven Days' Battle around Richmond, and when this bloody fighting was done, the gallant Georgian received a promotion and became a brigadier general.

His command was attached to the division of General Huger and fought through the battles of Frasier's Farm, Gaines' Mill, Malvern Hill, and James River Landing. In each of these engagements he distinguished himself both by his absolute fearlessness and his efficient generalship.

After Malvern Hill, his brigade followed the enemy on the retreat into Maryland and then met the Federals at the Second Battle of Manassas, where Lieutenant William A. Wright, son of General Ambrose Wright, now comptroller general of Georgia, lost his leg. In this battle, General Wright had his second horse shot from under him, but, fortunately, escaped injury. He was not so lucky at Sharpsburg, where historians agree the bloodiest fighting of the war took place, for here, after losing his third horse, he was wounded in the breast and the leg. He was carried from the battlefield on a litter, bleeding but protesting that his place was with his men. It was some while before his men saw him again, for the wounds were dangerous enough to send him home on a furlough.

Returning home barely long enough to be healed, he returned to Virginia and was assigned to Anderson's division, A. P. Hill's corps. This division saw eight days' fighting around Chancellorsville in May, 1863, and it was during this desperate fighting that Wright's brigade drove the enemy from their first and second lines of breastworks and captured an entire regiment, including the colonel, lieutenant colonel, major, adjutant and many cannon. On the day following this, Early's and Anderson's divisions, with Wright's brigade in advance, charged the enemy in their position on the river road and routed them, winning the compliments of General Lee, under whose eyes this charge was made.

Charge at Gettysburg

It was in this successful engagement that General Wright received his third wound, in the knee, from a piece of shrapnel. During the summer following he went with the army into Pennsylvania and there took part in the battle of Gettysburg.

If for nothing else in his whole career, General Wright would live in history for his achievements on the hills of Gettysburg. Here he accomplished—and failed—gloriously in the same attempt Pickett made upon the second day of the battle. Both men scaled the heights, although Wright penetrated farther— and both were compelled to retreat down the slope for want of reinforcements. General Lee, in an official report, gave a description of this feat, which was vivid even though couched in the terse military phraseology:

... About 4 P.M. Longstreet's batteries opened and soon afterwards Hood's division, on the extreme right, moved to the attack. McLaw's followed somewhat later, four of Anderson's brigades—those of Wilcox, Perry, Wright, and Posey—supporting him on the left, in the order named. The enemy was soon driven from his position on the Emmettsburg Road to the cover of a ravine and a line of stone fences at the foot of the ridge in the rear. He was dislodged from these after a severe struggle and retired up the ridge, leaving a number of his batteries in our possession.

Wilcox's and Wright's brigades advanced with great gallantry, breaking successive lines of the enemy's infantry and compelling him to abandon much of his artillery. Wilcox reached the foot and Wright gained the crest of the ridge itself, driving the enemy down the opposite side. But, having become separated from McLaw's and having gone beyond the other two brigades of the division, they were attacked on both flanks and in front and compelled to retire, being unable to bring off any of the captured artillery.

In the whole history of the war there is no more stirring or heroic incident than that of General Wright charging up the green slopes, slippery with blood, with his yelling men behind him. Sword in hand, he led the advance, amid a rain of bullets and swirl of cannon smoke that would have daunted a less fearless man than he. But fear seemed never to have entered his heart, for, calling to the color bearer to follow close, he waved his sword and cried to his men—"Come on! Follow me! Do you want to live forever?" (This cry was attributed to a Marine officer at Belleau Woods in the late war, but veterans of Gettysburg agree that it first sprang from the lips of the Georgia general.)

Best Fight of War

Sometimes he turned his back on the enemy to harangue his men, climbing the slope backwards, calling for the flag to follow after him as banner-bearer after banner-bearer fell and the standard was snatched by willing hands before it touched the earth. They reached the top of the ridge, sprang over the captured guns, cheering as the enemy retreated down the opposite side of the hill. But even in the moment of seeming victory, they stood alone, having outstripped all support. The federal batteries on all surrounding elevations focused their fire on Wright's men, and the top of the ridge becoming an inferno, the remnant of men fell back.

After the retreat began, Wright's brigade still further distinguished itself, for it was left to guard Manassas Gap until General Ewell could bring up his troops. So well did he perform his task that General Ewell exclaimed that Wright's brigade had "made the best fight of the war."

In the fall of 1863, General Wright ran for the state senate and was elected. In November of that year he took his seat in Milledgeville and was the winning candidate in the race for president of the senate. As senator he supported with great zeal every measure tending to strengthen the Confederacy and to prosecute the war with greater efficiency. Upon the adjournment of the legislation, he returned to the front and resumed command of his brigade.

From the Battle of the Wilderness to the lines before Petersburg, Ambrose Ransom Wright acquitted himself with untiring energy and unflagging courage and one coup, executed by him, stands out as one of the most brilliant of the war. While in front of Petersburg he stormed and captured an enemy trench, and then, turning, doubled up the flank of one of their army corps and captured more prisoners than he had in his whole brigade. It was during this battle that another horse was shot from under him, making the fourth that he had lost.

At the close of his campaign, serious illness, aggravated by old wounds, compelled him to return to Georgia, where he was placed in command of the post of Augusta. In the fall of 1864, President Davis sent to him his commission as a major general, and in this capacity he was present at the siege of Savannah and the subsequent retreat from that town. When the last sad days came, General Wright was with Johnson in North Carolina, and there surrender took place.

His Best Speech

The war was over and Ambrose Ransom Wright, with thousands of others, saddened by defeat, hastened home. But on reaching Augusta he found disorganization and misery. Thousands of tired soldiers, tramping home from Appomattox, had thronged the city, hungry, half-clothed, and bitter in defeat. The city had attended to their wants as best it could, but the numbers had grown to such proportions that there was hardly food enough for the inhabitants. At the time General Wright came home, Augusta was in the hands of a mob that was wrecking shops and opening warehouses in order that they might enjoy things of which they had been so long deprived. Some of the soldiers had found a storehouse of whisky, and the mob was beginning to be ugly and ominous. Women and children cowered frightened behind locked doors while the mob thronged the streets, yelling and breaking into stores.

General Wright sprang upon a dry goods box on Broad Street and there, according to witnesses, made the best speech of his life to "Soldiers of Bob Lee," as he called them. His ringing voice, his commanding figure, the eloquent sincerity of his plea that the unstained reputation of the Confederate soldiers be unmarred by lawless conduct, had the right effect. The mob knew him and his record, cheered him, and, putting back much of the looted goods, left for their homes.

Having saved the fortunes of Augusta, General Wright turned his attention to his private fortunes, which had fallen into a disheartening state. When he marched away with the Third Georgia, he had left behind a law practice not surpassed in the state, wealth, and property. When he returned home, he found all swept away except his home. For the first six months after the surrender he worked, as he had in his early youth, with his hands, in order to feed his family—and his lot was no uncommon one, for many a wealthy Southerner put his hand to the plow in actuality, after the war, following behind the horse that had borne him from Appomattox.

In the beginning of 1866, General Wright reopened his law office in Augusta with Judge Gibson as his partner, but this only lasted a short while until the judge went on the bench. In March, 1866, Henry Moore purchased the *Chronicle and Sentinel,* and made General Wright one of the editors of the paper. Due to mismanagement of a former owner, the circulation of the paper had dropped to almost nothing. But General Wright was one of the best known men in Georgia and one of the most popular, and in a short while the circulation had jumped astoundingly. In the bitter reconstruction days, the *Chronicle and Sentinel* and its editors fearlessly fought for the rights of the Southern people and denounced the carpet bag rule, until finally they saw the state emerge from oppression.

In 1872, General Wright was sent to the state convention of Democracy, and by that body elected a delegate from the state at large to the Baltimore convention. Later he received a nomination for Congress from the eighth district. There were strong rivals in the field against him, but General Wright "stumped" every county in the district, making hundreds of friends wherever he went. When election day arrived, General Wright won the race by nearly 3,500 majority.

However, the general did not live to serve his term, for he died shortly after his election. The press of the nation mourned his passing. Even the Northern papers, which only a few years before had blazed with bitterness, now said that Georgia's greatest man had gone to a well-earned reward. For he was a great lawyer, splendid citizen, a chivalric gentleman—and he served his generation well.

—December 13, 1925

General Benning, Hero of "Burnside's Bridge"

Henry Lewis Benning, after whom Fort Benning, at Columbus, Ga. was named, was the son of Pleasant Moon and Malina Meriwhether Benning. Born April 2, 1814, he moved with his family at an early age to Harris County, where he attended Dr. Beman's school. He entered as a sophomore at Franklin College (later the University of Georgia), from which he was graduated with first honor in 1834.

In 1835 he was admitted to the bar at Columbus, Ga., and in 1837 became solicitor general of the circuit. While solicitor general, he married Mary Howard Jones, daughter of Colonel and Mrs. Seaborn Jones. In 1853, when only thirty-nine years old, he was elected to the supreme bench, being one of the youngest men in the state to ever hold such a position. He served six years in this capacity and then resumed his practice.

When the election of Lincoln threw the South into tumult, Henry Benning was one of the first in Georgia to lift his voice in favor of secession. In 1861 he was appointed commissioner to the Virginia convention and was instrumental in passing the secession ordinance. His eloquence, his obvious sincerity as he spoke in behalf of secession, swept his hearers into enthusiasm. Returning home after having accomplished this, he waited not a moment to join the army. Although middle-aged and therefore not subject to call, Henry Benning raised a regiment, was elected colonel, and left immediately for Virginia, where his command was numbered the Seventeenth Georgia in Tombs brigade.

"Old Rock"

"Old Rock," as he came to be called by his men, made a remarkable soldier. He had had no previous military experience and had come from the quiet ranks of civil life, yet he applied himself to the business of being a soldier as he had that of lawyer, and he succeeded equally in both. He was a strong, solid soldier, courageous and just. He never commanded his soldiers to do anything which he himself would not do, for "what's good enough for the boys is good enough for me."

After the first year of the war, "what was good enough for the boys" was generally pretty poor fare. Parched corn and yams, roaster acorn coffee, hours in driving rain, beds in the mud, and sleepless nights in the saddle were what his "boys" were enduring, and they were what "Old Rock" endured with them.

Perhaps the most characteristic incident related of the general's courage and stubbornness occurred during the Battle of Chickamauga. Benning had been in the thick of the fight directing operations, dispatching couriers, and cheering on his men, seeming to bear a charmed life amid the deadly fire that was mowing down hundreds about him. His horse was killed. General Benning mounted another, proffered by one of his staff. When this mount fell mortally wounded, nearly carrying the general with him to the ground, Benning sprang clear of the dying animal and, refusing the second horse offered him by an officer, ran back to where an army supply wagon stood.

Hastily cutting one of the great animals from the harness, Benning mounted on its bare back, and galloping back to his position, urged on the fight with greater intensity.

Early in the war, he was promoted to the rank of Brigadier General and given Tombs's old brigade, which was later attached to Longstreet's corps. The tenacity and stubbornness of the commander seemed to communicate itself to the men, especially upon one occasion, when he held the bridge over Antietam Creek, known as "Burnside's Bridge." Hour after hour he held the bridge, under the enfilading fire of Burnside's men, while wave after wave of Federals swept up toward the bridge and fell back. The loss among Benning's troops was enormous, but it is said that that of Burnside's was double. Finally, the Federals retreated and forded the water some distance down the creek. When "Old Rock's" men fell back, they had only one round of ammunition left, but he brought up his other two regiments, the Fifteenth and Seventeenth Georgia, supplied them with more ammunition and returned to the fighting.

Wounded at the Wilderness

In the second day's fighting of the Battle of the Wilderness, General Benning was wounded in the shoulder. This bullet wound sent him home on furlough for six months. It proved very serious, and the general never fully recovered the use of his arm. Yet as soon as he was able to be about and to move his fingers, he returned to his men.

At this point in the life story of General Benning, it is only just to mention his wife, for her story is intertwined with that of her husband. She was a tiny woman, frail and slight, but possessed of unusual endurance and a lion's heart. The battles she fought at home were those of nearly every Southern woman, but her burdens were heavier than most.

Left in complete charge of a large plantation, this little

woman, who was the mother of ten children, was as brave a soldier at home as ever her husband was on the Virginia battlefields. She saw to it that the crops were gathered, the children fed and clothed, and the Negroes cared for. To her fell the work of superintending the weaving and spinning of enough cloth, not only to clothe her own children and servants, but also Confederate soldiers. While her husband was away, she buried her aged father (whose end was hastened by the war); comforted her sorrowing mother; cared for her bereaved sister-in-law, the widow of her brother, Captain J. A. Jones, and her brother's children; and nursed sick and wounded Confederate soldiers. And, hardest of all things in those trying days, she went three times to Virginia to bring home her own wounded.

She traveled to Virginia and brought home her husband on a litter, and after him her son, Captain Seaborn Jones Benning, a mere boy, whose health was ruined by his two wounds.

When Henry Benning recovered enough to return to his command he went into the Battle of Gettysburg where, strangely enough, he was unhurt, although his regiment was the storm center at Little Round Top. He reorganized his shattered command after Gettysburg, cheered them on with his own indomitable spirit, and fought through the rest of the war with the unyielding courage that shows his nickname to have been well merited.

Surrender to Appomattox

He was preparing to attack, at Appomattox, when a courier rode up with the news of Lee's surrender. The brave general, who endured hunger and wounds and weariness with unfaltering courage, bowed his head in heartbreak, for defeat was the only blow that could bend his gallant head. But so great was his pride as a soldier, that he lined up his ragged brigade in dress parade order and marched them to the rendezvous. Here he was able to say, "All present and accounted for, sir," when Lee turned sad eyes toward him.

"Old Rock" went home and to conditions that would have broken the spirit of a lesser man than he. He found his home burned; his land in ruins; and, added to this sad state, the care of his own wife and large family, the widow and children of Captain Jones, and the orphaned children of his sister, Mrs. B. Y. Martin. But Benning never complained, even after the death of his wife in 1867—surely as true a Confederate soldier as ever fell in battle.

Then, with the task of being father and mother and brother to so many girls, his only remark was "I feel as though I had the world on my shoulders!"

He resumed his law practice, and some time after the war ran for judge against Dawson Walker and was defeated. Later, when Governor Milton Smith offered the general an appointment to the Supreme Court bench, Benning refused it, preferring to continue his law practice. His practice grew again, as every one loved and respected the general not only for his marked legal ability, but for his war records, his sensitive honor, and his absolute integrity.

The entire South was shocked when on a July morning in 1875, he died while on the way to court to try a case. Praise came from both high and low, and even the papers of his former foes had nothing but highest compliments to offer. His brothers in arms assembled in hundreds to do him honor and to pay tributes. Perhaps the most fitting of these came from a former soldier who had served under him—

"Now I know why the Tenth Legion loved Caesar!"

—December 2, 1925

7

Bunko Gangs & Rum Runners

Mitchell's assignments sometimes took her into Atlanta-area prisons.
Pictured is the DeKalb County Jail as it appeared in the early twenties.

Gay Flowers Made
in DeKalb Prison Cell

A cell in DeKalb County Jail is the workshop where paper flowers are made to brighten the homes of people in Decatur and in Atlanta.

Hands that are stained with the blood of a fellow-man are forever cutting and twisting bright bits of tissue paper and fashioning them into flowers. Flowers grow in the cramped county jail because a convicted man's hands create them.

All preconceived notions of prisoners sentenced for acts of violence have to be revised after seeing Tom Ellis. He does not fit in with any of the conventional types. He is neither daring, defiant, and romantic; nor sullen and dour. There is none of the hardness of evil nor the weakness of dissipation in his eyes. It is difficult to associate "Tom," as everyone calls him, with the idea of crime as he sits in his cell painstakingly twisting together pieces of paper that will make a rose or a carnation.

Tom Ellis does not twist his flowers into shape nervously, nor with any special deftness so that his occupation could become a pastime to him. He plods away methodically at his task, because making paper flowers is the only thing he can do to earn a little money while he is confined in jail. Tom makes the paper flowers all through the day, and his wife sells them. The pennies and dollars they bring help feed his family and may help pay the lawyer who is working for Tom Ellis's release.

But the flowers that bloom in the prison cell have nothing to do with the case!

Last August, Tom Ellis was a tenant farmer on the truck farm of W. A. Chamblee. He was working the farm "on shares" and attended to the planting and cultivation of the crop. Not desiring to call on his employer or anyone for aid, he worked all night in a cotton mill, going back to Decatur on the first morning car. He would sleep for a few hours and then do his farming.

"It was last August when it all happened," said the prisoner. "It was Curb Market day in Atlanta, and I wanted to take in some ripe tomatoes to sell. But I didn't have no baskets. Mr. Chamblee had promised to lend me baskets, but when I asked him that day, he said he wouldn't lend me any. He got right mad about it. I went on down home to tell Nanny, that's my wife, that I guessed that we wouldn't sell no tomatoes at the Curb Market that day, and Mr. Chamblee, he kept following me, and arguing till we got home.

"It was there that the argument got hot and he started at me with an iron tooth off of a (narrow). I reached into the corn crib, where I generally sleep, and got my shotgun. I fired once, not to hurt him, but just to skeer him off. He thought that when the gun was empty he could get me, so he charged me again. But I run around and reloaded, and when he tried to kill me, I shot him."

The trial came up very speedily, in September, and Tom Ellis was convicted of manslaughter and sentenced to fifteen years.

William Schley Howard, who defended Ellis, has appealed for a new trial, and it will probably come up in the next month.

"Due to the fact that Tom was jailed before he had realized on his little crop, the family was practically destitute," said Mr. Howard. "So, of course, I refused anything for defending him. Tom Ellis is the best old man I know. But he and his wife are as honest and proud as the day is long, and they insist that they will pay."

So in the dark, dirty jail at Decatur sits a grizzled-haired old man with patient, fading blue eyes. The two other prisoners in his cell lounge on the cots and watch him apathetically as he fashions his flowers.

"My wife, she taught me how to make them," he said, holding up a remarkably life-like bunch of chrysanthemums and smiling at "Nannny," his wife, as she reached through the bars to take them from him. "At first, they were ever so hard to make, but then, I had to earn some money for Nanny and for the lawyer, too, so I kept on trying, till now I can make them just as good as Nanny can!

"Sometimes I have right good luck and sell all I can finish. Sometimes," sadly, "luck's not so good and I don't sell much. Folks in Decatur have been mighty nice to me, however.

"When I get out of here, I don't guess I'll do this the rest of my life—'cause I'm a farmer by nature and not a flower-maker. But I have to do something to help Nanny while I sit up here."

Pale pink roses and yellow-tinted daffodils have never bloomed in a more incongruous place than his little cell.

—*February 2, 1923*

Lifer Back in Jail Because He Told Truth

—◈◈◈—

Strange Story of Ira B. Hall Recalled by Mrs. Hall's Request for His Pardon by the Atlanta Prison Commission. During Eight Years After Escape, Hall Lived as Model Citizen.

—◈◈◈—

With an eight-months-old baby in her arms, Mrs. Ira B. Hall was in Atlanta recently to urge a pardon for her husband, escaped lifer, who since last November has been back on the chaingang, after eluding his sentence for eight years.

During these eight years he lived with his family under an assumed name, as a respected citizen of Wildwood, Florida. Romance was his undoing. Romance and an odd sense of honor. Nemesis overtook him, it is said, though his son-in-law-to-be, John Stevens, who is alleged to have disclosed Hall's true identity to the sheriff, after Hall, not wishing Stevens unknowingly to marry the daughter of a man who had slain another, confessed to him his past.

The story of Hall is one of those that dwarfs the imagination of diction by the stark realities of truth. It had its beginning in 1913, as shown by the daily record of the case on file in the office of the prison commission.

In the early spring of that year, Ira Hall was a storekeeper at Tifton, Georgia. Wishing to move to Florida, he sold his store and went south to look for an opportunity.

While he was gone, Mrs. Hall subleased part of their home to Dennis Hall before she went to join her husband. This, it is said, was strictly against Mr. Hall's wishes and against the request of the owner of the house. Mrs. Hall told her husband what she had done as soon as she saw him again.

Sentence to Hang

"I guess you will whip me when I tell you, papa, but I've let a family have three rooms of our house."

"Now, mamma, you oughtn't to have done that," is the reply. "Mr. Roe (the owner of the house) didn't want it subleased and, anyway, the two rooms left won't be enough for all of us."

"I've fixed that," said Mrs. Hall. "I've arranged with them to vacate on a two or three days' notice, whenever we want the whole house back."

But it was upon this very point that the trouble began. When the Ira Halls returned from Florida and wanted their house, Dennis Hall declared that he had an unwritten lease on the whole house and grounds for a year. In spite of strenuous objections by Dennis Hall, Ira Hall and his family moved into the two empty rooms, and the families continued to live under the same roof in very strained relations.

Quarrels were daily occurrences between the two men, and testimony brought out in the trial showed that the two wives lived in constant dread of trouble. Finally, the two men began to go armed.

One day there was a particularly violent quarrel. Testimony showed that insults were passed freely. Finally, Dennis Hall reached toward his hip pocket, where, the defense claimed, he had a pistol. Before he could use it, Ira Hall shot him.

Hall was arrested and tried in Tift County court. The defense alleged that Ira Hall was the legal occupant of the house and that Dennis was an interloper. The prosecution maintained that Ira shot Dennis in cold blood. The jury was out many hours and returned a verdict of guilty. Hall was sentenced to hang.

Commuted

This verdict caused a sensation. Because of some extenuating circumstances brought out, the sentence was afterward commuted to life imprisonment, and Ira was taken to the state farm. Later he was transferred to the Dodge County chaingang, and from there he escaped in May, 1916.

Hall disappeared completely. All attempts to trace him failed. It seemed as if the earth had swallowed him. Indeed, the world had swallowed Ira D. Hall, but suddenly disgorged Mr. Farrester, a truck farmer who acquired a small tract of land at Wildwood, Florida.

During his eight years of freedom in Florida, Ira Hall was a model citizen and raised a happy, healthy family of six children. According to numerous affidavits from the citizens of Wildwood,

Florida and the surrounding country, he "did well by his wife and family and worked hard on his farm. He was a law-abiding and valued addition to the community," until his rearrest.

When Ira Hall's oldest child, Robena, was nineteen, she became engaged to John Stevens, and the date of the wedding was set. Everything appeared to be going well, for as "Mr. Farrester," Ira Hall had lived eight years in Wildwood, undetected. There was nothing to point that he would not live out his life the same way. But Hall began to be worried by a consciousness of dishonesty.

Romance Brings Trouble

He had seen the romance growing between his daughter Robena and young John Stevens, and, while he was doubtless glad to see his child on the verge of what appeared to be a happy marriage, his conscience and sense of honor began to trouble him.

The young man had no idea that he was marrying the daughter of an escaped "lifer." He thought the Farrester family was all that it appeared to be—a solid, substantial family, highly respected by their neighbors and law-abiding to the last degree. Of course, John Stevens might have married Robena Hall and remained in ignorance of the true facts of the case until he died. However, the father-in-law-to-be took him aside, a month before the date set for the wedding, and told him the truth of the whole affair. It is alleged that following this confession, John Stevens informed the sheriff of Hall's true identity.

Honesty and a sense of duty impelled Hall to confide in Stevens. Was it an odd sense of duty also that caused John Stevens to turn the father of his fiancée, as it is said he did, over to the sheriff? Or was it disappointment at discovering that the antecedents of his bride-to-be were not all that he expected?

The fact remains that the deputy sheriff, after a month of

preliminary investigation, called at the farm of the "Farresters" and rearrested Ira Hall.

Mrs. Hall, who, with the aid of the four older of their six children, has been attempting to manage the farm since her husband's rearrest, told the prison commission earnestly that Hall was "needed at home." She further stated that he had proved, by his ability to live as a law-abiding citizen, his right to pardon. According to Mrs. Hall, her husband would be of a greater service to the community at home working his farm and looking after his large family than he would working on the county roads.

A psychologist would be interested in plumbing the depths of the minds of Ira Hall and John Stevens and discovering exactly what motives underlay the conduct of each.

What sense of honor or perhaps conscience led Ira Hall to confess his true history to John Stevens a month before his daughter's marriage was to take place?

And what motive led Stevens to turn up his future father-in-law to the sheriff, as the Hall family alleges that he did?

—April 6, 1924

Why More Boys and Girls Go Insane Now

More boys and girls around eighteen years of age are going crazy than ever before. According to Dr. R. C. Swift, head physician at the State Hospital for the Insane at Milledgeville, Ga., the increase in insanity among children in the teens is alarming. While sixty-five per cent of the total number of patients admitted in 1924 were between the ages of twenty and thirty-five, ninety-two of them were under twenty-five years.

What are the causes?

> Too much personal liberty.
> Dementia praecox.
> Pocket flasks.
> "Smut" magazines.
> Speed.
> Tantrums and tempers.
> Morbid emotions.

Atlanta psychiatrists and specialists in nervous and mental disorders give all the above-listed things as causes contributing to the increase of "child lunatics" in Georgia, as well as in the nation, for this increase in adolescent insanity is general. They declare that every child has a "breaking point," and that if constantly subjected to the strains of modern life and the morbid stimulations now within the reach of children, the mental make-up will disintegrate and insanity or abnormality will result.

One prominent Atlanta physician explained his "breaking point" theory more fully:

"In the life of every man or woman," he said, "there is bound to occur at some time, some emotional strain—a strain so terrific as to make the borderline between mental balance and insanity very shadowy and dim. The strain may be one of violent anger or an impulse to kill, a temptation to steal, a desire to have one's own way regardless of cost to others, and overwhelming passion that wrecks lives and disgraces families.

Running Amuck

"These impulses come into every life. If the fiber of character and control are of shoddy material, when the strain comes they fray like sleazy silk or crack as abruptly as rotten hemp. Their unstable emotions—undermined by excitement, speed, whisky, cheap sexy magazines, and indulgence in temper—go to pieces and they 'run amuck.' Sometimes the insanity is only temporary. But again the breaking of the barriers between the normal and the abnormal have been so complete that the patients never regain stability.

"If the children are brought up to discipline and control themselves, they bend but don't break when the strain comes. They ride through and gain strength of character. It's the undermining influences of the 'Jazz Age' that fill the asylums with youngsters these days.

"While I don't like to appear as one of those who is eternally criticizing the present age, I do believe that the modern mode of life has much to do with the increase of insanity among young people.

"But let's take two types of children and compare them—the average child of thirty years ago who was raised in the average normal family of that day, and the average child of today.

"Thirty years ago children were subordinate in the family. While the idea that 'children should be seen and not heard' was rapidly passing, children were not made as much of then as now.

"They learned obedience early either through love and respect of their parents, or through fear of a paddling. They also learned to hold their tempers and not fly into tantrums. They knew the hairbrush would be applied neatly and with dispatch if they aired any temperament.

Children Stayed Children

"Perhaps parents were strict about reading matter for children in those days. They allowed nothing cheap of sensational in the way of literature. This is apparent in the fond memories most middle-aged men nowadays have of the thrill of reading a forbidden *Old Sleuth* and *Young Wild West*. Why a boy of today would laugh at the transparency of such blood and thunder!

"Saloons were open and it was next to impossible for young people to procure whisky. No honest bartender would sell it to them, and should they somehow manage to secure the liquor, it was still more difficult to drink it surreptitiously. There weren't any automobiles for them to speed around in and get drunk. There were no movies to give them mature ideas before they were out of socks and kilts.

"There were no dances for children of 'high school' age and no jazz music. Boys were still given gold watches if they didn't smoke till they were twenty-one, and as for girls—well, no nice girl ever even thought of smoking.

"The result was that children stayed children till they were seventeen or more—and then they married.

"But take the average children of today. They are not to blame for their neurotic adolescences. Moving pictures and cheap literature give them distorted and matured ideas while they should still be spinning tops and playing dolls. If they are precocious, their parents laugh and are proud of them instead of reproving them for their pert remarks. Their whims in the matter of the selection of their clothes, their toys, their amusements, their all-enveloping desires to have everything they see, are humored to a greater extent than was formerly the case.

Temper Is Unrestrained

"If they fly into tempers and rave and become abusive in their childish tantrums, they are seldom whipped. They are either coddled or told to 'hush talking.' Children get into rages, lie on the floor, kick, and scream til they become purple and rigid, and their parents do not seem to understand the terrible significance of it. If the same conduct was observed in grown men and women, these ungovernable rages, tantrums, and hysterics would leave no doubt as to the presence of insanity. But instead of curbing these tempers with strict and swift punishment, parents think, 'Oh, the children will outgrow their tempers.'

"Yes, they sometimes outgrow the outward manifestations, but the inner tendency remains to break over under strain, and when the strain occurs, there is no barrier of control to hold them in the road."

"I have only one idea on the causes of increasing insanity among children," said another well-known Atlanta nerve specialist, " and that is that the reduction of the number of older patients suffering from alcoholic psychoses has decreased and thus thrown the insane young people into greater prominence. There is more drinking and less drunkenness now than ever before in the history of the country, and there are fewer patients committed to asylums from alcoholic excesses. Formerly these people were over thirty years of age. The decrease in these patients makes the number of young people proportionately larger."

Another psychiatrist laid the blame for the increase of youthful insanity to the fact that dementia praecox, that form of insanity which manifests itself in early adolescence, is more apt to appear when the sufferer is subjected to constant excitement.

Dementia Praecox

"Scientists now believe that dementia praecox is congenital and due to a subnormal or abnormal development in the physical make-up. It is unfortunate but in most cases the poor children seem predestined to insanity. Dementia praecox appears between the ages of thirteen and eighteen and probably accounts for most of the atrocious crimes committed by children hardly in their teens. The papers these days are full of accounts of little girls who give ground glass to their brothers and sisters, boys who shoot their playmates 'just to see what will happen,' Dorothy Ellingsons who kill their mothers and go blithely on to wild parties, Leopolds and Loebs who kill for thrills, and Frank McDowells who become religious maniacs and burn and shoot their families.

"Not all those suffering from this form of insanity go completely insane. Many people who were born predisposed have grown up normally, married, had normal children, and lived out their lives like their neighbors. But these people are the ones who during adolescence were not subjected to strains, stimulations, and morbid excitements. They were coddled in cotton wool, so to speak, or were grounded, early in life, in self-control. The weak spots in their temperament were not strained and battered.

"Modern life and the personal freedom permitted children are largely responsible for the increasing number of dementia praecox patients committed to asylums. Formerly when life was more slow moving, there was a greater chance of a smaller number becoming absolutely insane.

"But today, when children in their teens are allowed to drive high-powered cars, attend dances, listen to jazz music which pounds their nerves to shreds, drink bootleg whisky out of pocket flasks in washrooms, 'pet' indiscriminately, read the cheap smut magazines that have sprung up everywhere, what little resistance they possess is broken down, and if the latent dementia is in them, it comes out under the excitement.

Paddling Might Have Prevented Murder

"And when it does, their families and friends are stunned to see the children, apparently rational and normal, go suddenly to pieces, become violent, or commit crimes. Dorothy Ellingson was a fair example of this. Had her mother paddled her a few times when she began to show signs of weakness and willfulness, probably Dorothy would have never reached the unstrung state she was in when she shot her mother.

"The fault lies at the door of the parents, not the children," declared a psychiatrist who uses psychoanalytical methods in the examination and treatment of his patients. "I find in most histories of insanity occurring under the age of twenty that bad home influences are to blame. By bad, I do not necessarily mean immoral. I mean influences that contribute to making a child morbid, hysterical, and nervous.

"Many mothers frighten children into obedience by threatening them with 'buggabears' if they do not behave, and nurses further the mischief by telling ghost stories well calculated to harrow childish emotions. Jazz parents who are in the habit of going out to parties or theaters every night and leaving children alone in dark houses are responsible for the emotionally unstable personalities the children develop at fourteen and fifteen. Spoiling and indulgence develops self-centeredness, introspection, and morbidity which is unnatural in a normal child.

"Constant fussing and wrangling between parents, wherein the child first takes the side of the mother and then of the father has a very bad effect on its nerves and outlook on life. Home influences should always be soothing and steadying instead of uncertain and irritating.

"These early influences all contribute toward making the child irritable, nervous, morbidly emotional, erratic, and furthermore establish a craving for unhealthy forms of stimulation and amusements. Then modern life reaches out and grabs them, and their mental structure crumbles."

—April 12, 1925

Federal Prisoner Finds Con Man King of Crooks

---∿∿∿---

This is the second of a series on inside stories of life in the Federal prison in Atlanta, as related by a former inmate to a *Journal* staff writer.

---∿∿∿---

"The confidence man is the aristocrat of the criminal world," according to Henry M. Thornton of New York, just released from the Federal penitentiary in Atlanta, where he found that social distinctions of the outside world were as nothing compared to the rigid lines drawn by prisoners themselves.

"The difference between the skilled and the unskilled worker—the man who uses his brain and he who uses only his brawn has constituted the basis of the social scale since the beginning of things. It is especially true in Crookdom, for the crook who uses his brain to separate the trusting citizen from his cash to have ten times the social standing of the thug who, for lack of brains, resorts to such crude methods as the blackjack and the holdup.

"For this reason, the confidence man, some time called the 'bunko' or 'con' man, is the king of the criminal world. His returns are the largest for the smallest amount of energy expended, and he never uses clumsy methods or violence. He remains the 'smooth gentleman' throughout all the transactions and is frequently a cultured and well bred man 'gone wrong!'"

With the "con" man leading the list, the social scale, according to Mr. Thornton, runs as follows:

➤ The confidence man.
➤ The Big League Bootlegger and Rum Runner (not the small fry of "runners" and retailers who are held in contempt).

➤ The cracksman (Gerald Chapman's type).
➤ The train robber and mail bandit.
➤ The pickpocket.

These five types comprise the upper stratus of criminal society and ranging downward are:

➤ Second story men and garden variety burglars.
➤ "Accidental" criminals (those who had no criminal records but who when in positions of trust, embezzled funds or forged checks).
➤ Small forgers who traded on the trust of their friends to cash their bad checks.
➤ Highwaymen.
➤ Kidnapers.
➤ Blackmailers.

Prison Cliques Bar Climbers

And, at the bottom of the list, the white slavers whose crimes are held more in contempt by fellow crooks than any other.

"The 'con' man is naturally the aristocrat among criminals," said Mr. Thornton, "because he pulls down thousands by simply pitting his wits against the cupidity of these foolish people who want to get something for nothing. He makes more money than any other type, and the punishment is lighter. He uses his brains. Some of his schemes are most ingenious and plausible. He has no scruples about taking the money of some farmer who has worked all his life to collect a few thousand dollars, for he feels that the man who wants to 'clean-up' a million on the market and fake horse races is potentially as much of a thief as the bunko man himself. Anyone who wants to get 'something for nothing' is unconsciously a thief.

"These bunko men are often cultured, refined fellows. They

have to be, for their smoothness is their stock in trade. They are the envied class at the pen, and, during the hours on the yard, the bunko crowd can always be seen, talking and laughing together over their exploits. Their's is the close clique in the pen and all 'climbers' who try to insinuate themselves into their midst with tales of millions cleaned up on bunk schemes are met with cold aloofness. Cliques in the penitentiary are far more merciless toward social climbers than any 'four hundred' set outside of prison. They don't welcome outsiders, and discourage them by coldness and well-bred ridicule. The bunko men feel that they are superior to any other class of criminals.

"I knew one old man in person who had been a confidence man all his life, and except for his utter lack of scruple about bunkoing boobs, he was one of the most honorable, truthful and clean minded old man I ever knew—and the world's best chess player. I know that sounds paradoxical but is true.

Cracksmen "Operate" on Safes

"Next in the social scale come the big bootleggers—such as George Remus and his comrades. They are really the *nouveau riche* of the half world, and unless they have made an overwhelming success at their game, they don't rate very highly. In fact, the petty bootleggers are almost as low in the scale as the footpads—and that's very low!

"The most admired criminals of all are the cracksmen. They must be cool-headed, iron-nerved men, who do not get flustered in emergencies. They must possess a high degree of mechanical skill and a lightening-quick brain. Gerald Chapman is of this type.

"The safe cracker usually started life as a skilled mechanic and, after falling in with crooks, was taught the art of safeblowing. When a cracksman sets out to blow a safe, he takes three men with him. Two are posted outside of the building to give the alarm, or to kill or silence any guard or watchman who might surprise them. The cracksman and his assistant enter the room where the safe is, and after laying out their kit, proceed like a surgeon operating.

"The assistant hands the cracksman the tools, like an operating room nurse assisting a doctor. Assistants and lookouts have all the respect in the world for a master safe blower and feel themselves privileged when working with one well known in crime circles.

Old-Fashioned Methods

"Cracksman who use old-fashioned methods bore holes in the safe near the combination and put in the 'soup' (nitroglycerine). More up-to-date blowers use an acetylene torch, which is quicker. They put in the soup, muffle the noise with a blanket and when the door is blown off, rifle the contents. If they are surprised, it is the lookouts or the assistant who do the shooting or blackjacking, while the master cracksman makes his escape.

"Though this is the most admired line of the whole crook profession, it is one of the most poorly paid, for the cracksman never knows whether or not he is going to get a million or two cents for his time, risk, and trouble.

"Cracksman make model prisoners. They are usually quiet, pale, small men, soft spoken and well mannered, and once in prison, they seem to forget the outside world and devote their time to being good prisoners, so that they can get time off for good behavior. They are always in demand in the pen because of their mechanical turn and have good jobs—repairing plumbing, doing carpentering, and making themselves generally useful.

"The train robber and the mail bandit are usually desperate men, and in many states the death penalty accompanies the conviction of a train robber because, potentially, they are murderers. The train robber must have courage and cold nerve, even as the cracksman, for his job is still more risky.

Pickpockets Low Type of Crook

"How the pickpockets get into the upper crust I do not understand," continued Mr. Thornton, "except that they insist so loudly that they belong there. They aren't a very high type of crook. They depend mostly on the quickness of their hands. They don't make much money, as, like the craftsman, they can never be sure of how much they are going to get on a haul. They are usually a boasting crowd who believe themselves superior to everyone else. But no one else shares their opinion!

"Crooks" Who "Come Back"

"The rest of the criminals enumerated are usually looked down on by the upper crust as being too clumsy to make their living any other way save by killing, knocking people in the head, or taking advantage of trust placed in them by friends or women. I'd like to say more later about the criminals' attitude toward women.

"The 'accidental' criminal, for instance, is seldom given much respect. By 'accidental' is meant a man who didn't commit crime because he was forced to it by circumstance or because he was a professional crook. He is the man, who being placed in a position of trust, was not strong enough to withstand temptation, and so embezzled money in his care or defrauded the public in some manner. They are not professionals and get scant sympathy or respect from the others. You might say that they are 'non-union' men!

"Yet these accidentals have more chance of 'coming back' than any other type of criminal because they haven't been bred to lives of crime. Most of this type try to come back, but it's usually hard, because they are seldom trusted by their associates. They have to work for one-tenth of what their former salary was and so spend their lives in drudgery.

"A high-class safe cracker has the utmost contempt for a footpad or a burglar, because they descend to violence. They think a man is of little worth if he can't talk people out of their money, or crack safes, or sell them whisky, or have the nerve to pull off robberies on a large scale. Besides at heart, a footpad and a burglar are killers. They are prepared to kill their victims if they resist or refuse to give up their money. High class criminals know that even association with murderers, potential or otherwise, is unlucky and so they haven't much use for them.

"Kidnaping and blackmail are always the lowest depths to which the criminal can sink. Particularly is kidnaping despised because it is usually a futile affair and the risks are high and the returns low. There is nothing a good crook despises so much as a clumsy job, and kidnaping is always clumsy.

Criminals Protect Women

"Blackmail isn't considered honorable, even among thieves, nor is white slaving. Both of these offenses usually involve preying on women, and though people won't believe it, none but the lowest type of criminal will injure a woman, unless it is absolutely necessary for him to save his life.

"Crooks are usually good to their women. This can easily be seen by the faithfulness with which their wives, mothers, sisters, and sweethearts of men in Federal pen wait and visit and write letters to their loved ones behind the bars. It is those waiting women who keep up the courage of men serving long stretches, and it's the letters they write every day that boosts the spirits when they drag. It is surprising to know that nearly every man out there at the pen has someone who writes to him. I never knew of a single man who didn't have someone on the outside who either loved him or felt sorry for him. Every night, long before the mail is due to be distributed, the men are waiting at the doors of their cells impatiently for their letters."

—*April 19, 1925*

Gallows Room at Tower Used as Pantry

The famous gallows room at the Fulton County tower, the merest whisper of which, in the days that are past, brought terror to the hearts of many a prisoner under sentence of death, is no longer a chamber of horrors.

With the substitution of the electric chair for the noose, this small dark room that so often has echoed faintly to the faltering last words of men who died for crimes of violence, has become a pantry—an innocuous storage place for sacks of meal and potatoes.

But despite its present use, a bit of the old foreboding still clings to this room, which is characteristic of gray stone pile with dark barred windows.

Before the entrance of the tower, on Butler Street, there are always four or five tired-looking women, waiting admission to visit prisoners. The "talking cells," where prisoners are allowed to see their family and friends, resemble chicken coops. They are iron-barred cells, heavily covered with thick steel bars, so closely woven that even a hairpin could not go through the meshes. The prisoner is locked in this cell and his friends allowed to sit in the next cell and talk. They can talk, can see each other vaguely outlined in the gloom through the wire—but there can be no kissing, holding of hands—or passing of saws, knives, pistols, or poison.

On the first floor, the cells are divided into four wings, all of which open onto a wide, concrete court, called the "run around," where privileged prisoners are sometimes allowed to exercise under the eyes of the guards. Through the four entrances of the "run around," cells can be seen, wherein are prisoners moving about and looking through the bars, in a pathetic attempt to see something which will catch their interest.

Door to Death Cell

These cells, built in the middle of large rooms with iron-barred windows, are locked by a double combination lock. "Uncle Jack" Smith, the turnkey, has to unlock an iron box on the outside of each cell and fiddle with an intricate system of levers and bolts before the door of the cell will open. Just how Satterfield made his dramatic escape no one is exactly sure, but the outside window bars where he sawed his way through now show the signs of soldering.

The top floor of the tower is brighter than the other floors, for the skylight, stretching half across the ceiling, throws a semblance of dimmed sunshine down through the open court to the five floors below. On this floor are a few cells where unshaven bootleggers play poker with an air of ennui, also the kitchen, storerooms, hospital ward—and the death cells and gallows.

The door to the death cells is different from the other doors of the tower in that it is solid and not barred. It is a door of steel, gray painted and heavily bolted. Beyond the door is a small room, in the middle of which are two cagelike cells. These cells, which are used only by prisoners awaiting execution, are narrow and cold in appearance, furnished with single iron bunks.

The sunlight from the window falls across the cells in bars and checkers and makes odd shadows on the concrete floor. The view from these windows could not be pleasant to a man who loved green things and the out-of-doors, for it overlooks a railroad yard and the smoked and grimed tops of buildings— but perhaps those who sit on the hard bunks with only a few hours to live treasure any bit of sunlight and freedom, no matter how tawdry.

On the opposite side of the room from the death cells is a heavy steel door—the door that leads to the gallows.

The Gallows

It is only a few feet away from the cells, only a step or two, but to many a pair of dragging, faltering feet that little walk must have seemed interminable and beyond human accomplishment.

When the bolts of this door are shot and it swings noiselessly open, the gallows room is disclosed, a small, dark room full of shadows out of which the scaffold rises.

In former days, before the electric chair superseded the noose, this room on the day of an execution was packed with newspaper men, jailers, and physicians who whispered and moved their feet nervously as the door swung open to admit the condemned man and the guards who walked on either side. Near the door are steps leading up the platform to the gallows, and as they are slowly climbed, the first object that strikes the eye is the lever controlling the trap. This lever, which resembles nothing so much as an overgrown Ford brake, is as delicate a bit of mechanism as a hair-trigger pistol, for though it takes three men to close the heavy trap, the slightest pressure on the lever suffices to spring the trap and jerk the prisoner into eternity.

A turn in the steps and the platform is reached and with it a full view of the spot where so many criminals have stood and looked their last on daylight. A light ladder, for use in adjusting the noose, leans against the wall below the steel girder onto which the other end of the rope is attached.

Potatoes and Meal

But all this is changed now. There are no occupants in the

death cell, and the concrete floors do not resound to their cease-less tread. The gallows room is still and a spider is attempting to throw a gossamer rope where once a hempen one swung.

Where the reporters and doctors ranged the walls are now shelves and pine tables on which are potatoes, and leaning against the scaffold are bags of meal and flour. Where once jail-ers and hangmen went about their grim business, Negro cooks go in and out under supervision of a fat and jolly-faced white man who wears a long apron over his overalls.

Next door to the gallows room is the barred door of the hos-pital ward, where more space is allowed to prisoners. One side of the ward is given over to a large room with a table and sev-eral chairs, where weak and convalescent prisoners can sit and talk and eat, or exercise; the other side is full of cots for the sick. These rooms, being on the top floor and the outside, have plenty of sunshine and a breeze, although the air in them, as in all other parts of the tower, is pervaded with the odor of strong soap and disinfectants.

The Killer

In this ward, on one cot lay a bandaged figure, head hidden by gauze wrappings, sheet drawn high under the armpits. He lay as still as death except for a low intermittent moaning. He had shot and killed his wife and then fired a bullet into his own head. The bullet had been extracted, and he had been moved from Grady Hospital to recover at the tower and await trial—a trial that will never be held, for death later visited the man hid-den under the wrappings of gauze.

The other occupants of the hospital ward, a one-legged Negro who hopped noisily about the floor with a dripping mop and bucket of soapy water, a bewhiskered elderly man who was held for vagrancy, a white-faced young whisky distiller with heart trouble, and a tall convalescent with resplendent "galluses," gathered sympathetically about the cot, in an attempt to make the sufferer more comfortable. Ill fortune does more toward breeding desires to be helpful than does good fortune, it would seem.

The elderly man with the whiskers, George Washington Drake, by name, aged seventy-seven, was a mass of rags and tatters and unkempt hair, but there was something gentle and educated about his speech and manner that arrested attention.

According to his story, George Washington Drake, who studied geology and mineralogy at New York Institute and Toronto University and took degrees in both and Sweden and Switzerland, has had a most varied life. After finishing college, he joined the Angler party, who were going to Africa to capture wild animals for the old Barnum circus.

Capturing Elephants

"Barnum was certainly the prince of showmen and one of the greatest of American press agents and publicity men," he said. "Of course, they didn't call them 'publicity' men then. He sent us to Africa to catch lions and tigers and elephants and herds of small animals like monkeys, little deer, and bright-feathered birds. I just missed being in the party that taught Jumbo, Barnum's famous elephant—the one that he bought from the English zoo. The tropical glare had affected my eyes and I had had to undergo treatment and remain in my tent with eyes bandaged the day Jumbo was caught. I think they captured him as we did most large animals, by digging a pit into which the animals fell and were unable to get out. Then we kept them there, without food, until they became tractable enough to be drawn out and put in cages.

"I was one of those who captured the elephant that Barnum used to keep out on the front yard of his home in Connecticut, so that everyone on the passing trains could see him and mirate.

"I went to Alaska in the Klondike gold rush in 1899 because I knew with my experience in mineralogy I ought to have some success—enough to give me a start on the stock market, where I cleaned up enough money to make me speculate foolishly and lose it all. I think my biggest thrill, in all my prospecting career in Alaska, Nevada, and California, was working a claim next to a prospector who dug up a lump of gold—it was too big to be called a nugget—worth $50,000.

Amateur Cracksman

Mr. Drake said that he had ten living children and had forgotten how many grandchildren, but that it irked his freedom-loving soul to live with any of them, when he had been used to the open road for so long. However, he remarked sadly, his money had given out and it seemed that he had fallen into hard times.

Jack Whyte, the seventeen-year-old "lone bandit," who was taken red-handed by the police as he was leaving an unsuccessfully "cracked" safe at Cooper & Duke's Billiard Parlors, 57-1/2 North Broad Street, is probably the youngest prisoner the Tower has lodged in many months. He is good-looking in a swarthy foreign way, soft-voiced, and unembarrassed. He had left his home in Paterson, New Jersey, and traveled south, because he said he heard work was easier to get in the South than in the North.

It was his first job, he declared, and this assertion is borne out by the amateurishness of the methods employed.

"If I'd known anything about safecracking, I wouldn't have tried to crack that safe with a hammer and chisel," he declared. "But I didn't know how to do it. I just knew that I couldn't get work and was broke and going to be hungry soon—and I just had to have money.

"I'd pounded the pavement for a week in Atlanta, trying to

find a job as a steam fitter's assistant, but I hadn't had any luck. I'd been hanging around this poolroom and couldn't help noticing the safe, so I got a hammer and chisel, broke into the place, and started to hammer the combination off. I didn't know anything about nitroglycerine or acetylene torches, and, anyway, if I'd had the money to buy them then I wouldn't have been safe cracking.

"I was awfully scared at first—heart just hammered. But when I got started, I calmed down. I got the combination off and hammered both my thumbs to jelly, but that was all. I had thought that if the combination came off I could easily push the pin through and get in. But it didn't work, and so I was sneaking out when the police got me."

—May 31, 1925

"Honest Man" Wakes to Find Himself a Thief

Charles Clements played in hard luck.

Even the police will admit that, now that they have him under lock and key.

The young Englishman, whose case excited interest all over the country when he was found wandering in the streets of Atlanta with his memory gone, has been identified as an escaped prisoner from a Florida prison camp.

After being at liberty and "living honest," according to his own story, he woke up trustingly to the first policeman he saw, to whom he confided his predicament.

"I think that subconsciously I must be an honest and an honorable man, and utterly without criminal instincts," declared the young prisoner as he stood behind the bars at the Atlanta police station awaiting the Florida officers who were on their way to escort him back to the camp from which he escaped. "I have had memory lapses ever since I was thirteen years old, and every time I have one I go hunt up a 'bobby' and ask him to take care of me. Just like a child, I seem to feel vaguely that policemen stand for law and order and that they'll make everything all right."

Mental Blankness

The Atlanta police made everything all right within a very short time. The fingerprints, measurements, and photographs of the prisoner were broadcast, and from the Department of Justice in Washington came a wire identifying him as a fugitive from Florida.

When the identification was made certain, efforts were begun to have Clements deported to England instead of being returned to the Florida prison. Doctors pointed out that his physical condition makes it doubtful that he can survive five years' imprisonment— the term that faces him. The British consul in Atlanta then took up with the Florida authorities the matter of securing a commutation of Clements's sentence in order that he might be deported to England, and there given a chance to start life anew.

When the telegram was received in Atlanta from Washington confirming Clements's identification, the young prisoner, who had been sitting disconsolately in his cell trying to recall something of his past life, was astounded. It was impossible for him to reconcile himself to the idea of crime. When questioned by mental specialists and fellow prisoners, he could recall nothing. He could read and write in both French and English, but he had no recollection of his name, his home, or anything that might have happened to him in the past.

"It was like looking into a mirror and instead of seeing your face there was nothing but blank mirror reflected back," he said. "Although I have had other spells of forgetfulness, whenever

I am having one I always forget that I have had others, and it's just as terrifying and confusing each time as it was the first time."

The doctors tried repeating names and dates and towns to him, but all he could say was "I don't know. I don't know." Childlike, he kept asking that they help him as he wandered, groping in a mental blankness, hunting for his identity.

"The doctors said I was neurotic," he continued, "and subject to hysterical states, and it didn't sound at all familiar to me, although now that I recall everything, I know that many doctors have diagnosed my case as hysterical. I'm undoubtedly neurotic, but exactly what started me off being that way, I don't know. Psychoanalysts say that if you can ever discover the original impressions, occurring in childhood, that brought on the first attack, sometimes amnesia can be cured.

Confused and Unhappy

"You see," he admitted, "I've read up a lot on my case to see if there wasn't something I could do to cure myself. When I try to recall the first time I ever lost my memory, I don't remember the exact circumstances surrounding the matter. I was at school and I got some kind of a shock or scare or mental upset and completely forgot everything.

"Of course, my family was very much alarmed and didn't know what to make of my condition. But the doctors they called in to attend me told me that I would probably come out of it in a short while. They said, too, that many people lost their memories under nervous strain and never recovered it. And that some people forgot only things happening in their past and could recall things studied or read. Some unlucky ones had to be taught to read and write all over again like children. Of course, this worried my family very much, but in a short while I came out and seemed none the worse for it.

"Whenever I am 'out,' I seem to have a different personality. I am frightened and confused, like a child waking up in a strange dark room, and when I see a policeman I feel relieved, for the police then mean safety and assistance to me. My subconscious mind is very trusting, believing that the world is going to help me. Doctors always go through the same procedure with me, suggesting names that might be mine. Always there are wires from all over the country, from police and from people who have lost members of their families, all hoping that I may be the person they are hunting for. But no name suggested ever seems to be familiar or to do anything more than make me more confused and unhappy.

Memory Recalled Accidentally

"The way I came out of it this time was merely accidental. But for a careless remark of one of the boys in the cell with me, I might still be wondering who I was. They had told me that I was Charles Clement, an escaped thief, and I couldn't believe it. I had thought and thought till it seemed as if my brain was going to pop.

"Then, one of the boys looked at his watch and said, 'Well, it's 7:30 P. M.,' and I said, 'Is it? I've an engagement at seven-thirty,' and then it all came back to me. I remembered buying a hack saw and cutting my way out of the convict camp and working slowly up to Atlanta, always trying to get farther away from the section where I was known. I was playing straight and honest and wanted to get far North in New York, where I could get a decent job. I had decided that I was too clumsy ever to be a crook, and moreover I was wanting to be a useful citizen and not be eternally in fear of prison.

"I remembered coming to Atlanta with a little money in my pocket and meeting a man on the train. He told me to meet him in an Atlanta hotel at seven-thirty. I met him and a woman at seven-thirty and they gave me one drink. That was all I remembered about that part of my life until it came back to me. As it was, I found myself on some Atlanta street, bruised, cut, and robbed, my clothes torn, and as innocent as a newborn babe about my identity. Just like being transferred to another world on the moon or a star.

Subconscious Mind Honest

"But when one of my mates said 'seven-thirty' I thought in a very natural way, 'Why, I'll be late for my engagement,' and then with a rush it all came back to me, who I was and what I was. Then I called the police and told them that I was Charles Clements and that I wanted to go back and finish my term, so that I'd be free for good and all.

"That was the worst luck in the world, getting away from the police and then walking right down to the station and into their hands! The doctors agree with me that my subconscious mind is an honest mind and that my conscious mind has criminal tendencies. However, I am through with stealing, consciously or otherwise.

"Doctors say there's no sure cure for my amnesia and that any shock or strain similar to the one producing my first childhood attack will bring it back on me and that it will be as if there were a blanket laid down over part of my brain—what part, they cannot say. It may affect one part of my memory or another. While I am not actively afraid of these spells, it's not a pleasant thing to look forward to."

Clements came to this country two and a half years ago and worked his way to Florida, where he obtained a position as a house-to-house canvasser. While unsuspecting people were not looking, he was in the habit of picking up odds and ends of jewelry, small bric-a-brac, and valuables.

"I was a rotten thief," he admitted, "I always left a card with my name and that of the firm employing me at every house and so that made my arrest easy. Then, too, I never would figure just how to dispose of the stuff after I had collected it."

—*July 19, 1925*

8

"News of Books & Writers"

These Barren Leaves

After finishing a volume as replete with polished portrayals of the frailties of human nature as Aldous Huxley's third full-length story, *These Barren Leaves* (Doran), one is impressed anew with the unfortunate fact that Huxley has wasted a wealth of penetrating wit and undeniable talent on characters who are colorless and scarcely worth the effort.

Despite this, *These Barren Leaves* is excellent reading. The motley group of characters who are pinned on bits of cardboard and whose wrigglings and squirmings are studied microscopically are set down with a mercilessly scientific hand that would have done credit to Aldous Huxley's more famous relative, who dealt in natural science alone.

Mrs. Lillian Aldwinkle, who is not as young as she would like to be (not by some twenty years), gathers in her Italian villa a house party of young moderns who, she believes, will best set off her deathless charms. Among them are Miss Thriplow, who yearns to be "simple but deep"; Mr. Calamy, a squire of dames whose indifference drives Miss Thriplow to depths of despair; the poet Chelifer, on whom Mrs. Adwinkle casts amorous eyes; Falx, a solid Guild Socialist, astonished at the company in which he finds himself, but secretly feeling that his presence there means a step up on the social ladder.

A well-written, carefully handled book, but, to my mind, not as good as *Antic Hay* or *Young Archimedes*.

—*February 28, 1925*

Numerous Treasure

R obert Keable went to Tahiti to write his novel of the South Seas, *Numerous Treasure* (Putnam), and while it falls short of *Simon Called Peter* in shock of high voltage, it possesses all the poignant beauty captured by Rubert Brooke in his Tahitian poems, and the vividly drawn characters live and move against a background almost tangible in its warm laziness.

The story of the South Sea idyll begins when the young hero, Ronald, newly graduated from Oxford, comes out to the South Seas to visit a family friend, George, who has been living in the islands for ten years. George is frankly an expatriate from England, frankly a cultured cynic, and frankly in love with the easy-going atmosphere and morals of the little island on which he lives. At George's plantation home, Ronald meets the heroine after whom the book takes its title, *Numerous Treasure,* a half-caste Polynesian child whose drunken white father had named her after a popular brand of Chinese cigarettes.

Treasure, with whom Ronald falls in love, is a playful, child-like, and charmingly irresponsible young person. Ronald wants to marry her, which is an immaterial matter to Treasure, but he is prevented by George (who covets Treasure for himself); Kiriti, a giant Danish planter; and Tony Verclos, who is, in reality, the dominating character of the book.

Tony is French and an artist, casual, frank to brutality, a blood sister to Julie of *Simon Called Peter,* and Pam of the *Mother of All Living.*

It is the last five chapters of the book that save it from being just one of "those South Sea stories." Tony and Ronald, who go to fight for France in 1914, return to the islands in 1918. It is when Tony, blinded while nursing in France, turns sightless eyes to green Atoae, that the full depth and tragedy of the story are apparent, because, "There, I can always feel the sun shine, even if I cannot see it. There, I will feel no strangers staring —

there Kiriti will take care of me for ever — and, perhaps, even love me a little."

The pilgrimage back to the only paradise they knew by these two relics, who cling together in bewilderment at a world in ruins about their ears, is done in masterly style and brings the book to a close that is somehow heartrending.

—March 29, 1925

Soldiers' Pay

Since 1918, thousands of stories have been written of the return of the soldier, and the bitterness and disillusion that changed conditions produced in him. *Soldiers' Pay*, by William Faulkner (Boni & Liveright), strikes an entirely new note in post-war fiction, for it tells of a different sort of homecoming—a homecoming that will be especially interesting to Southerners, as the scene is laid in Charlestown, a small town twenty miles or so from Atlanta, Georgia.

Donald Mahon came home to Charlestown and did not even know he was coming home, for "in his mind, Time and Space had stood still" since a machine gun bullet from a German plane had scarred his face and battered his skull. On the southbound train, Donald's dazed and fumbling movements and his terribly scarred face attract the pity of two fellow passengers, Joe Gilligan, recently demobilized enlisted man, and Mrs. Margaret Powers, a young war widow. This woman, whom "Aubrey Beardsley would have loved to paint," and the philosophic roughneck take the fumbling boy in hand and bring him home to his father, a minister.

His homecoming is a bombshell in the small Georgia town, for he has been mourned as dead by his father; Cecily, his shallow-witted fiancée; and Emmy, a country girl whose lover he once was. The rest of the story revolves around the quiet soldier, who lies on the shady lawn, remembering neither town, father, nor fiancée. Joe loves Margaret, Margaret loves the unknowing Donald, and Cecily, blowing hot and cold, jealous one minute of the strange woman who has brought her fiancé home and loathing him the next minute for his scars, makes the action about the Timeless Donald.

The three minor characters, Emmy; George, who is one of Cecily's boyfriends; and Januarius Jones, a fat, satyrlike creature "with eyes as yellow and old in evil as a goat's," are exceptionally well-drawn, and their affairs, though subordinate to the main theme, are told with penetrating satire.

Soldiers' Pay has obvious crudities and many loose ends of the plot are left, but the story, as a whole, is intensely interesting. The treatment is modern, and the vividness of character drawing is intensified by the adroit manner in which Mr. Faulkner tells the coincident thoughts of his characters along with the entirely different words they utter.

The atmosphere of the small Southern town where the duck-legged Confederate monument ornamented the courthouse square, the red dust of the road settled thick on the magnolia blossoms in the hot afternoon, and the summer somnolence pervading everything except the hearts of the characters, is perhaps the best thing in the book.

—*March 28, 1926*

Former Atlanta Woman Writes Novel

H*eat,* by Isa Glenn (published by Alfred A. Knopf), is a remarkably vivid story, told in a realistic style against the most romantic of backgrounds; its theme a tropical love affair between a young army officer and a gardenia-like Spanish girl.

Isa Glenn is the daughter of the late Thomas Glenn, who was at one time mayor of Atlanta. After a brilliant debut and social career in Atlanta, she married General Bayard Schindel. As the wife of an army officer, stationed in various countries of the world, her experience has been colorful and rich, and although she has a natural gift for writing, she did not take it up seriously until the death of her husband. Her short stories, published in *The Century, Scribner's,* and other well-known magazines, have already established her reputation and prepared the way for *Heat,* which is her first novel.

Like Somerset Maugham in *Rain,* Isa Glenn has made an impersonal natural element the villain of her novel. The heat of the Philippines pervades the entire story, from the moment Tom Vernay, the young lieutenant fresh from West Point, steps off the army transport in Manila and sees the shivering heat waves rising from the mudflats—to the last tragic scene wherein the heat has caused his final disintegration.

The scene is laid in the islands in the early nineteen hundreds, at the time when the hatreds of three races lay like open sores in the hot, poisoned beauty of the tropics. The Spaniards, still smarting under defeat, despised the Filipinos and boycotted the Americans. The natives swaggered and were insolent under their new freedom and hated equally their former oppressors and their new saviors. The army, toiling and sweating in high-collared uniforms under a sun that sucked their vitality, hated both Spaniards and natives.

Young Tom, whose repressed imagination is beginning to blossom under the influence of the crumbling ruins of the Spanish civilization, and Charlotte, a young school teacher with a native uplift complex, are thrown into the midst of the narrow army clique. It is in the handling of the lives, conversations, parties, and scandals of the army women that Isa Glenn shows her true genius for characterization.

The colonel's lady, the major's martinet, and the captains' wives form an ironic Greek chorus against the background of the heat, which, as the story progresses, becomes a living and diabolic force wrapping itself serpent-like around the young lieutenant. When he lands in the islands, he is in love with the matter-of-fact Charlotte, but the heat, the haunting scents of ylang-ylang, the plaintive notes of guitars from walled and moonlit gardens, all conspire to turn him from her.

The dark-eyed daughter of an aristocratic Spanish family inflames Tom's imagination and becomes for him the incarnation of the spirit of old Manila and of all his boyhood dreams. For this sheltered and uncomprehending child of the walled city, the heat-enveloped young lieutenant sacrifices all that makes his life worth living.

Heat is a colorful, logical, and perfectly plotted story, and on closing the book, the reader has the rarely attained satisfaction of feeling that the author had her subject thoroughly in hand and had lived among all the things of which she wrote.

—April 11, 1926

Acknowledgments

Many people have generously shared their time and expertise in helping bring together this selection of Margaret Mitchell's journalism. Roger Kintzel and the *Atlanta Journal-Constitution* have been kind to grant permission to return these articles to print. Don O'Briant and Jennifer Ryan of the *AJC* have been particularly generous with their help. Mary Rose Taylor, executive director of the Margaret Mitchell House and Museum, has provided able advice and practical assistance, as has Mitchell House Communications Manager Heather Hjetland. Mary Ellen Brooks and her staff at the University of Georgia Libraries' Hargrett Rare Book and Manuscript Library, particularly Chantel Dunham and Nelson Morgan, have been generous in sharing their materials, time, and encyclopedic knowledge of Mitchell's papers.

I wish to thank Amal Bane and the Atlanta Press Club for their interest in remembering and sharing Mitchell's journalistic legacy. The executors of the Margaret Mitchell Estate, Eugene and Joseph Mitchell, have kindly assisted in making this book a reality. The advice of estate attorneys Paul Anderson and Thomas Hal Clarke is greatly appreciated. I would also like to thank Michael Rose and the staff of the archives of the Atlanta History Center, and Greg Eow and the staff of the DeKalb Historical Society for their assistance in photographic research. Many thanks go out to Joyce Allen, Karlene Allen, Heather Blasingame, Jane Eskridge,

Dr. Tom McHaney, Alison Moran, Jason Orlovich, David Owen, Jeremy Pope, Elizabeth Steeby, Amanda Storey, Mark Studel, and Bob Sweeney. Thanks also to Aces and arb.